(handwritten inscription) ... _2014_

With love from Mich.

This book is dedicated to the memory of those, Salcombe born and bred, who went before, and to my father Peter James Murch, a son of Salcombe. With love.

My sincere thanks to all the members of the "Salcombe History Society", but particularly to Ken Prowse, Edward Hannaford, and Tony Leete for their patience.

I would like to acknowledge the help of Mrs Peter Marshman who donated photographs from her collection. I am very grateful to have these and to be able to share them. Similarly I owe a huge debt of gratitude to the Frith and Fairweather photograph collections. These two men recorded the history of Salcombe. Without Len Fairweather's gift to the Murch family of very many of his photographs, this book would not have been possible.

Last but not least I am grateful to the late David and Mrs Muriel Murch for firing my passion to learn more about my home town, for always answering my questions, and for allowing me to quote from "The American and British Naval Forces in Salcombe and Slapton 1943-1946". My thanks also to my cousins, Capt. Julian Murch and Nicola Gaulter who kindly spent time with me and helped so much by producing photographs and information.

As always, and for always for John

An environmentally friendly book printed and bound in England by
www.printondemand-worldwide.com

Mixed Sources
Product group from well-managed forests, and other controlled sources
FSC   www.fsc.org Cert no. TT-COC-002641
© 1996 Forest Stewardship Council

PEFC Certified
This product is from sustainably managed forests and controlled sources
PEFC
PEFC/16-33-415   www.pefc.org

This book is made entirely of chain-of-custody materials

DANCING SEAGULL PUBLISHING

SONG OF SALCOMBE
Copyright © Virginia Murch 2014

A catalogue record for this book is available from the British Library

ISBN 978-178456-004-1

First published 2014 by
DANCING SEAGULL PUBLISHING
An imprint of Upfront Publishing of Peterborough, England.

"There was a spirit, a shining in the old Salcombe folk. You couldn't put it into words, but it was there, so strong. Mebbe it was their strength or the way they pulled together in times of trouble. Mebbe it was their common blood...Or mebbe it was just the town that bound them together."
Edwin Chant.

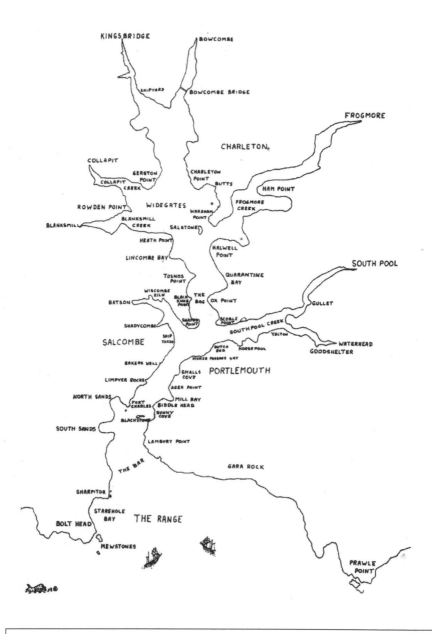

Map of Salcombe and Kingsbridge Estuary. Muriel and David Murch

SONG OF SALCOMBE

Virginia Murch

CHAPTER 1

I was born in Batson, near Salcombe, Devon on 10th December 1886, the second son of Aaron Francis Murch and his wife Ellen Elizabeth Cranch. Two months later, dressed in a robe lovingly made by my mother from a Trants flour sack, I was christened at the Island Street Wesleyan Chapel.

After the ceremony my parents led a party consisting of some twenty friends and relatives on foot back through the mud and driving rain of a bitter February morning, my mother carrying me, my father striding beside her with my eighteen months old brother Francis in his arms.

The party crowded into our tiny tied cottage overlooking Batson Creek to partake in a celebratory cup of cider and the pasties which my mother had been baking since early morning. With their wet clothes steaming in the heat from the Lidstone range, a cheerful, convivial atmosphere soon prevailed. Mugs were raised and prodigious toasts were called for. The gifts laid out on the window seat for inspection were admired and their relative values privately compared. The cider was a present from farmer John Adams and his wife Mary, pressed at nearby Horsecombe Farm. Other gifts included a sack of potatoes from my uncle, farmer William Henry Murch of Dove Cottage, Higher Batson; a small twist of salt in a piece of brown paper from our neighbours, kindly old Sam Pepperell, a retired mariner and his wife, Sarah. My grandparents James and Jane Cranch, who lived nearby, gave me a square of stout cloth to make my first pair of breeches. There were other small gifts from my many uncles and aunts which mostly took the form of contributions to the christening feast: some bottled plums; a large pat of butter; two freshly baked loaves, a quart of rich buttermilk and a tub of clotted cream. There was also, in pride of place, a bible inscribed with my name in copperplate writing, which was a gift from my father's employer, though he being an important man, and not having the time or interest to ascertain exactly my newly given name, had inscribed it incorrectly to "James Crunch Murch". He had added a line of instruction below this misspelling, in which he abjured me to strive always to be an upstanding, God-fearing man, lest the Devil and his sins take me. Needless to say, encouraged by contemplation of this dire epistle which confronted me every Sunday, I did my utmost to avoid such an end. The fact remained however, that his master had done my father a huge honour in recognising both his – and my – existence, and giving the gift. It was unheard of then for gentry folk to concern themselves over much in the lives of those who toiled for them. With the exception of my parents' bible, my own was, and would remain for the majority of my life, the only book in our household.

"Buckley", Lower Batson. c 1900 J Fairweather

It was said that the hamlet in which we lived was ancient, and that its name, Badestone or Batson meant "the place where a Saxon called Bada first placed his stone". Whether 'twas true or not, it is a fact that Batson was a thriving farming community long before its neighbour, Salcombe, was settled.

Tucked away in our little creek, nestled amongst the hills where our farm animals grazed, we were remote from the world, and saw almost nothing of the by now far larger and much more important town further down the estuary. But in the tranquil peace of our home we occasionally heard the sounds of the busy, bustling port as its inhabitants went about their business.

When the wind was in the right direction we could hear shouts as a cargo was unloaded or the flap of canvas as a ship prepared to set sail. Sometimes we heard hammering, or the breeze might blow in to us from the yards at Shadycombe the sound of whistling or laughter.

Once I heard a man's voice lustily singing:

"A lofty ship from Salcombe came,
Blow high, Blow low, and so sailed we..."

But the lie of the land and the bulk of the rolling hills about us kept us remote even though the two settlements were less than a mile apart.

"Buckley", where my family lived at that time was a thatched 17th century stone building. Forming an L shape with a store on the short side, and three cottages on the long, it sat on rising ground beside the cart track that led out of the hamlet towards what was then Ilberstow, but is now known as Snapes Point. Though gas had by this time reached Salcombe with the big gasometer built at Gould Road in Shadycombe in 1866, our two up two down cottage boasted no such modern convenience. Our sole source of heat came from the black leaded range in the kitchen, which in the winter was almost continually bedecked with drying clothes. Our lighting was by kerosene lamps, or occasionally candles. Generally however we kept resolutely to the old ways, up at dawn, bed at dusk when we climbed the wooden steps to the two rooms above the kitchen, one for my parents, t'other for us boys.

Our lives revolved around the kitchen and more particularly around the big black cast iron pot in which my mother did most of her cooking. The smell of wild rabbit or fish, or once in a while a piece of broiling beef coming from that pot held us captive, just as the pies baking and the crusty bread browning in the oven kept us from straying too far. Very rarely was the pot empty, but we lived with the fear that it might one day be. Poverty and the threat of hunger kept us company like spectres at the feast. When my father said grace before our one main meal of the day he concluded with the words, "..... and in Thy mercy Lord, grant us food to eat..."

We ate at the rather rickety table which my father had made, after first washing our faces and hands in a bucket of cold water in the yard. My father sat on a big grandfer chair which was the only thing he owned that had belonged to his father, my mother on a slightly smaller chair that had been thrown out of a grand house in Salcombe. It had a story to it that chair. Discarded by its wealthy owners because it had a broken leg, it had lain neglected at their gate awaiting disposal until my father plucked up courage to approach the cook and ask if he could take it. He carried it home almost two miles – and it was an awkward chair to carry.

Then he had made another leg for it but as his skills were not up to turning he had simply replaced the missing Georgian flared leg with a straight piece of wood, meaning to ask a turner to match the leg at a later date. The chair was serviceable even though five years later it still had one square leg – mother wouldn't part with it long enough to have its leg mended and I suppose they couldn't have afforded it anyway. On its seat was a red velvet cushion Ellen had made, which boasted incongruous faded gold tassels at each corner. The materials were left over from a sewing job my mother had done. It was the only pretty thing she possessed, and she treasured that cushion and her chair and allowed no-one else to touch them.

We boys sat on a form on the fire side of the table, but later when our youngest brother arrived there would be two forms both made by my father. Aaron was a careful rather than a skilled carpenter, and these items, forming our family's only furniture except for my parents' bed, the low trestle my brother and I slept on, and a couple of stools, were serviceable rather than beautiful. But my mother loved them, and she polished them with beeswax which she procured from the hives belonging to a distant Cranch relative, infusing it with the lavender flowers that she grew outside the kitchen door, so that its fragrance scented the cottage and became one of the memories of my early years.

Our kitchen floor was thick slate flagstones. My mother kept these spotless. The first rule of the house was that our dirty boots and outer garments must be taken off out in the porch. With the rough sacking that she wore for jobs such as this tied firmly around her waist with a piece of twine, she'd get down on her hands and knees daily to pay her floor homage, scrubbing with a stiff brush wielded with both hands into all its nooks and crannies. The slates were so uneven with age that when she threw water onto them, the peaks were dry before the pools of water in the valleys had even started to evaporate, something which always intrigued me as a child.

The floor of the other room on the ground floor was just beaten earth which we kept covered with straw. Some of our neighbours kept livestock, but we couldn't afford animals, so we gained a room. We kept firewood there and coal, and my mother's preserves, home-made medicines and liniments which were ranged along a high shelf. The room got very muddy in wet weather though, especially as heavy rain sometimes started off the small spring that rose at the back corner of the house. A great Uncle, Tom Murch kept his donkey in a similar room in his cottage. Through the years that beast had learned to walk sedately through his main room past his family sitting at their table on its way to its stall. It never fouled the room. Uncle Tom reckoned that that animal had better manners than most people.

Across the other side of the lane, perched necessarily above the creek's end were the water closets which served the cottages. There was a wooden pail of earth or fire ashes beside the hole and a little shovel with which you covered what my mother primly referred to as "excrement". My younger brother could not say that word, which was big for a little tacker. He called it "scream" which made for some amusing times when he first went to school!

Wading in the estuary we made sure the tide was incoming. We used to avoid first thing in the morning too, timing our swim for when no-one had used the closets, otherwise the effluent appeared in the water around you. I swam in Kingsbridge Estuary years later, and there because of the many houses, the problem was much worse and the waste came bobbing in and out on the tide. When someone complained they employed a man to scoop some of it out, and dispose of it, but it was a losing battle. The smell was something terrible in a hot summer.

Our water came from the pump in the centre of the village. In winter, despite the thick covering of straw and sacking that the men tied onto it, the pump often froze, and then we had to hack a hole in the ice and take our water from the little stream that tumbled down the hill.

There was Higher and Lower Batson. Higher was farming territory; Lower mixed farm workers and fishing, with several other trades thrown in for good measure. Lower was generally where things happened I decided early on. The cottages there were cheek by jowl together rather than spread out, each nestled in their own fields, as they were in Higher Batson. And Lower had gentry, in the spindly shapes of Mrs Catherine Weymouth and her sister Miss Elizabeth who lived with her, both descendants of an ancient family. Habitually dressed in assorted colours of mauve and purple, the elder wore a pince nez on a long chain around her neck. To be polite, people described her as "vague". Her sister certainly had all her marbles though, and she guarded the Victoria plum tree in their garden at "Perrotts" vigilantly. Scrumping a single plum from their tree was worth five apples from Farmer Wood's orchard at Batson Farm, because farmer was a kindly old man and would usually turn a blind eye as we boys crept across his fields intent on helping ourselves to his bounty

As well as the cottages and houses in Lower Batson, there was a square, open-sided smithy, a bakery owned by William Clark, an alehouse called "The Victoria" and a post office staffed by two women and a post boy. The water came right up to a sandy, stony beach in those days. It wasn't silted up and reedy like now. You could tie a dinghy to your front door latch if the tide was high enough.

The "Victoria" sold "White Lightening", an ale first brewed in Kingsbridge and said to be so potent that it brought even seasoned scrumpy drinkers to their knees. They said drinking "White Lightning" made you blind. Maybe it was just the Temperance folk who spread that rumour, but I once saw a procession of three old blind men each holding onto the shoulder of the one in front, making their way into the pub. Mind you they used to say the same about cider. They never stopped anyone making cider – there would have been a revolution if they had – but they did eventually ban

"White Lightening". It was a long time later that we learned that "White Lightning" made of malt wort, eggs and wheaten flour also contained a secret ingredient called "grout" Rumour had it that "grout" derived from pigeon dung, but my father always maintained that it was guano, which ships brought into Salcombe harbour in vast quantities at that time for use as a fertiliser.

William Henry Murch, grand-daughter and g.granddaughter at Buckley. c 1910

My father Aaron Francis was then employed as Under Gardener at "Ringrone House" – which later became the "Marine Hotel".

The great house, which had gardens fronting the sea, was the private residence of Baron Kingsale and it took its name from his family estates in Ireland with which country the title was largely associated. The family was established there by Sir John de Courcy, created Earl of Ulster in the days of Henry II. It was interesting that the Baron, who held at least eight other titles was the only member of the nobility who enjoyed the hereditary right to keep his head covered in the presence of the monarch.

My father was told this by the Head Gardener along with the reason for it, which I forget, except that it was to do with some big favour one of the Baron's ancestors had supposedly done a reigning monarch – I think it had to do with a loan of money. Whether 'twas true or not, it gave my brother and me much sport, each of us in turn pretending to be the proud Baron, wearing my father's cap and refusing to doff it to the other playing the part of the monarch. On account of the gift of my bible which I figured gave me a sort of distant association with the great man, I usually claimed the right to play the Baron, though the game always ended in rough and tumble, and sometimes degenerated into actual fisticuffs which necessitated our mother wading in to separate us. Though I was smaller than Frank I always gave at least as good as I got. He took after our father: he was sunny natured and preferred an easy life. I was stubborn and pig headed, and I refused to give in, so I usually won.

The fact was though that Lord de Courcy who became a great benefactor to Salcombe was rarely in the town in those days, and for the most part my father worked for his overseer whom I remember only as a tall, lean man habitually dressed in a dark suit, a white, starched high collar, and a bowler hat. This man occupied an uneasy place between "gentry" and "working people" which must have been an uncomfortable place to be.

Besides "Ringrone House" there were other grand villas in Salcombe. Drawn by the climate, said to be the mildest in Devon, as well as the outstanding natural beauty of the surroundings, a handful of incomers had commissioned these homes in the late 18th century. "The Moult" built by John Hawkins and described as a "mere pleasure box", was the first in 1764. Then in 1797 came "Woodville" later to be renamed "Woodcot" which was set in a prime position in Cliff Road, then later, "The Grange".

Early lithograph of Ringrone house

Such houses were rare however, for even in 1822 a visitor writing in a "Guide to the Westcountry", described Salcombe as a "fishing towne with three shipwright's yards…and a Whitsuntide fair for trinkets, sweetmeets, etc."

By the 1750's the manors of Batson and Shadycombe were held by William Bastard of Kitley in Yealmpton parish. This family were to remain owners over several generations. Towards the end of the 14th century Salcombe was one of a group of seven manors, five of them in Malborough Parish, granted to Hugh, Viscount Courtenay, the Earl of Devon.

Ordinary people like us did not own their own houses in those days. Nearly all our neighbours were tenants in property owned by rich men, who used such cottages to house household staff which could number up to twelve or fourteen. Our small cottage came with my father's work, its size reflecting his relatively lowly status.

My father's life had perhaps been more directly influenced by the rise and fall in Salcombe's fortunes than any of the rest of his family. Born to Thomas Murch and his second wife, Susanna Oldridge, he was the youngest of ten children. The first child, the only infant of Hannah Trout, was named Elizabeth. After the second marriage, there followed five boys, Thomas, Richard, John Henry, William Henry and James, then three girls, Sarah Mary, Susan and Grace, and finally Aaron, born twenty five years after his eldest half-sister.

Thomas was a tenant farmer of some standing. He farmed 14 acres together with a productive orchard, and he owned three cows and two horses. Thomas, his eldest son worked the land with his father to whom he had been legally bound in apprenticeship. All the other siblings had been apprenticed in their turn and taught trades: Richard as a painter and decorator with a firm in Plymouth; John Henry as a shipwright in Devonport Dockyard; William Henry apprenticed as a boat builder. Sarah Mary went into service. Susan married Samuel Farr, a builder from West Alvington who was later to bankrupt himself building Cliff House. In time both sons and daughters married and many moved away, looking to find work and better themselves

My Uncle John Henry who had sailed before the mast on the tea clipper route to the Far East, went to Australia. There he settled down with an American named Ellen Cairns, who, so family lore had it, had previously lived with a gold prospector who had got himself squashed under a boulder.

After many years without any contact John Henry took it into his mind one day to communicate with his family back home in Salcombe.

Next page - Lower Batson, 1896. Smithy is square building in centre, with "The Victoria" behind. "Buckley" is on right above wall. Post Office is in white house on left. J Fairweather

---

Being for the most part illiterate, he employed the offices of an itinerant Irish preacher who happened past at the opportune moment. Understandably wishing to render a good account of himself and his doings in a foreign land, Uncle John Henry gave instructions to his scribe that he was to paint his achievements in the best possible light.

Since at this juncture John Henry had actually achieved very little, being possessed of only the clothes on his back, a tumble-down, heavily mortgaged shack and several acres of poor scrubland, this presented the preacher with something of a dilemma. With no alternative he chose to concentrate on the only things in his employer's life that could conceivably be described as assets: a bad-tempered, elderly mule, an equally bad-tempered wife - though admittedly younger than the mule - and five barefoot, snot-nosed children. In a flowery missive penned throughout in purple ink, the clergyman claimed grandiosely that John Henry had married well, owned livestock and had founded a dynasty.

The service the preacher offered had included securing the letter on board a boat bound for England, but the money he had earned very quickly began burning a hole in his pocket. He reminded himself that he had not actually agreed a date for the letter's delivery, and on the strength of this decided that there was surely time for a drink to celebrate the successful completion of his commission. With that he hit the bar in the nearest town, and launched himself on a three week drinking spree.

Tucked in his saddle bag, nestled against a greasy and rapidly decomposing slice of ham which he had bought for a meal and then forgotten about, the letter accompanied the preacher as he made his increasingly unsteady way around the local watering holes. It fell into the hands of a red-headed barmaid who passed it on to a sailor whose ship was leaving for England the following week. But the sailor started drinking with the preacher and so the barmaid, who had had a Lutheran up-bringing and was quite conscientious, took it back, and passed it to a handsome Italian captain with gold braid on his hat. The captain however despite the gold braid was morally rather lax, and the letter drifted into the hands of a one legged black whore and onto a couple of gentlemen of her acquaintance before arriving by a circuitous route on the very ship it had originally been intended for and beginning its long journey back to Devon.

By this time the greasy, dog-eared, faded, beer and salt water stained missive that Aaron and Ellen – who suffered from a similar affliction regarding their lettering as John Henry – had deciphered for them some ten months later, could just as easily have conveyed the information that Uncle John Henry had acquired a dynamo, and married the donkey.

After this Uncle James shipped out to the United States.

He told everyone he was going to make his fortune, but I guess he failed, because in all the intervening years there was only word of him once. That came from a Cornish tin miner who had been in America and was on his way back to Penzance. "Jimmy says to say he's well", he told the assembled relatives waiting breathlessly for news.

"That's all…?" Grandfer Thomas asked finally.

The man nodded. He took off his greasy cap and scratched his balding head. "Yep…" he said.

The miner stayed on for two days until his ship left and he drew us a map of the United States of America in the sand and put a cross somewhere near the middle and said that that was where Uncle James was, in Acron, Ohio.

To my eyes that little cross looked lonely and a bit miserable all by itself, and I wondered if that was why Uncle James had never sent a message before. Certainly he was a long way from the sea which all agreed was not proper for a man born in Batson.

Grace the second youngest and the black sheep of the family, ran away to London on board a trading ship and was never heard of again. It was said she followed a man with black curling hair and a gold earring in his ear but that was all we knew of him. It took us boys years to make sense of them all and their families and our multitude of cousins.

Born in Batson, Aaron was educated at Harry's School in Courtenay Street until he was nine, when as was usual then, he was taken away to begin work on his father's farm. He received a little more schooling after this, but it was spasmodic. Thomas Murch died when Aaron was thirteen. He had gambled and drunk away the little money he had earned in his lifetime, but he passed on the tenancy of the farmland he worked to his brother William, on condition that he apprentice Aaron when he was old enough. His uncle kept his word and in time Aaron was apprenticed as a shipwright in Bonkers yard in Salcombe.

I think that boat building must always have gone on in the estuary. My father used to tell us stories of a mythical race known as the Sewr folk who lived around Bolt Head at the dawn of time. He said that Soar Mill Cove, or as we knew it Sewer Mill Cove, was named for them and that although they built their settlements on high ground as protection from raiders from across the sea, they used the estuary and its creeks as their main thoroughfares.. He maintained that these people traded with the Continent and beyond, even then. It was many years later that a Bronze Age wreck containing French made weapons and jewellery was discovered off the coast of Salcombe, which proved that the old folk stories that Aaron had told us were true and that ships carrying a variety of goods from across Europe and further afield had traded with Devon from the earliest times.   But it was Portlemouth – literally the "mouth of the port" – surmounting the hillside on the eastern side of the estuary which had at first been the more important boat building centre, our father told us.

In the course of his work at "Ringrone" he had several times met the eminent historian J A Froude who was then living at "The Moult". This gentleman admired the work my father had done in Ringrone's rose gardens, and asked for tips on how to look after his own roses, so in time despite the differences in their stations, they often talked together. They shared a common interest in both fishing and sailing boats which helped. Aaron had an excellent memory and he remembered all Mr Froude told him, and passed it on to us word for word, giving us second hand the sort of history lessons only afforded to boys from the best schools. Thus it was that we came by the information that in 1342, in the first recorded mention of the Haven, Portlemouth had supplied 12 barges and a ballinger or whaling boat, to transport English soldiers and archers to Brittany as disputes about land held by the English crown in France rolled on in what would eventually come to be known as the One Hundred Years War. Typical of Aaron was his irreverent delight in the apocryphal story that after disembarking the troops at Brest, at least two of the Portlemouth boats had deserted and returned home. Aaron always maintained that the estuary was the best place in the whole world to be.

Batson Creek. c 1910. Murch

It was from Aaron's conversations with Mr Froude that we boys learned about the French Campaigns in 1346, and the vast fleet that was raised from all the English ports to transport the ten thousand English bowmen who won the day at Crecy. East Portlemouth had supplied five ships and 96 men for this campaign, a figure that reflected the considerable size of that village before its much later partial demolition by its owner. But I have to admit that for both Frank and me these facts paled into insignificance when, after making us swear never to tell our mother, Aaron showed us how to make the victory sign that these English archers had made at Agincourt to show the French - who habitually cut off the first and second fingers of captured bowmen – that they still had their bow fingers!

The boats being built in our estuary back then were mostly small fishing vessels Mr Froude told my father. Even by 1580, Salcombe was registered as having only one ship over 100 tons weight. Twelve years later however, a list of 130 ships accredited to Devon showed Salcombe with five vessels over that size. By 1588, when called upon, the towns and villages around the Haven were able jointly to fit out 16 sea going vessels to sail with Drake to repulse the Spanish Armada which had been first spotted from the tower of a local church.

There had always been plenty of fish around our shores to feed the town and outlying hamlets, and to supply passing and harbour bound ships. The roads in and out of Salcombe were notoriously bad even by the standards of the day, and though some shellfish and salted herring were sent further inland, transportation of fresh caught fish beyond the immediate area was rarely attempted. But as the population increased and Church influence encouraged the eating of fish on Fridays, boats from further around the coast began fishing Devon waters, forcing the estuary boats to travel further for their catch. Built for our own waters but already seine netting as far away as Ireland, the Salcombe fleet began to sail further and further during times when the fishing was poor, until finally they reached the shores of Newfoundland and discovered the plentiful cod on the Grand Banks.

Cod with its firm, dense flesh was the prize. Ideal for salting and drying it was a staple food for victualling ships for long journeys and it found a ready market in Europe. With salt cod in their holds, and a virtual monopoly on the trade, the Salcombe fishing fleet began to prosper as never before.

By the third quarter of the sixteenth century the tiny number of Salcombe boats leaving annually for Newfoundland had turned into a fleet. Our small estuary boats with their traditional fore and aft sails were highly manoeuvrable, ideal for the narrow rocky creeks and bays of the northern coasts. Sailing at first to Spain or Portugal to load salt, they went straight on to the fishing grounds.

The catch was transferred to larger vessels lying offshore and salted at sea before being taken ashore, tied in pairs and hung out to be dried by the sun and wind. The nature of this trade required men to stay on shore to keep guard over the huge drying racks during the months after the spring and summer catch until the boats left again for home in the autumn. Facing long months without companionship, some of the men brought out their wives and families, and often settled in the country for years at a time. In many cases they cut their ties with their homeland altogether. It is why today so many families in Newfoundland and the eastern seaports of North America can trace their ancestry back to Salcombe.

The dried fish came to be separated into three grades depending on size and quality, with each grade best suited to a different market. Ship owners arranged cargoes for the return voyage at each stage, for the masters rarely set sail without a full hold to pay for the journey. Thus when the Grade I fish went to Europe and Spain, the ships carried back oranges and lemons bound for the London markets on the return run. Grade 2 fish were destined for the Mediterranean from where the home bound cargo was dried fruit. Grade 3 was earmarked for the South American markets, where the boats loaded pomelos and the much prized pineapples from the Azores which fetched high prices in the London markets for their novelty value. From London, on the third leg of what became a triangular voyage, the ships took on cargoes of candles, soap, cloth, lamp oil, groceries and other necessities for the trip back to Salcombe.

With the numbers of settlers in Newfoundland growing, boats going out to the fishing grounds began routinely to carry essential supplies and orders. Iron castings, cooking pots and boat parts from the Lidstone factory in Kingsbridge, including the ranges similar to those on which the settlers families had cooked in their old homes were taken out, as was flour, sugar, malt, cider, ale, sails, ropes, clothing, shoes, paper, even small boats … in short everything that was needed by an embryo society which as yet manufactured nothing, As some settlers moved on south to the American East Coast states of New England, the trade expanded, continuing and enlarging during the next century.

And all the time that this far off trade was taking place, the coastal ships which were the life blood of the harbour continued plodding around the coast in their steady and undemanding way, hauling primarily bulky, low value cargoes, exporting slate from the Charleton and Frogmore quarries to the Low Countries; pilchards, barley, cider, potatoes, malt, grain and livestock around the southern coast, and bringing in coal and anthracite from South Wales. Devon was the leading importer of culm, small hard pieces of anthracite coal which was used to fuel the kilns to produce the fertiliser lime, which besides being exported, was used as paint to protect cob walled cottages, and put on the fields to lighten our heavy red Devon soil.

Throughout the 17th and 18th centuries piracy was rife along the South Devon coast. It was particularly bad in Salcombe which was known as a place so lawless than the king himself was petitioned to do something about the gangs of men up to 200 strong that controlled town and harbour, and the boats that lurked in the creeks ready to waylay any ship that passed.

Ships in home waters had often been subjected to boarding and attack, but now with the ending of the wars with France, the English navy was free to concentrate once more on the seas around its coast, and the problem of piracy was tackled and ended. With the shipping routes safe, there was an explosion of trade. Britain with her strong Navy now ruled the waves, and her ships criss-crossed the globe exporting and bringing back a multitude of trade goods.

To sustain this increase in trade more shipyards sprang up in Salcombe, and this in turn created the need for the many associated trades, sailmakers, spur and blockmakers, stevedores, riggers, carpenters, shipwrights and ships chandlers, to name but few.

Ship building yards, Salcombe. c 1878. J Fairweather.

Rope making had been carried out in Kingsbridge from 1783 to satisfy demand from the Royal and Merchant Navy which had barracks in Kingsbridge, the Haven shipyards and the Newfoundland and Labrador fisheries. By 1820 there was need for an additional Rope Walk. By 1837, when the Kingsbridge shipyards began building ships the two rope walks alongside the estuary were employing in the region of 30 men and boys. The industry brought increased trade into the town and more butchers, grocers, bakeries and dairies sprung up together with additional public houses to quench the thirst of the sailors, and the female companions who always appeared where the ships tied up.

But it was Salcombe, ideally placed at the end of the English Channel, with a harbour that provided shelter no matter what the wind direction, that was the natural refuge for ships beating their way up or down the south coast. In bad weather in the 1840's Grandfer Cranch told us, it was not uncommon to see upwards of 200 ships riding at anchor or victualling in the port from abundant local supplies. A multitude of cargoes passed through the town, or were transhipped on as vessels replenished their stores with West Country fresh meat, dried fish, cider, ale, bread, salt tack biscuits, flour, salt beef, cheese and rum.

Flushed with this new prosperity, the yards began building bigger boats to take advantage of the trade, even though until 1839 Salcombe still came under the customs registrations of the Port of Dartmouth.

The "Endymion" 251 tons, built by Evans, Salcombe.
Launched 22nd November 1870

But there were dark clouds on the horizon. Trawling was by now being used much more extensively following practises being adopted by ports such as Brixham and Dartmouth, and now other boats began to follow the Salcombe fleet to the Grand Banks. These fleets brought their fish back to ports near the large urban conurbations in the North East and Midlands where the now improved road and new railway links had opened up access to untapped markets. It was inevitable that these boats also loaded the salt cod that had for so long been Salcombe's traditional cargo.

The railways were now expanding rapidly throughout the country, and Salcombe consoled itself with the belief that the line, which had already reached Kingsbridge, would soon arrive and transform the market for its fish, crabs and lobster. The sight of the sombre-suited, top-hatted surveyors measuring the land around Snapes, only further convinced everyone that a brighter future was just around the corner.   Enthusiastic investors had already put money into excavating a road around to the point... Then abruptly hopes were dashed, as following delay after delay, it was announced that the railway would by-pass Salcombe.

It was a bitter blow. To add to this Salcombe cod fishers now discovered that the Newfoundland salters, who had recently formed a co-operative, had now started to build their own ships with the expressed intention of cutting out foreign fishermen.

Seeing the way the economic wind was blowing, a few astute Salcombe investors began pushing service industries and lines of credit to the Newfoundland and North American settlers. But it was obvious that this alone was not enough to replace the lucrative cod trade. Already used to bringing back fruit as a return load, the ship owners began to investigate the possibility of increasing this trade

They started to convert boats specifically for the purpose and were rewarded by excellent returns.

Brig. "Phantom" 249 tons. Built by Joseph Evans, Salcombe.
Launched 14th December 1867.

Employing the knowledge they gained, the yards gradually began turning out bigger, faster boats with an optimum cargo capacity, and so the famous Salcombe fruit schooners were born.

Speed was everything if the fruit was to reach the London markets in top condition and command the highest prices. As a youngster I stood on Bolt Head one summer afternoon and watched one of the last of these windjammers flying up the Channel on a following wind. The breeze carried the creak of the sheets in the tackle blocks, and the hiss of water as the ship's hull sliced through the waves. The sun shone on the billowing sails, and I thought that I had never in my life seen anything so completely in tune with its environment.

Competition was fierce and the boats raced each other to be the first of the season to land their cargo. There was extensive betting on the end result.

My father told us that as a boy he had several times been sent out to the cliffs with a spyglass to try and make out the name on a ship as it passed the harbour entrance. He was then tasked with running as fast as he could back down through the street to where his father sat in the Ferry Inn together with several cronies who had heavy bets placed on the outcome. Since the names of the boats were sometimes deliberately obscured to lengthen the odds, it was a ploy that was not always successful.

Fruit ships in harbour in Madeira. c 1870

The Channel run of these fruit ships to the capital was one at which the Salcombe boats excelled. Our masters were so skilled that they could get right up to London Bridge under sail with no pilot, my father told us. As they came up the Thames, he said they would fix a pineapple on the bowsprit to advertise their wares.

Demand for the produce was high and the profits to be made by the successful boats were even higher, but it came at a dreadful cost, for almost half of all the boats engaged in the fruit trade were lost, many with all hands. But there would always be those who would risk everything for profit, and so the estuary yards were busy replacing the lost ships and building ever more.

The success of these boats was almost solely responsible for bringing money and work into Salcombe, and the town began to grow rapidly The construction of the Holy Trinity Church in 1843 meant that Salcombe finally shook off the mantle of Malborough to become a parish in its own right. By the mid-1840's trade had increased enough for it to be awarded the status of customs post, and the foundation stone for the solid, four-square quayside Customs House was laid in 1847.

Holy Trinity Church, Salcombe. J Fairweather.

The Salcombe yards were all busy, and to keep pace with demand, boat building expanded on reclaimed land on what had formerly been known as Shabbycombe, but which now became Shadycombe Creek.

A customs return dated 1848, showed 355 vessels entering the port with a total of almost 17,000 tons of cargo, mainly coal, fruit, groceries and slate. The remaining vessels sailed in ballast.

Trade reached its peak in the 1850's. During 1855 and '56 records show that vessels from South Devon entered the Port of London on 419 separate occasions.

They brought tea from Shanghai, wool from Buenos Aires, sugar from

Old photo.of Shabbicombe now Shadycombe. Att. to J Fairweather

Demerara and glass from Antwerp, but the vast majority of the craft arriving between October and February on the by now celebrated triangular voyages, carried oranges and lemons from Seville, Gijon and St. Michael's in the Azores, or currants and raisins from the Greek Islands of Zante and Cephalonia.

There were by now around 150 vessels registered in the port, trading regularly with Newfoundland, South America, India and even as far away as the China coast. In total during the 19th century nearly 300 sailing ships were built around the shores of the Haven, almost all for local owners. . Ship builders John Evans and John Ball of Salcombe and William Date of Kingsbridge had begun to build large numbers of craft from the 1830's – three boats the "Water Witch", the 200 ton "Phoenix", and the 150 ton "Renovatio" were launched by John Ball's yard in one week alone. It was Salcombe's golden age.

In 1872 when my father Aaron was apprenticed at Bonker's Shipyard it seemed as if nothing could stop this inexorable rise in the town's fortunes.
He must have truly believed that he had achieved the goal of every Devon man: to earn his keep – maybe even riches - without having to leave the beauty of his own home town. If so, he would indeed have been a happy man, for Aaron loved Salcombe with every fibre of his being.

Outwardly the prosperity of the Haven continued. In 1864 there were 98 foreign going vessels and as many harbour and coastal ships in the estuary. The registered tonnage had gone up from around 11,000 tons to almost

Fruit ships in Salcombe harbour. c 1868. J Fairweather.

18,000, though this was largely because of the increase in the size of the vessels. But things were changing in the outside world, and fickle Fate chose this moment to play her hand, as disease struck the fruit trade. The advent of the steam engine and iron hulled boats had already brought massive changes in the rest of the country, and gradually, inevitably, the fall out reached Devon and the Estuary.

Orders for new ships declined rapidly. The shipyards became quieter and the sound of hammering and sawing that had once reverberated around the haven, was silenced. Joseph Evans launched his last vessel, the 289 ton brig "Creole", built for R H Sladen of Salcombe, in 1878, and as orders dried up my father was laid off. By 1880 the number of vessels launched from Salcombe yards was down to 80, and by 1885 it had fallen to 61. By 1890 it had dropped to twenty. Ancilliary workers began packing their tools and heading out with their families. Businesses dependent on the ships for their livelihoods had already seen a serious decline in profits, and some of their owners were eyeing up other, bigger and more prosperous ports. With many already heading to the naval dockyards of Plymouth and Portsmouth and others to the yards around the Tyne and Wear, they now began deserting the town like rats from a sinking ship.

Competition from first iron and later steam driven boats began to take the trade from the remaining sailing ships. The East Coast shipbuilders started to produce sturdy, reliable boats that were ideally suited to the coastal trade.

Their strength of course was that they were not dependent upon the weather. They did not have the speed of a racing clipper, but equally they could keep puffing along steadily when the winds had died and a sailing ship would have been becalmed, at risk of losing most if not all of its precious cargo.

Belatedly seeing the way things were going, the Salcombe shipyards tried to change. Five steam ships were built in the estuary, but the area was not best placed to develop these new designs. Lack of capital, a skill base of wooden shipbuilding, as well as limitations of space and a shortage of locally available materials made it impractical for Salcombe to compete with the yards of Northern and Eastern England and Scotland. Besides, the town's heart was in its sailing ships. The sight of a steamer belching smoke, chugging along the shipping lanes, could not compare in our eyes with the sheer majesty of a tall ship under way.

Almost overnight orders for Salcombe ships ceased. The town's brief heyday was over. The last sizeable wooden ship was launched in the estuary about the time of my birth. Thereafter Salcombe reverted to boatbuilding for fishermen and, increasingly, for leisure use, as tourists and day trippers carried on the railway to Kingsbridge began to arrive in the town in charabancs, and the new motor coaches and automobiles, and then the first paddle steamers to ply the Estuary. With them came a new breed of gentleman sailors who discovered for themselves the attractions of the harbour. Hot on their heels came visitors who found the unspoilt beauty of the landscape irresistible, and wanted to remain. There were still few of them, but gradually their numbers increased and they moved seamlessly into the homes that the shopkeepers and boat owners had vacated. To meet this new demand, the owners of the larger houses, such as "York House" with its grounds running back from the sea wall and looking across to Snapes, began tentatively turning themselves into bed and breakfasts and hotels.

Work of any sort was becoming scarce and for a while Aaron worked on his uncle's farm. But William Henry, now married and with his own growing family, did not welcome another mouth to feed, and so my father went to sea, shipping out first on the schooner "Daring", then in 1879, signing on as an O.S. on the barquantine "Brizo".

His widowed mother was by then living in a small cottage in Island Street, Salcombe. While Aaron was away, she took in a feisty young lodger, the daughter of neighbours in Batson, to help pay the bills.

Aaron and Ellen had known each other as young children, but the pair had not met for several years, as, with her parents earning barely enough to support themselves, eight year old Ellen had been farmed out to her married sister in Charleton. But when Aaron returned from sea, Ellen Cranch took one look at the big boned, handsome young man with the guileless blue eyes, and decided that she wanted him for herself.

My father went back to sea once more, this time just for a summer. Ellen made it a condition of the marriage that he "swallowed the anchor", in other words, came ashore. She wouldn't have stood for him being at sea. She knew well enough what the sea did to men. Related to the Trout sisters who later so heroically rescued men from the ocean – as indeed was my father - she had already lost a brother to the sea. Years later, in her soft Devon burr, I overheard her warning a girl who had her heart set on marrying a sailor, "Don't 'ee forget the sea is a more exciting mistress than any maid." No, Ellen wanted her husband at home, and what Ellen wanted she always got. Only eighteen when they married she was already a skilled dressmaker, and a determined, forceful young woman. The fact that the "Brizo" was later lost with all hands in the North Sea, only reinforced what she saw as the right decision having been made.

"Ringrone House" from East Portlemouth. J Fairweather.

So Aaron obtained his job as Under Gardener at "Ringrone House", and married Ellen, digging and planting with one eye on the harbour and the ships that came and went. His duties included maintaining his employer's general purpose boat, and most days he spent some hours down on the waterfront. There were times, especially in the summer or during the autumn party season when he rowed across the harbour several times in the course of the day or evening, taking the family and their friends to the beach, to dinner or entertainment with friends and acquaintances living on the East Portlemouth side. He was, I think, a deeply contented man.

Almost two years after my birth we moved house. The new cottage called "The Nook" was barely eighty yards away, further inland than the cottage where I had been born, set on the same high ridge and overlooking the centre of Batson and the creek. It was again a tied house that went with his work, so I suppose Aaron must have pleased his employer to gain this advancement. His position was now that of "Gardener".

"The Nook" was a detached house, much bigger than our last, and with a garden enclosed within stone walls. Like our previous cottage it backed onto the rolling green hills behind, where the noises of grazing sheep had often kept my brother and me company through the night. But "The Nook" had its own toilet in the garden which meant much greater privacy. The other wonderful thing about "The Nook" was that the small attic room where my brother and I slept, was to us just as we imagined a ship's cabin to be. In storms its ancient roof timbers creaked and groaned just as my father said the old boats used to, and the rain pattered against the lead lights of the windows creating a cosy safe haven of the bed where we lay.

It was while we were at "The Nook" that our youngest brother Frederik was born. Strangely for me this major event paled into insignificance beside the fact that at about the same time Frank burned his arm on my mother's flat iron. I have to say that Frank had in the meantime convinced me that the new baby would not be staying in the household, so I really felt I had little to gain by showing any particular interest in him. Whereas Frank, with his scorched flesh and piercing shrieks provided an absorbing spectacle. But it was the aftermath of my brother's accident that stayed in my memory most clearly.

The home remedy then for a burn was to wrap it in milk-soaked cloth, leaving the wrapping in place until the burn had healed, so as to minimise the risk of scarring. My mother grabbed the first piece of material that came to hand to use for the emergency, which was a piece of pale pink silk wedding dress lavishly embroidered with flamboyant darker pink roses that she was working on at the time. Dunking it in the milk pail, she bound it tightly around Frank's arm. The widespread teasing and subsequent agonies of embarrassment that my brother endured in the days that followed caused the whole family no end of amusement.

When we were very small, my elder brother and I played in the fields or the foreshore below the cottage with the other children of the hamlet. We were boys, full of energy that could not be contained, and we were into everything. While Frederik, whom my mother assured me tersely was definitely to remain in the household, slept in his cradle, Frank and I got into mischief. As we grew older, no matter how frequently my mother swatted us with her dishcloth, hauling us apart amid dire warnings of what would befall us if we did not behave, my brother and I often fought. I still carry the scar as a reminder of an argument which erupted about which one of us should be in charge of wheeling our small wheelbarrow containing a barrel of salt which we had been charged to bring back from the quay at Shadycombe. I was barely two years old then, so I must have been truculent early in life.

People then had big families, and there were always little knots of children gathering at the slightest indication that something interesting might be happening. The older ones looked after the younger, but we knew everyone we met and they knew us, and like all youngsters then, we almost certainly gained from the open handed policy in which all the hamlet seemed to feel it incumbent upon them to contribute in some way to our upbringing.

Children then seemed to belong to all. I lost count of the number of times that we were rescued from scrapes or impending disasters, returned to our mother covered in mud or soaking wet from a tumble into the creek. Once I was rescued from the top of the lime kiln by Ilberstow Manor which Frank had dared me to climb.

Another time we were both picked up off rocks where we had become marooned by the rising tide. Neighbours summarily dispensed rough justice then, not hesitating to clip a child around the ear or paddle their backsides when they deemed it necessary, although more often than not this was tempered by the gift of an apple or a piece of pastry after our tears had been wiped away and a handkerchief pressed to our small noses with the firm instruction to "blow" into it.

Hamlets then were not deserted for most of the year as they are now. I remember them to have been always full to bursting, teeming with noisy life. Cottage doors seemed always to be open with people continually coming and going. My memories are of old women in aprons sitting in doorways shelling peas, slicing beans, plucking a chicken, or peeling potatoes, tasked with keeping a weather eye on crawling babies; a woman knitting, or mending, or braiding a child's hair, patching a pair of trousers, or turning the collar of a shirt as she gossiped with passers-by. The men usually only met up in the evenings when they came back from the fields. You would see a man honing a sythe, repairing a crab pot or a fishing net, but more often than not they retired to the pub to ease aching muscles and parched throats with a much needed drink. They died young generally, these farmers and seamen, worn out like pack horses, though some went on until they shrivelled into little more than sun burnt sinew and bone. These old men in their smocks had their own place on the seashore further around towards the point. They seemed to us children hardly to talk at all. I remember them gathering with their white clay pipes, lengthy puffs punctuated by sparse remarks, then more companionable, lengthy puffs. They had known each other all their lives so I suppose they had little left to talk about. A wedding, a new baby, or a change in someone's circumstances or behaviour was the trigger for a babble of talk amongst the women who met by the pump. The loss of a ship, the launch of a new fishing boat, or the arrival of the grooms from the Shadycombe stables where the gentlemen's horses were kept, occasioning the close examination and discussion of the finer points of some thoroughbred seemed to be about the only things that stirred the old men to conversation, though a cargo unloading at the quay, a mettlesome horse at the smithy, or the aftermath of a drowning, fishing or sailing accident attracted all comers and always drew a large crowd.

Staff outside Batson Old Post Office. C 1897. J Valentine

Most of the villagers were away in the fields or at work in Salcombe during the day, but in the evening they returned, and often then you would see young couples walking in the twilight in the direction of Shadycombe, or climbing up into the fields towards Snapes, their heads bent together, completely absorbed in each other. Sometimes in the warm summer gloaming they made babies in the shelter of the hedgerows, or the thick warmth of a haystack. They said that many children owed their existence to the warm, light summer nights.

People in those days did not shut themselves off from their neighbours: whatever affected one, affected all. If a cottager was sick or injured, or was going through hard times, others helped out...It was needed if families were to survive, and survival was the best that any of us could hope for.

Nearly all our neighbours were farmers or agricultural labourers, and these families relied upon every pair of hands however small to help with the household finances. The Education Act of 1870 which decreed that children should stay at school until the age of 12 had not been welcomed by most Devon families. Opposition to the Act had been as fierce as it had been to the initial introduction of schooling for the masses, when land owners in Devon had joined with local employers in arguing that education would make the labouring classes think, and that once having begun that process, they would in all likelihood find their lives dissatisfying. Even so, in Devon, the harvest, a wreck, or family need still took preference and resulted in a child being kept back from school.

Both boys and girls worked from as soon as they were able. Apprenticeship was one of the few ways out of poverty, but it was only available to those whose parents could afford it. If the parents were in trade it gave the lucky ones a ready-made job. There were few enough jobs for men, fewer still for women. It was an economic choice for most girls to marry early. For their hard pressed parents, it was one less mouth to feed. Lives followed a set pattern; all was inevitable, unchanging and unchanged through the centuries, the passage of time marked by the visits of the journeymen, knife grinders, or pedlars with their trays of desirable, brightly coloured wares.

It was those who brought news of the outside world who were most welcomed, but there were characters who were interesting enough in their own right to attract a big following.

One of these was an ancient traveller who said he had fought in the Crimean War. He was on his way through to Exeter to meet up with an old comrade he said. Though in the next breath he said he was walking to London to take tea with the queen. He told us tales of battles in the Crimea, and sea battles with dreadful monsters. But it was his badly deformed face that drew us children, and kept us spellbound in front of him, because there was a large, gaping hole where part of his chin and cheek should have been. He had been struck in the face by a musket ball he told us. The ball had removed all his teeth and a portion of his jaw. He couldn't afford new teeth, he said, so as he had been a carpenter by trade, he made himself some new ones. Those teeth fascinated us. They were made of wood painted white, and were as big as tombstones. Owing to the hole in his face you could see them clearly. They clacked when he swore, which he did a lot. He cussed non-stop in a loud, broken voice invoking not only doubtful parentage, but farmyard animals and strange practises which went totally over our heads, but we children thought he was marvellous, and followed him around throughout his stay. It was summer and he made himself a bed in the hedgerow near the style that led up into the fields. He stayed for two, mebbe three days. Then just as we were beginning to get used to having him around, he disappeared overnight with the money that Prowse the pig sticker had earned working down at Batson Hill Farm.

On another memorable occasion, a hurdy gurdy man with a monkey in a little blue jacket with shiny brass buttons walked into the hamlet. He had performed in Salcombe and was making his way through to Kingsbridge. He set up his pitch on the beach and began turning the handle to make his tinkling music. It attracted a big crowd as everyone came out of their cottages or barns to listen, and watch the antics of the little monkey who held out a cup so prettily to collect money. But the hurdy gurdy man soon found that no-one had any money in Batson, and he packed up bad temperedly and went on his way.

But these visits were few and far between. For most of the time we lived in a still backwater, far removed from the power and force of the sea and the doings of the world. It was a place where life went on it as it had done for hundreds if not thousands of years, set to the old diurnal cycle, and even from our youngest years, we children grew used to its daily routine.

We were awoken by the cockerels crowing on the farms around us, and soon after heard the cows being brought down from the top fields for milking. We knew the sounds the different women used to call the chickens, Mrs Ford's "cooee-cooee", Mrs Chant's "cluckety cluckety" followed by the rattle of the pannikins, and then Mrs Weymouth's "whooo whooo whooo", which we tried hard to imitate but never managed. We heard farmer John Ford's morning whistle for his dog Rustler, and the collie's anticipatory excited yelps. By the time we had eaten our breakfast the wild cats had been called for their food by the mad old woman at the top of the hill who fed them and watched them multiply and grow fat on the huge numbers of rats in neighbouring barns, and the first cart of the day was rumbling down the lane on its way to Salcombe with milk for the town's breakfasts.

Gradually my world expanded to take in the hills and lanes just beyond Batson's huddled stone cottages. The banks of the lanes were filled with wild flowers in the spring, so plentiful that my mother used to say that you could not put a hand down without it touching a blossom. After the rains, rivulets of spring water ran down these banks as dark red run off from the sweet smelling soil. I remember the cool, shady green tunnels that the trees formed overhead and the little streams tinkling down the hill over the stones, where horses and dogs drank on summer days. When I was just a little bigger, I followed that stream one day and found to my astonishment that it flowed into the sea.

At first the sea for me was only the water that lapped at the sea wall near our garden gate. I knew Batson creek as well as I knew my own home, the cottages and beach at its heart, the tall elms and craggy oaks on the hilltops, the sandy stony foreshore below the overhanging blackthorns that wound around to Shadycombe. I knew the position of the lime kilns and Snapes

Manor, the big house nestling in the fold of land, on the eastern side of the creek. I had once ventured far enough from home to glimpse the masts of a barge, and the roof of a boat shed in Shadycombe. I had seen cottages huddled under grey slate roofs and had a confused impression of a big circular red construction that must have been the gasometer, and above it the solid, square tower of the church set in a green churchyard dotted with white grave stones. A part of me was aware that somewhere close to us were many other people whom I did not know, living in another place which I knew of as Salcombe, but this was part of a secret world that as yet I could not enter.

Then one day we boys walked with our father out from the hamlet behind the big house and on out to Snapes Point and I discovered to my utter amazement that my little, familiar world was only a small part of a much greater whole.

We stood together on a finger of land jutting out into an estuary so much greater than the one I knew, that I felt I was looking at a vast ocean. I was perhaps two and a half. My youngest brother was in my father's arms, my elder brother had just turned four and was already going to school, so I suppose he must have seen this before, but for me it was as if my world had suddenly exploded, changed from black and white to a riot of glorious colour, as if everything that had hitherto been silent was now charged with a fantastic diapason of sound.

Awestruck, I drank in the sight of the harbour and town spread out before me, the myriad ranks of grey slate roofed houses straggling down the hillside, the deep blues of the sea and the rolling green hills with the yellow beaches at their feet. The beauty of the place touched me in some indefinable way. My breath caught in my throat and my heart expanded with a feeling so all-encompassing and complete that it was as if there was no room in my body for anything else. I knew suddenly that this was not just my home, but the one spot on God's earth where I belonged.

I looked down the harbour to the twin, towering cliffs at the entrance. They were dark, lowering shapes even in the sunshine and I glimpsed for the first time the sparkling, dancing ocean beyond. Aaron had sailed out past the houses and the beaches and the cliffs into the brilliant, enchanted sunlight that dissolved into a line of pure blue under the sky.

At last, as I stood in silence staring, I understood where my father had been when he had gone to sea. This place, this magical entity outside the harbour entrance had nothing to do with the gentle sea that lapped the beach near my home or even this estuary.

I was awestruck, no, more than that, I was consumed by the vision. Beside me Frank too, was staring as if he could not get his fill and I knew that he too had been stricken by the same sudden intense longing to journey outside that habour, beyond the narrow entrance and out into the open

Salcombe and Harbour from Ilbertstowe c 1900. J Fairweather

ocean. I guess our mouths must have been hanging open as we stood and stared, because I remember my father giving a short bark of a laugh, unlike his normal sound, and saying, "The call of the sea... You're only babes yet, but you can feel it too, can't you?"

He was unusually sombre as we walked back. I think he knew then that one day all three of his sons would go to sea.

CHAPTER TWO

My father had always been in work. Though there were many times when things must have been difficult for our parents, we boys always had food in our stomachs and clothes on our backs. It helped that we were so close in age, because our shirts, jackets and trousers were not completely worn out when we each inherited them from an elder brother. It was not until Fred had also outgrown them that our well patched clothes were washed and given to poorer children than us, because my mother instilled in us that there were always people in greater need than ourselves. Our boots followed a similar trail being finally donated to the Salcombe Boot Club, which dispensed footwear for children who would otherwise have gone without. We wore boots all year round unlike many children around the Estuary who went barefoot in the summer. It was my misfortune though that Frank's feet grew quicker and were much bigger than mine when I was small, so that I spent most of my formative years with my footwear packed so plentifully with newspaper that it seemed as if they had a life of their own independent of my feet. Even worse though was when my feet took on a sudden spurt when I was older, and ended up being bigger than his!

Now that I had seen Salcombe for myself, I was consumed with the desire to go there. The town had become a Mecca for me, promising all that was exciting, forbidden and unattainable. It was I suppose inevitable given the strong willed child I was, that I should try on several occasions to make my way there by myself, only to be brought unceremoniously back by some adult with a firm grip on my ear or the seat of my trousers. I was due to start school when I was three but I already considered myself old enough to follow my elder brother, so it was more than frustrating to have to wait.

Frank was now away at school during the day. Fred was still too young to provide any source of entertainment, so along with the other Batson youngsters I was left largely to my own devices. But life was full. Like the shoaling minnows we caught in the stream in the woods, quick silver and fast moving, we flowed through the hamlet, running and shouting and tumbling in our games until the need for food or sleep stopped us in our tracks.

We possessed no toys, but we had no idea that people might consider us deprived. We utilised the oddments lying around for our entertainment. An old fish box, a plank of wood or a tangle of discarded rope kept us amused. We climbed trees and built dams in the streams. We gathered teasels which had a market with weavers who used them to comb out wool. We traipsed through the fields and made dens in the crop fields when the wheat, barley or corn had grown high enough. We made slingshots and tried to hit targets. Once in a while a discarded iron cart rim came our way and was bowled gleefully up and down the lane with the help of a stick; stacked crab and lobster pots made climbing frames. More dangerous was the game of setting off the gin traps that had been placed for rabbit or badger that resulted in several serious accidents. The girls had their own games, hopscotch and skipping or playing house which they tried unsuccessfully to get us to join in. One or two of the smaller girls owned cloth dolls that their mothers had made.

Lower Batson. White building on right, shown end on is "The Nook". Torre Hill Farm buildings are directly above. c. 1896.J Fairweather.

There was beachcombing which sometimes yielded mysterious treasures, a seed that my father said had probably come all the way from South America; a piece of driftwood with part of a boat's name painted on it; a stave from a barrel or a keg or something that had washed overboard from a ship. Once Frank found a piece of a flesh coloured wooden arm that we guessed must have come from the figurehead of a wrecked ship. Rock pooling whiled away many hours. Completely oblivious to anything else, we crouched silently over tiny marine worlds, carefully moving aside rocks to reveal the flash of a hidden fish, transparent shrimps or a shuffling hermit crab. But for the most part our entertainment revolved around the everyday events that went on around us, fishermen bringing ashore their catch of shining, flapping fish; a new brood of piglets at one of the farms; the endlessly fascinating hatchings of tiny ducklings, and fluffy yellow chicks; the mending of a plough or harrow, or the hitching up of a shire. Once in a while a farmer would lift us up onto his horse to ride in front of him, or one of his farm hands would let us climb onto a cart going up the lane; we hung around the Smithy, watching the blacksmith made superhuman by flying sparks and firelight as he hammered white hot metal on his anvil, or forged horseshoes or farming implements; we circled lobster as they were landed, lost in wonderment at that majestic doyenne of the seas; we dared each other to prod the snapping claws of large crabs that were strong enough to have easily chopped off our fingers if not our skinny, grubby arms.

After the autumn storms had torn the seaweed from the rocks we struggled to help the farm boys lifting armfuls of the slippery, slimy stuff onto the donkey cart then followed it to the fields where the farm workers spread it out on the land as fertiliser. We walked behind the geese as they waddled through the hamlet, collecting their feathers and the fluffy white down they shed as we had been taught, and taking it carefully home to our mothers to use in plumping out the family bedding. We taunted the gander to see him stand tall, hissing and flapping his powerful wings in a display that was meant to see us off. We watched the swans sailing in proudly like white ships on the full tide. We gathered to see whatever was happening in cottage gardens or doorways; we watched Mrs Strawbridge and her daughter Mary both laundresses, as they plunged their big, muscular arms up to the elbows in washing suds, pumping up and down at the clothes or twirling the dolly stick vigorously between plump soap-reddened hands.

Sometimes the bigger children were tasked with turning the mangle handle as the women fed the dripping garments through, or sometimes we little ones were given the job of holding up the pegs for them as a lady or gentleman's clothes were hung out on the line, for the pair walked backwards and forwards from Salcombe two or three times a day with laundry that was delivered or collected from the big houses. Batson was well off for laundresses. In a neighbouring cottage lived Sarah Ash and her married daughter Bessie Dunn who also took in washing. Between the two cottages there was always linen hanging and the smell of lye drifted out on the waves of steam coming from inside. Just a little further up the lane in Higher Batson Cottages, was Lydia Moor also a laundress, who lived with her four year old niece Florence, a child who was a particular friend of mine since she was fearless and could climb any tree just as well as a boy.

Lower Batson c 1896. J Fairweather.

Evening milking time found us gathering at whatever farm we happened to be near in the hope of a mug of warm milk straight from the cow to share between us. We whiled away many hours watching men working. We sat around one legged, old John Collings the stone breaker who lived at Malt House Cottages as he hammered rocks, copying his habit of spitting dust out of his dry mouth, or now and then wiping his bristly, dirt caked face with the grimy neckerchief he wore around his neck. Sometimes if he was in a good mood he told us stories of things that had happened to him long before, but mostly he just chipped away in morose silence. Once in a while if we annoyed him he would lob a piece of limestone at us.

More rewarding was the occasional event such as a fire, which brought men shouting and running with buckets and wet cloths. We villagers dealt with such emergencies by ourselves. Even if the owner had insured the cottage, which you could tell by the iron badge fixed to the building which showed the name of the fire protection office that covered that home, the fire engine would have taken too long to reach us. It was down to every man, woman and child to do their bit, forming a chain stretching up from the beach to get sea water to the site. Fires were not rare, open fireplaces, oil and kerosene lamps, candles, ranges and thatch all played their part in making sure of that, but the fact that there were always so many people around helped to deal with them swiftly when they did occur.

The thatchers came in the wake of the fire or sometimes just because the roof was old and rain drenched and needed renewing. They always seemed to me to be large, confident men with ready laughs and sunburnt faces. They wore big buckled belts and had twine tied around their trousers legs which they said was to stop mice running up them. They came mostly from out of the immediate area, arriving with a cart loaded down with ladders and bundles of bright golden reeds, usually with a couple of mangy, half-starved dogs running alongside. They were paid by the job and so they started work immediately.

Guaranteed a good show we children would set up camp around their cart, determined not to miss anything as the men set their ladders and swarmed up onto the roof with the hooks they used to pull off the thatch.

Cottages at Shadycombe. c 1895 J. Fairweather.

They bestrode the roof as naturally as if they were walking on the ground, striking poses if ever a young woman walked past, and it was not long before the skeleton of twisted, blackened old roof timbers were revealed.

When all the old thatch was off and burning on the seashore to the accompaniment of shrieks from the washerwomen who berated the thatchers for the smuts that assaulted their washing, the men took a break for their dinner, bringing forth huge pasties wrapped in cloth from battered tin boxes. They ate with gusto, now and then tossing a piece of crust to the slavering dogs who fought over it viciously, washing the food down with a flagon of ale or cider which they passed from hand to hand with much smacking of lips.

Then, with a final wipe of their mouths on the backs of their grimy hands, a belch or a visit behind a nearby bush to relieve themselves it was back to the job again.

Salcombe boatyards c 1887. J Fairweather.

While two of the men stood on the roof timbers, sturdy legs spread wide to keep their balance, the others threw up bundles of reeds. The men on the roof stacked them where they were needed, then took them up one by one, tied and twisted them into place and pegged them down. The whole task was done in such a smooth, easy motion that it made it look as if anyone could do it. Before long the thatch was spreading further and further across the roof, and the amount of exposed timber correspondingly lessened. The thatchers worked so quickly that if you looked away for a moment and then back again you could see that they had covered several feet more even in that short time.

Sometimes when they had finished the thatching they fashioned a cockerel or a fox, a badger or a pheasant to sit on the roof for they all had their own individual signatures. But this happened seldom because the cottages were largely for workers to live in and very few masters would pay extra for ornamentation for a worker's home.

The roofers were working men and earned respect for their craftsmanship, as had all those who had served their apprenticeship and become tradesmen. But the thatchers had a particular place in communities like ours which was so cut off from the world, for they brought in news of friends and family from as far away as Kingsbridge, South Pool and

Malborough. They were noisy and lusty and they had knowledge of the wider world, and so their opinions were sought on many matters. They drank in the pub and they slept beneath their cart for the short while they were in the hamlet, and then they were gone again, swaggering off down the road to the next village and the next roof, with money in their pockets and sometimes the heart of a simple village girl as well.

The Workhouse men who came to toil in Batson occasionally were very different beings. They seemed to me to be enveloped in a grey cloak of failure and a sense of impending death. These lines of ancient grey clothed men settled like flies around the pyramid-shaped piles of stones that old John had left beside the lane when the potholes were bad. They picked over the stones, sometimes splitting them down further much to the old man's irritation because he was convinced they did it just to annoy him. Unlike the roofers who were in the lusty prime of life, these men had given up and they worked as a rule infinitely slowly despite the overseer who shouted and bawled at them, calling them slackers and good for nothings. But you could not deny that after they had patched up the lanes walking was much easier than before when you had to pull your feet up out of the mire at every step, even though for days afterwards everything was coated in a fine layer of lime dust.

Sketch of Kingsbridge and District Workhouse.

The dust drove we children to the water, or up into the cool green of the summer meadows. We hung around as farmhands repaired gates or fences, dug out overgrown ditches or coppiced hedges. We followed the plough horses as they plodded slowly up and down the furrows. We tried our hands at a hundred different tasks, and us not old enough to do any one properly except perhaps to scare the birds from the germinating seeds.

We were almost the only ones of God's creatures who were permitted idleness. Perhaps our unfettered joy at life and the sound of our happy, piping voices as we played was some recompense for our hard pressed parents.

Now and then visitors from outside came into the hamlet, as strange to us in their elegant clothes and expensive belongings as beings from another planet. I saw two ladies in big hats carrying sketch books, who settled down for the afternoon on the shore on chairs brought out for them from nearby cottages. A tall man in a dark suit, who people said owned the newspaper in Salcombe came with a camera, and took pictures of us. Some days later he came back and showed us images of ourselves just as we looked, wearing the clothes that we wore, and it was so strange that it frightened us all. He told one of the old men he photographed that he was taking pictures around the Estuary, and that he would see the photographs in the newspaper, and he did too. Afterwards we often saw Mr James Fairweather as he was called, sometimes with his son Ernest whom he was training, but almost always with his big camera, the plates protected by their wooden cases, and the black cloth he put over his head when he operated his machine. You'd see him everywhere taking photographs.

One year about this time some gentlemen came to Batson to fish. They had formed a club in Kingsbridge which people said was called the "Piscators", which was a funny name in itself. They wanted the local fishermen to take them out and they offered good money for it, so there were always plenty of takers. All you had to do was row them to places where outcrops of rocks made for good fishing and sit around while they smoked and dangled their lines in the water, blissfully unaware that only a few feet from where they were fishing in what we considered an averagely good area, there was a particular crag of rock, or a sunken boat that marked really good fishing.

Often as not they had great hampers of food with them, and the local men used to boast amongst themselves of the food their fishermen had partaken of – cold lobster, chicken and meat pies, washed down with wine. Very rarely did the fishermen themselves get any of the food. But it was enough that they had the vicarious glory of being the transporters of these diners. We saw them several times over the course of a few years but then the club disbanded and the fishermen disappeared. I don't think they caught more with their expensive rods than we boys did with our hook and line sinkers. It was the same with the few yachtsmen who appeared in the harbour. They might have had smart boats, but they didn't know their way around the harbour, or the tides and the mud banks and they often had to be rescued, so were for a while another excellent source of local income and amusement.

One day I saw a gentleman's steam yacht moor up off Shadycombe.

Fishermen at Ditch End, East Portlemouth J Fairweather.

There was activity on deck and after a little while two white clad crew launched a small dinghy. Three female figures in light coloured dresses holding parasols were helped into the boat and one of the crew rowed them ashore just a few yards down from where I was investigating a deep and particularly interesting rock pool.

I watched the boatman help the three passengers out onto the shore one by one. Two of the women were elderly, but the other was very young, just a girl, with long, yellow hair tied back with a blue ribbon hanging down her back. Her parasol tilted back as she stepped daintily out onto the muddy shore and she looked across at me and smiled under its shade. But I could only stare at her in wonder. It occurred to me that she must be an angel because she was the cleanest person I had ever seen. She had delicate little feet in pale kid shoes, and I thought it was a shame that she should have to place them on the rough stones. It was years later that I heard of the exploits of Sir Walter Raleigh, but I swear if I had owned a cloak then, I would unhesitatingly have placed it at the feet of this enchanting creature.

But there were more interesting things in life even than angels with pale kid shoes. High on the list of exciting interludes were the periodic rat hunts that took place in the hamlet. The one in Farmer Adams big barn was the first one I remember. Aided by a posse of feral farm cats which looked furious at the idea of sharing their sport with humans, about fifteen men and boys rounded up and cornered perhaps forty rats. They were bunched up in a dark corner of the barn, and you could see their red eyes shining horribly. Then the older boys ran at them with wooden staves, smashing their skulls and throwing them screaming and bloody to the ravening cats. One terrified rat ran up the trouser leg of a Hannaford boy, and he yelled and jumped and danced around. It did not bite him, but his performance made the rest of us laugh until we nearly fell over.

There was almost always something going on in the farmyards, whether t'was animals causing a ruckus, or a cart shedding a wheel. One dark October afternoon Farmer Masters of Torre Hill Farm had a cart horse that was lame in its back leg. He had tied it to a ring in its stable, and was trying to examine its hoof, but the horse was having none of it. Kicking out at the stall's planking, bucking and generally making a fuss it soon attracted a small crowd, including us. Farmer Masters needed help, and he needed it fast. He eyed up the assembling company and decided it was all too puny to be of much help, so he collared my twelve year old cousin James Murch, and Robert Brown from Shadycombe Farm, who happened to be passing. With Robert holding the horse's bridle, he instructed James to take a candle from the shelf and light it, then hold it close to the animal's rear leg so that he could see the problem better. Robert was good with horses, and he was stroking the animal's cheek and talking softly to him, and the horse calmed down as if he sensed that what was going on was for his own good. Seeing things were quiet, Farmer Masters began cleaning the mud off the hoof. He took a folding paring knife out of his pocket, opened it and bent to his task. Gathering quietly in the circle of the candlelight we all drew nearer, craning our necks to see what was happening.

Close to we could all see that the flesh above the shoe was puffy and inflamed. Pulling up a milking stool Farmer began to examine the hoof carefully. Finding a split in the horn which seemed likely to be the source of the infection, he began cutting away at it. It was growing darker in the barn, and he couldn't see properly. Afraid of cutting too deeply and injuring the horse, he instructed James to hold the candle closer. But just then the horse broke wind and the gas hit the candle flame and exploded, knocking Farmer Masters off his milking stool and sending James shooting backwards against the barn wall several feet away, to howls of merriment from all of us watching.

Another time Farmer John Yeoman lost control of his prize bull when he was moving it up to the top pasture where the cows were grazing. It was a huge beast that one, heavy set and brown coated with a white blaze crooked over one eye. It had a reputation that bull. Ask anyone about John Yeoman's prize bull and they'd tell 'ee that that beast was the debil incarnate. He'd gored one man in the leg and broken another's arm, and that was when he was just a youngster. Now, weighing in at several tons and as mean as hell, 'er scented freedom and just took off.

That bull really went on the rampage. 'Er tore through the hamlet, scoring deep grooves in the lane and breaking up the wooden fencing around two gardens, before tangling with a heap of crab pots and sending 'em flying. The crab pots slowed 'er down a bit. 'er pawed the ground and snorted and huffed like a steam engine as if 'er were thinking about it for a while, then 'er put 'er massive head down, swaying from side to side for a bit, and then 'er was off again. Men were jumping every which way, trying to catch him and trying just as hard not to get gored. A pile of kids had taken shelter behind some milk churns. One of the farm boys from Torre Hill Farm was swinging a rope around, as if he meant business, but running like a singed cat whenever the bull looked in his direction. Others were just running. Well when that bull was finally captured down on the foreshore, Batson looked as if a hurricane had swept through it. Everywhere there were people up trees, hiding in doorways or behind walls. One boy had climbed up onto the roof of the Smithy and was laughing so much he couldn't get his self back down again, while old Mother Trute had locked herself in the privy and couldn't be persuaded to come out until several people had yelled through the door that it was safe. Even then she emerged brandishing the shovel and the clinker bucket as if she intended to do battle with them.

There was a great deal to get involved in once I had escaped my mother's vigilance, but for me by far the best part of the day was when first my elder brother and then my father returned home. Frank was now part of a scholarly world that had for the moment firmly excluded me, but when he came back to Batson he brought with him news of Salcombe and the comings and goings of the outside world. Frank's friends were older, and once their chores were completed and their evening meal eaten, they were free to roam much further afield than I was permitted to go alone, and they usually tolerated my presence even though they had a habit of abandoning me if I couldn't keep up.

Tagging along with them, with Frank keeping a weather eye out for me, I scrambled over the muddy foreshore to Shadycombe, and followed the group as they paddled or fished for crabs off the quays, played on the towering stacks of crab pots, or hung around the fishing boats and barges, exploring the narrow streets and alleys off Island Street with their workshops and boat stores and fishermen's lofts. Thrilled to be included in their number, I copied what they did, trying my hardest to whistle as they did, to spit and to swear (both of which habits my mother later beat out of me), and generally to emulate their ways. One thing which always defeated me was the trick of stretching a blade of grass between their thumbs and blowing on it to make a piercing shriek like the sound of a hunting buzzard. It was doubly annoying because Frank learned this easily.

But always my father's return brought us both back. Frank could tell the time by the church clock and he always knew when Aaron was due home.

Winter or summer we ran to intercept him. The times I remember best were the warm summer evenings when Frank and I, later joined by Frederik, went to meet him as he walked along the path through the fields above Shadycombe.

Aaron was a big, spare man dressed habitually in the drab browns of the countryman, with a battered, sweat stained felt hat pulled down over his eyes. He wore a rough jacket patched at the elbows, and a weskit and neckcloth with a flannel shirt below. He strode out in heavy brown hobnail boots with polished, lace-up leather leggings that protected his legs from what we knew as "brimbles". He wore leather straps around both wrists to strengthen them when he was lifting heavy loads, and a wide leather belt with a brass buckle kept up his patched and worn trousers. When we went to meet him it was usually the end of a hard, twelve hour day, and he was hungry and weary, but when he saw us his shoulders would straighten and a smile spread over his weathered, sunburnt face. His very steps seemed lighter as he came towards us over the dusty, stony track, and we vied with each other to be the first to reach him, each keen to be the one chosen to be lifted up onto his broad shoulders for the walk back to the cottage.

But Aaron was always fair and however much we clamoured he always remembered whose turn it was. Riding up there, holding onto his shoulders, laughing as our heads brushed the new green leaves and the sharp thorns and pure white starriness of the blackthorn blossom, we breathed in the salt, mud smell of the estuary and the soft, verdant meadow grass and we were sure that we were the luckiest boys alive.

My father was not wise in the ways of the world, for he was incapable of seeing the bad in any man, but I know that others loved him for this character trait. He was widely regarded as a kind, God-fearing man of peerless honesty and integrity, and he was the best possible father to his sons.

We boys adored him and followed him around like shadows, helping him as best we could as he chopped wood for the fire, tidied and dug in the garden, emptied the lavatory pail, raked the clinker path and cleaned the whole family's boots. Like my mother's, his work was unending. We learned so much from him. Under his direction we dug and planted the little patches of ground that he had marked out for us. We learned how to sow seeds, and to prick out the tiny seedlings when they sprouted and carefully transplant them into the vegetable patch, marking them with twigs cut from the hedgerows. We learned how to grow and care for our crops, how to tie up runner beans, hoe around cabbages, pick out the tiny weeds from around the delicate froth of the carrot tops, and dig up the smooth, creamy potatoes that lay like pale buried treasure in the rich earth.

There were many agricultural workers and farm labourers in Batson, but few domestic gardeners. At that time besides Aaron there were two others,

William Legassick and Isaac Finch, both working in Salcombe. Sometimes my father got together with them in the evenings and they swopped cuttings and seeds, smoking their pipes companionably as they tried to work out what Old Moore's Almanac advised for the coming weeks. Most of the men in the hamlet grew their own vegetables, even if they only had tiny bits of ground, or in some cases had been given permission to grow things on common land. For all of us it was food. The rabbits fattening in their hutches, the chickens in their run, if you were lucky the salted joint of pork wrapped in muslin and hanging from the rafters, the jars of pickled eggs and the dried, smoked fish, each one more hedge against hunger. We were not supposed to make pets of the animals but we always did and inevitably there were tears when they were killed for the pot. We were too young to understand that we could not afford the luxury of sentimentality. But even so Aaron could not bear unkindness to any animal, and he looked after the rabbits well, though the chickens were always my mother's preserve. It was Aaron who taught us to love the land and the growing things, and we learned the names of the plants from him. The Latin names were incomprehensible to us, as they largely were to him. He spoke the long, difficult words if at all, with his soft Devon burr, but it was my mother who taught us the names of the wildflowers, giving them their Devon names, "Lady's Mantle", "Shepherd's Purse", "Bread and Cheese" and "Ragged Robin". It was she who instructed us in the medicinal uses of the plants: "Sneezewort" which cured the common cold; "Knotgrass" which she picked for her father's arthritis; "Good Henry" which we sometimes ate as a vegetable, though it was a little insipid for my taste, as opposed to "Bad Henry" which was poisonous. There was "Herb Robert" for blisters and wounds; "Jack-by-the-Hedge" which helped sore throats, and the bright green young nettles and clinging cleavers which our mother picked in the spring and made into a tonic for us every year to clean out our systems. Taught by her mother and grandmother before her, the names and the uses of plants came naturally to Ellen because she loved the flowers so.

Jane and James Cranch, Ellen's parents, lived in Batson at Ilbert Cottages almost next door to us, but my mother's brothers and sisters were all scattered. Ellen was the youngest of four – three girls and a boy. Her father was an agricultural labourer, the lowest class of worker. James Cranch had never earned much money, and as he got older even this amount decreased. People who employed agricultural labourers always chose young, fit men. By the time Ellen was born the family were used to going hungry.

Ellen was recognised as a bright child, and it was agreed that she would go to live with her brother in law Joseph Harvey and his wife, Ellen's much older sister, Mary. The family lived in Charleton which was where Joseph had been born. Ellen was to help her sister. It seemed a sensible move, since Joseph, although also only an agricultural labourer, was a big, strapping lad who always had plenty of work. It was considered a good

Ilbertstowe House. c 1900.J Fairweather

chance for Ellen as she would attend school in Charleton and thus see a bit more of the world. But Mary was lazy and she saw this as an opportunity to sit back and do very little. So before long the eight year old was cleaning and running the house as well as taking care of her young nephew and niece, John aged two years and Mary, three months. Ellen never spoke of this time to us, yet even as an adult it was as if there was the shadow of childhood unhappiness hanging over her. But at least she was fed which was probably her mother's objective. She must have known what Mary was like, but reckoned that she had done the best she could for her youngest child. People said that James and Jane Cranch and their children had always existed near the bread line. But they were proud that they had never been in the Workhouse even in hard times, and James continued to work even into his 70's when he could, though he was riddled with arthritis by then. Ellen once told me that the Cranch family were descended from wealthy Huguenot merchants who had come to Britain in the wake of religious persecution in Holland. I remember thinking that if this were so and if there was any money left anywhere in the Cranch name, it would best be served by helping this, the lowliest of this house.

Ellen's brother had been a ship's carpenter. He had been lost at sea off the Azores Her sister Polly had disappeared to London and had never been heard of since, though some said that she had found her way to Australia.

Her sister Elizabeth, always known as Lizzie had married into the ancient Weymouth family, members of an old Celtic clan farming Lincombe and Snapes at Batson even before the Normans seized the land. I never met Lizzie but after we learnt how she and her husband William had narrowly escaped being arrested for piracy on their wedding day, I always had a soft spot for her.

Aaron told us the story one cold March night as we sat around the range with the wind howling outside. My father was in his big chair, my mother in her own chair on the other side of the fire, sitting with her sewing box patching my father's trousers. We could see that Aaron was in one of his story telling moods. His blue eyes were dreamy and far away and he had stretched out in his chair, his stockinged feet towards the open door of the range, enjoying a rare moment of relaxation. We had come like puppies to his feet, and we waited, Frank on the stool, me sitting cross legged on the rag rug my mother had made, Fred at my mother's skirts, distracted for the moment by the tassel on her cushion. A cold draught came in from the gap under the kitchen door, despite the straw stuffed sacking that was placed there, but our faces were rosy and scorched by the blazing fire. There was no sound from outside but the gusting wind and from time to time the eerie hoot of a hunting owl.

"I'll tell 'ee about Lizzie," Aaron said. My mother frowned at him and pursed her lips disapprovingly. Ellen didn't like us to hear stories of people like Lizzie. If my mother had had her way we boys would only have learned about the great and the good, preferably heroes who had pursued some noble calling, so that we could aspire to be like them. But t'wasn't like that in our family. We were ordinary folk. And scratch ordinary folk in Salcombe in those days and you would find pirates.

Sure of his audience, Aaron took his time over his preparations. He picked up his pipe, tapped it against the fire door to empty the ashes, slowly took out his cutting knife and scraped at the bowl, then reaching for his old yellow oilskin pouch from the mantelshelf, began stoking up. Tonight it was Frank who had the coveted task of lighting a taper from the fire and touching it to the tobacco.

We waited as our father got the pipe going to his satisfaction. Knowing that once Aaron had it in mind to tell a story, no-one could rightly stop him, Ellen bent her head over her mending. I think in her own way she took a sort of pride in her sister. At least Lizzie was different. She was not like everyone else, having kids and working 'till she dropped. Lizzie had seized life with both hands.

"'Twas a cold and windy morning – April 't'would have been…" Aaron began. "The Preventives had had a tip off about goods looted from the wreck of the "Gossamer", from someone who said he'd seen barrels being brought accrost the land in the dead of night, and they laid siege to

46

Lincombe farm. There were a dozen of 'em Customs men - mebbe more – armed to the teeth, they was, an' they came a-creeping 'crost the fields t'wards the house…

Well the Weymouths was inside with their friends and relations all dressed up in their finery. 'Twas the morning of their wedding, and the young people, your Aunt Lizzie and her husband William Weymouth, they was a-drinking and eating and laughing and jest enjoying theirselves. The noise they made was enough to cover the sound of the Customs men as they surrounded the house and came through the yard and right up to the door. No-one heered the dogs barking, nor the geese clacking a warning as the sergeant threw open the main door and the men with their pistols in hand ran into the house."

Fred had fallen asleep on the mat, and Aaron lifted him up and settled him on his lap, smoothing back his silky black hair from his rosy face. Fred slept like the dead once he was asleep. Frank and I held our breaths, our eyes fixed on Aaron's face, waiting …

"Well, everything came to a halt sudden like… " Aaron continued… "The talking stopped. Glasses halted on the way to mouths… Lizzie was wearing a scarlet silk gown looted from the ship. William was dressed in a captain's frock coat. Blue, 'twas with gold buttons a-glinting in the sunlight…

A dozen guns were pointing at them. There was nothing they could do. They were caught red handed. With their suspicions confirmed the sergeant instructed his men to take them both into custody and several pairs of hands reached for the handcuffs and chains they had brought with them.

'T'was William who recovered first. He laughed and pulled his young wife to him his arm around her slender waist. Lizzie was wild and beautiful, untamed. But William, people said he could charm the birds off the trees.

"'We'll cause no trouble,'" he promised the sergeant. "'We'll come quietly… but first as it's our wedding day, you'll perhaps drink a toast ..?'

The sergeant was relieved. He had come from Plymouth and the night before he had heard talk in the pub about the lawless pair and their tight knit family and he had been prepared for trouble. It was cold outside but a fire was burning brightly in the hearth to ward off the damp of the old farmhouse walls. The room was cosy and the thought of a glass or two of wine and maybe some food was very inviting. The sergeant agreed, and the Customs men gladly un-cocked their weapons and stacked them against the wall, piling their handcuffs and chains on the floor beside them. One drink to the health of the young couple was certainly called for. It would be churlish to refuse such an invitation, all agreed.

Completely absorbed, Frank and I stared up at Aaron. The wood crackled and shifted in the range. We could tell that even Ellen was listening though she pretended to be absorbed in her mending.

With the consummate skill of the seasoned story teller, Aaron took his time. He puffed on his pipe contentedly. He knew he had his audience's whole attention and he was enjoying himself hugely.

"So a temporary truce was agreed," he went on after a moment. "William and two of his brothers and Lizzie helped the officers to wine and food and insisted they taste the uncommonly good brandy.

The Customs men ate and drank deeply. They stuffed their pipes with tobacco looted from the ship, and they drained their glasses and held them out to be refilled with more of the contraband alchohol.

Sunlight flowed in through the windows and hazed over the smoke from their pipes. The Customs men had been given seats by the fire and they were warm and very comfortable. Several of them had taken off their jackets. The sergeant had his pistol beside him on the settle. Lizzie came to sit by him and talked to him, and flirted with him. He laughed and suddenly began to feel like a very fine fellow indeed. He didn't notice when she spirited his gun away, concealing it in her skirts.

The drink continued to flow freely. One of the Preventives was sound asleep by this time. Another was holding forth expansively in a corner, telling anyone who would listen about the troop's past successes. Several of 'em had forgotten what they came there for. Some of the others had trouble standing up..."

Ellen who had been brought up Temperance clucked her tongue loudly at this, stabbing her needle hard into the trouser patch in condemnation of such behaviour.

"But lookee see, this is what those Customs men didn't know ..." Aaron continued, bending down to us, his voice low and conspiratorial... "They were the only ones drinking. The others were all pretending to drink but they were really getting ready to spring an escape..."

Frank and I exchanged glances our eyes wide. On Aaron's lap Fred snored gently in the warmth of the fire.

"Well, after a bit one of William's brothers began to sing a rollicking song and another guest joined in with his 'armonium 'till they was all bellowing it out. As they yelled out the chorus another of William's brothers slipped away. He crept accrost the yard and went to the barn where "Satan", William's horse was stabled. 'Er was a big, jet black stallion. Sixteen hands high 'er was. Fastest in the county some reckoned.

Well, 'er saddled him and led 'im out, and minutes later William and Lizzie ran accrost the yard... They mounted 'im and William dug his heels in and that 'orse, 'er fairly flew... 'er raced across the fields and jumped the hedge to the lane and off up towards 'Xecuter... and never seen agin..."

It was a true story I found out years later when an old newspaper cutting came to light. A small boy had seen them. "I seed that big Satan," he told the examining justice solemnly.. "'er was going like the wind. They wus on back and 'er was laughing…"

"Is there anything else you can remember, young man?" the magistrate asked him sternly. "Be careful how you answer and tell the truth now."

The boy thought for a bit. "…I remember her dress sir. Scarlet t'was and flying out behind 'er like a banner"

No-one saw them again. They had by all accounts left the county that day and possibly even shipped out abroad. They had evaded capture altogether. But often afterwards I thought of the beautiful wild girl with her flowing red silk dress. For me she and William were what pirates should be, people who bent the rules and took what they wanted. They were far more interesting than the dull, hard-working, law abiding men whom my mother was so keen for her sons to emulate.

Strange to tell – though mebbe not since Salcombe people had always married within their own community – that Weymouth-Murch marriage was only one of several both before and after. The homes of both families were so close. Generally speaking if you were in Batson you were in Murch or Weymouth territory. Many years later my own first born son would marry a Weymouth daughter.

My father's brothers and sisters, being largely so much older than he, had mostly long since moved away, but they left behind them a legacy of second cousins, and third cousins, and men and women whom we called uncle and aunt, because they were, though no-one could by now remember how they were related. It was just how the old Salcombe families were united.

Frank and I learned to swim about this time. In that we were different to most of the fishermen's children because they feared the water and never swam. It only prolonged dying if your boat was wrecked, or if you fell overboard, they used to say. If you couldn't swim you just drown-ded. Quick, easy and painless, it was all over. If you swam it just took longer. It gave false hope and hope kept you cruelly alive to go mad and die slowly of thirst and exhaustion. Death was still inevitable, because way out in the ocean no-one would find you. It was all part of the magic and wonder of going to sea. The men who sailed in the boats brought back with them so many tales.

It seemed to me in those days that our lives revolved around such stories. We lived on tales of huge seas, and topgallants carried away, of anchors dragging in storms. We knew about ships springing a plank, and men lost overboard, about burial at sea, and captains who lashed themselves to their wheels in raging seas. We heard about St. Elmo's fire, and about the huge sea albatross that was the sailors' friend. And we absorbed almost unconsciously the stories of the pirates and smugglers and the press gangs which had frequented our harbour through the centuries.

To have Aaron, or even sometimes both parents to ourselves for a while was a great treat, for they worked all hours God sent to provide for us. So Sunday afternoons were a special time. It was then, after morning church and the Sunday School that was compulsory for us children, and before evening Vespers, that my parents had their only rest. All of us dressed in our Sunday best, scrubbed clean from our Saturday night bath in my mother's wash tub, we often walked up the lane to Snapes and on the hills around towards The Bag. It was on these walks that Aaron introduced us to our world.

He would spread out one of his huge, heavily calloused hands and mark off the creeks: Widegates, The Bag...My thumb is Blanksmill, my forefinger, Collapit; the main finger Kingsbridge, the next finger, Bowcombe, and the little finger, the long, thin inlet of Frogmore. We followed the direction in which he pointed, seeing the little clusters of farms, the scattered hamlets that nestled at the ends of the creeks, the cows and sheep grazing on the hills over Quarantine Bay where the sick had been put during the time of the plague and the Napoleonic Wars; South Pool Creek, leading to South Pool, Gullet, Waterhead and Goodshelter where Crispin and Weymouth families lived; and Blessed Saltstone, bared now at low tide, where the brave martyrs of the Wesleyan faith had first prayed, secure in the knowledge that this barren rock at least was outside the jurisdiction of the law.

After our walk we would find a sheltered spot out of the wind which gave us a good view of the estuary, and my mother would unpack her basket, bringing out fresh crusty bread and hard boiled eggs. If we were lucky there was blackberry juice that she had bottled the autumn before. She and my father drank cold tea. Now and then their hands would touch as they reached for the stone bottle and they would glance at each other and smile a smile that excluded us boys.

With appetites sharpened by the fresh air and the walk, we ate until we were full. We generally stayed out except when the weather was very poor. We collected kindling for the fire, and berries from the hedgerow. In season we looked for mushrooms and picked blackberries or sloes. Sometimes if my parents just wanted to rest, we boys would play hide and seek. But almost always before we packed the dishes back into my mother's basket and went home, Aaron would tell us another tale, continuing the story of our heritage as told through our ancestors' eyes. If we were lucky, he would tell us our favourite ...

I still remember all those years ago, sitting with my brothers on the heavy old oilskin coat that Aaron had from his time at sea, shielded from the bite of the sharp breeze by his body, feeling the tingle of anticipation running down my spine as he began ...

"The Spanish ships were in the Channel... Cap'n Drake he was on the

Hoe… Henry was a bit of a boy then, no more'n nine when he went to sea with the Cap'n…"

Our chins lifted and our small chests puffed unconsciously with pride as we heard of our illustrious ancestor. Far below us I saw the ferry packed with passengers, rounding the point and begin toiling stoutly up a choppy estuary. Her decks were piled with barrels and boxes of goods. In a pen on the foredeck were a couple of goats. Their bleating rose above the sound of the new-fangled steam engines and the splashing of water from the paddles and reached up to where we sat, as my father related the story of the Spanish Armada approaching, of the game of bowls, and the courage and daring of England's hero. Frank and I had discussed the story of Sir Francis Drake at length, and we had only recently solemnly agreed that we would fight and if necessary die for our country, should the Cap'n's ghostly drum sound to summon us. Dreading yet also keenly anticipating that event, I had to admit privately that when Frank and our father had played a trick on me one evening and banged a metal milk can under the bedroom window, calling out to me in ghostly voices, I had nearly died of fright.

The "Reindeer" Paddle Steamer. J Fairweather

The passengers on the "Reindeer" caught sight of us as they passed far below, and several of them waved, one gentleman even going so far as to take off his shiny black top hat and hulloo up at us, as, our story finished and the time for Vespers rapidly approaching we got to our feet to begin the walk back to the cottage.

Our father taught us to fish as soon as we were able. Fish supplemented our table, and we learned never to leave the house without the fine cotton thread that we had filched from our mother's sewing basket, with its hand-made hook on the end, or the wooden square which held our crab lines. Aaron taught us the countryman's ways. He instructed us that the good Lord allowed us to kill to eat, but that it was a sin to take more than you needed, or to kill one of His creatures just for the sake of killing it. Not that there was much chance of that, at least when we were small. Fish came to Frank's line more readily than to mine. I was too impatient to sit still for long. But because I had once slipped down the entrance to a warren up in the fields above the hamlet and somehow accidentally managed to sit on a very old rabbit, which my father's quick thinking had managed to secure for the pot, I rejoiced at this time in the title of best family rabbit catcher.

Aaron had a crab pot which he put out off Snapes, which was a good crabbing area. Some of the crabs he caught were big, and once or twice he caught a lobster there. He had a special lobster pot made by a friend in return for a day's work cutting reeds over in Mill Bay valley, and that pot went on to earn him quite a bit, for he always sold his catch in Salcombe. Once though he caught a lobster with a badly damaged claw, and since rich folk didn't want to eat deformed creatures, we had it for our tea. The taste of it was wonderful but it was so rich after our normal plain diet, that we all had stomach aches that night.

Left to our own devices Frank and I would go down on the beach, paddling or spending endless hours searching in vain for the elusive message in a bottle that one of our older cousins had promised to throw overboard from his ship for us. But when Aaron was with us, he told us about the ships, the barques, brigantines, schooners, barquantines and brigs that had once filled the harbour, drawing pictures of them in the sand with a stick and naming the sails, the fore gallants, and top gallants, the mizzens and mainsails, top sails and jibs. He told us about the great herds of cattle that had once been driven from the fields on the East Portlemouth side and shipped across the estuary, or had been taken through the streets to the slaughter houses in Salcombe. Other cattle had been herded from market in Kingsbridge and penned in a field at Bonfire Hill to fatten and await the time when they too would be killed to feed the sailors. Many hogsheads of beer and cider had been loaded on the ships; sacks full of ship's biscuit and cheese had been stowed, with crates of brandy and wine, pilchards and salt cod. He told us about Salcombe's golden age and how the town and the quays and the public houses had all buzzed with the vibrancy of passing sailings and trade and talk of other ports and countries...

But there was little enough time for such day dreaming. Little by little, inexorably, we were being groomed for the work that would be our daily lot.

Our tasks began as soon as we were old enough to be useful. Frank was already carrying water, and now I began to help him. We spilled a great deal at first because we were still so little, but Aaron built us a wooden square to steady the heavy buckets and gradually we got better at it. We both helped regularly in the vegetable garden now, scrubbed potatoes, cleaned the family's Sunday boots, scoured the knives with sand to remove stains, and carefully washed the hens eggs, any excess of which my mother took to sell in Salcombe. Both my parents subscribed to the theory that the Devil made work for idle hands, and so they made sure that he stayed away from our door.

Sometimes if it was fine, Ellen would sit out on the steps with us, the dress or coat that she was making or the skirt that she was letting out or taking in for a customer, spread out on a piece of clean linen to make sure it did not get marked. When I think of my mother, I remember that she was always busy. She was not the sort of woman to sit doing nothing even if she could have afforded it. As we now had to do, she had had to work hard all her childhood, and she knew no other way. When and how she had taught herself to sew I do not know, but it was something she had always had a gift for. She was much in demand amongst the ladies in Salcombe and even as far away as Malborough and Kingsbridge, though she had little time with all of us to take care of. She had the ability to see a dress or costume shape in a bolt of cloth, and her clever, square, strong little hands would whisk over it until the outfit appeared as if by magic. Usually she went to the big houses where her customers lived, but every now and then, a carriage would draw up and a smartly dressed lady would come to our cottage, and all of us "men" would be banished until the coast was clear.

It was at times like these when my mother was not around, that my father would tell us tales of the sea.

The "Brizo", which to all of us was always Aaron's ship, was a 231 ton three masted barquentine, built by Vivian's Yard for Balkwill and Company in Kingsbridge, and launched in March 1877. We boys knew everything about the "Brizo". We knew that she was 121 ft long and 28.8 feet in width, that she drew 13 ft, that she had a raised quarterdeck 32 ft long. That she was the last vessel built by James Vivian.

From 1877 to 1886, the year of my birth, her master was John Pepperell who owned six shares in the "Brizo".

In 1879, as well as my father Aaron Murch, who was an Ordinary Seaman, her crew was : Caleb Gillard, the mate; Roger Pepperell, bosun; John Murch, my uncle, Cook/Steward; William Hannaford, Able Bodied seaman; F Petersen, also A.B and John Pepperell, O S. We knew too, that she was wrecked on Samphire Reef, near New Province, the Bahamas on 11th April 1886 when she was lost with all hands   Aaron had sailed a long way before the mast – but perhaps not as far as we believed. He had gone, he told us, to lands with magical sounding names. He had rounded the Horn in seas higher than any building we had ever seen. He had docked in Valparaiso, and danced the hula in Hawaii. He had fished for giant squid

The "Brizo"

off Newfoundland and he had been on the India run. He had even gone as far as Australia. There were so many stories Aaron told us always out of hearing of my mother because she grew angry when he talked this way. We did all go to sea when we were grown. I don't know how much of it was because of Aaron's stories, and how much just because we were Devon boys.

All we knew as we danced the hornpipe in the vegetable patch at my father's instruction, piping the chorus of "Oh….Rio, We're bound for the Rio Grande" in response to Aaron's rumbling bass "Farewell and Adieu to you Ladies of Spain ..." was that one day we too would lie in hammocks on rolling seas, would climb far aloft to look for land, or would take the night watch under the diamond bright stars of a tropical sky. We too, would be a part of that magic of sailors and the sea.

I know my father missed the sea, but I don't think he minded toiling the land. He was just carrying on the old traditions: Land or Sea, those were the choices for Devon men. And sooner or later, all men retired from the sea. They either left because their wives nagged them to, or because the sea had turned against them. The sea made so many weeping widows and orphans. Some years when the sea claimed many lives, were worse than others. In the 1840's my father told us, the "Beau Ideal", an 85 ton schooner sailed from Salcombe bound for St. John's Newfoundland loaded with limestone. Neither the schooner nor the crew were ever seen again.

Waiting for the tide, Salcombe. J Fairweather

In the November gales in 1851, seven Salcombe vessels, including the "Speedy", a replacement for a ship of the same name, were lost off the Azores. In 1859 the 147 ton "Mary" sailed from St. John's, Newfoundland with a cargo of oil, bound for Greenock. She too disappeared. . In 1866 the 139 ton schooner "Cynoshore", the masters of which were all from the local Yabsley family, relations by marriage, was lost at Safi, Morocco where once the Corsairs had enslaved hundreds of Devon and Cornish mariners.

In 1887 when I was barely a year old, the "Zenobia" was lost at sea with all hands. The numbers of sorrowing and grieving relatives seemed endless, my mother told me once quietly, especially so since our lives were all connected. Most of us were related, distantly or closely. Salcombe and the Estuary was a tight knit community. If the men of your own immediate family returned safely, you still grieved for those others, the men of the town who were not coming back, and after such a tragedy people were solemn and quiet for days afterwards, their faces reflecting the common loss.

But there were good years too during this period, when the weather was clement and the ship owners made good money and more boats were built.

Boats in those peak years were commonly owned by many individuals, in up to 64 shares. Sometimes they were part owned by their masters,

The Harbour, Salcombe. c 1900 J Fairweather

sometimes by traders, such as the butchers and bakers who supplied them. Widows sometimes owned shares, or the crew occasionally had a percentage of their wages paid in shares. Loads were spread between ships in a damage limitation exercise, so that if one ship went down its loss might be compensated for by other cargoes which did manage to make it to their destination.

As Salcombe's decline began, a Captain Hill, a quietly spoken man renowned for being a hard disciplinarian but a just master, began what he called the "Salcombe Shipowning Company", hoping to halt any further downward trend in local ship owning. Shares to the value of £5,000 were offered in the company, in 64 lots, but only three fifths of them were ever taken up.

Cap'n Hill had started his business in 1868 with two vessels, a new ship, the "Lord Devon" and the second-hand "Lady Bertha".

By 1875 the company operated six vessels. All went well for the first eight years, then the Cap'n's luck changed, and within five years he had lost four vessels. The shareholders wanted to wind up the company when the "Lady Bertha" was lost, but it was not until 1901 that the company became defunct with the sale of the "Lord Devon".

For Salcombe the downward slide had now become inexorable. Despite the opening up of the West Country by railway, ferry, motor coach and the

Captain F W Hill of "The Salcombe Shipowning Company" and the 96 ton Schooner, the "Lady Bertha".

new-fangled idea of holidays for the rich which had brought a new breed of yachtsmen to the harbour, it did not compensate for the loss of the town's trading ships.

Everything I heard about the town only served to pull me towards it. I was desperate to see Salcombe for myself. I began pestering my father and my elder brother, and as soon as my legs were long enough we walked there together one Sunday afternoon.

At last I got to see for myself the wharfs and quays and the bustle of the town. Even on a Sunday, when no ships would sail for fear of disaster befalling them, it was a hive of activity and noise. After Batson, it was a metropolis, and it filled me with excitement. That night I could not sleep. I lay in my bed tossing and turning as all the things I had seen drifted through my head, until Frank pushed me out to sleep on the floor.

When I was just over three I was sent to the Church of England Infant School with Frank, and at last joined the procession of children who walked through the fields from Batson every day, the proud possessor of the title of "Scholar".

Dressed in my smart new school clothes, my hair neatly brushed and slicked down with water, I joined the group of local Batson children and the half dozen or so children who came in from outlying farms and gathered in a noisy gaggle in Batson each morning for the walk to Salcombe. Parents paid 1d for each child, and although there were mutterings about schooling being a waste of time and money, it was in some ways child care, since, knowing their children were safe, parents could devote themselves to their work. And, like the beasts of burden, it was work that was their reason for being on earth

It was March 1889 when I went to school. It had been a bitterly cold winter and there was still no sign of a thaw. The ice had only just melted on the stream and hoar frost had stuck to the inside of our bedroom window for weeks. Beneath my new trousers which my mother had made especially for this auspicious day from the cloth my grandparents had given me, my knees were blue with the cold. Frank's nose was running, and I saw him wipe it on his sleeve, though I knew that mother had made him a pocket handkerchief. It was an offcut from one of her sewing jobs though, and I was aware that once again it had flowers on it, so I forgave him this sin. I think in her desire to equip us properly my mother sometimes overlooked the flowers.

As one of the newest and smallest boys in school I stayed close to Frank on that first day. Following his example I lined up with the others when the bell outside the school door was rung, and like them was silent.

Once inside we stood behind a line chalked on the floor for prayers, reciting the Lord's Prayer which I already knew by heart. Then we sat on the floor for some biblical texts. We new pupils had to stand up as our names were called so that we could be introduced to everyone. A young woman with curly brown hair caught back in a tortoiseshell hair clip, made marks in a book which Frank told me later showed that we had come to school. I knew three of the other new pupils as they had come from Batson but several who had come from outlying farms, I did not know at all.

The head mistress, Mrs Rosamond Neil, was assisted by two unpaid pupil teachers, one of whom was the young woman with the curly brown hair. Our learning was by rote. We started with the alphabet which we dutifully copied onto our slates in our best imitation of our teacher's beautiful copperplate writing, learning from the start to make the small and the big letters just as she did. Maths was also taught by rote and we began with the two times table which was chalked on the blackboard, repeating it over and over until before long we could and did say it in our sleep. It was cold in the school but no colder than in our homes. Sometimes in the early morning our breath fogged in front of us as we sat at our desks. There was an open fireplace in the main schoolroom, and Mrs Neil's desk was immediately in front of this. We pupils might occasionally get to see a flicker of flame reflected around her ample form, but we got no heat. On the white painted walls of this room hung several biblical pictures, mostly of saints with upraised hands on the point of being transported to a heaven already densely populated by other saints. But there was one, to me by far and away the most interesting which showed Daniel in the Lion's Den. This picture featured a white clad Daniel with clasped hands and an other-worldly expression on his face, seemingly completely unmoved by the slavering jaws and huge teeth of the half dozen or so lions which appeared ready to make a meal of him. I puzzled over the picture many times, but the fact that Daniel was apparently doing nothing at all to save himself except praying, engendered in me a lifelong mild contempt for the saint. I spent many an idle moment when I should have been studying, imagining how, if I had been in the same situation, I would have defeated the lions by wrestling them with my bare hands or jamming one of the logs depicted lying on the ground nearby, between their jaws.

The only other print was more cheerful. It was a large, colourful picture of Jesus with a bright yellow halo, smiling at a group of children with clean, scrubbed faces dressed in garments of such a brilliant white that I was certain their mothers must have been at the dolly tub for a week.

With the advent of my school career came additional responsibilities. I was never much of a one for my mother's skirts. I wanted to be a man. My everyday role models, beside my father, were the fishermen and farmers I saw around me. I longed to work on the boats and haul in fish, or move heavy hay bales and get the big plough horses to obey me. I was now four years old, but I was already wiry and quick witted, and so I pitted my small strength against the tasks I was set, running errands, helping in the garden, trying in any way I could to contribute to the family income like a grown man. The other thing of moment at this time was that Fred learned to swim, instinctively taking to the waves like a fish. If left to his own devices though he preferred to swim underwater, which astonished Frank and me.

But in the meantime as we walked backwards and forwards to school, there was Salcombe, the place where I had longed to be for so long, and like the majority of my school friends, I took every advantage to explore it and enjoy the excitements it offered, particularly down on the quays where the fishermen and sailors gathered.

One day when we were on Customs House Quay watching barrels and boxes being craned off a barge that had come up from Plymouth, I saw a particularly large cotton bag landed. It came close to where I was standing, and I dodged, but one of the ship's deckhands laughed and told me I needn't have bothered, as this particular bag was so light I could carry it by myself.

I must have looked doubtful for he challenged me to try and lift it. My classmates egged me on, and I took hold of it though it was far bigger than I was. My surprise when I discovered that it weighed nothing at all made the crew and the other children laugh uproariously.

"They's ostrich feathers, my lover," he said, his form of speech marking him as a Plymouth man. The deckhand who was a big, jolly looking man with sun bleached curly yellow hair, pulled back a flap of the gunny sack covering and showed me what was inside, and I saw to my astonishment a mass of grey, white and black feathers all tightly packed but of course weighing nothing at all.

That evening I told my mother what I had seen, and she said that the

Standing off Customs House Quay, Salcombe. C 1900 Fairweather.

feathers were probably destined for the wife of the same Mr Fairweather we had seen taking photographs. Mrs Fairweather she said, washed, combed and dyed the feathers and then re-packed them for transportation up to London where they graced the hats of society women or   were sold on to local milliners.

There was Martha Hodges who lodged with retired mariner Edward and his wife Rhoda in Courtney Street and her daughter in law, 17 year old Bessie Arundle, who was learning the business from her.   Then there was Hannah Barton, daughter of Mrs Barton, the dress maker who lived in Union Street, who was also a milliner. They were all good hard working hat makers who often bought feathers from Mrs Fairweather, my mother said.

There was another, altogether different type of woman I fell in with on a visit to the Town Quay some months later. I had been running an errand for my father in Harvey's Row. Frank had gone on home, but I lingered, and that was when I met her. She wore a low necked bright blue gown and a feathered hat, which is what had attracted my attention because I wondered if these feathers too had come from Mrs Fairweather. I must have been staring at her because she came up to me. She chucked me under the chin, and smiled at me. She smelled strange, an overpowering scent that with my youth and inexperience I failed to recognise as a potent mix of gin and cheap perfume. I liked her and was prepared to stay and talk. It was not until a buxom fisherman's wife dragged me angrily away by my shirt collar, muttering that the woman was "one of the sailor's doxies", and that I was to go straight home to my mother, that we parted company.

Needless to say, after this encounter, I looked eagerly for the woman in the blue dress the next time I was near the quay, but I never saw her again. I expect she had shipped on and was maybe drinking in one of the taverns in Plymouth or Dartmouth. Sometimes these women travelled on to London following after some sailor. Once in a while they would return, older and more haggard looking usually. When I learned much later from Frank about my aunt Grace, I often wondered if that was what had happened to her. For all I knew my friend in the blue dress could have been her...

The street often flooded but I remember this year the floods were particularly bad. Spring tides bought havoc and people were out in Fore Street in boats. It was good fun for us children but the sea came over the boards that householders put up and many of the houses and shops were flooded to a depth of several feet.

The mother of a school friend who had saved up the necessary one penny to take a bath at Snell's got trapped there by the high tide and in the end had to hold up her skirts and wade bare footed back through the street, cursing loudly because there was mud and silt in the street and she got all dirty.

It was at this time that we first heard rumours that "Ringrone House" which had long been without an owner, was to be sold. The name Major Bennett came up frequently at home. People said that he was to convert the big house to a hotel to be named "The Marine".

 Building work started and we saw scaffolding being erected and builders swarming over the great façade, which seemed to go on for a long time partly because for the first time the house now had proper bathrooms.

Major Bennett's agent was seen all around the town. He was hiring people to work in the new hotel, and I know Aaron was concerned about his job. Then came the glad news that not only was my father's job secure, but that he had been promoted from Gardener to Head Gardener, responsible for the grounds of "The Marine Hotel", which was a considerable advancement for him. It was yet another sign of how well thought of my father was.

The promotion meant moving house again, and what was most amazing

of all as far as we boys were concerned was that this time we were to move to Salcombe. We were to live at No.7, Robinson's Row, just off Fore Street. On the strength of this promotion my mother talked of having the leg on her chair repaired. This never happened, but she did achieve one of her other ambitions which was to have a geranium in a bright copper pot in her front window.

We were due to move in the middle of September 1891. The weather was fine and it looked as if it would hold, which was ideal. My father had borrowed a horse and cart from his brother William, and we loaded it with all our possessions. We owned little, but even so, with my parents' bed and the one that my brother Frank and I shared and the little truckle bed that we had slept on and which had now passed to Frederik, the three thick straw, feather topped mattresses as well as the household goods, the chickens and the rabbits, we had to make three trips. We had help from relatives and friends, but even so it was a busy day. Frederik stayed with Ellen but Frank and I wemt round with my father in the cart, thoroughly enjoying riding up beside him, as we went up Fore Street and through the arch into Robinson's Row, where my mother was waiting to welcome us into what after hours of hard work was a spotlessly clean cottage – though she was happy to tell everyone she met what a state it had been in when she first came to it.

That first night mother had prepared a rabbit stew for us as a special treat, and we ate until we were ready to burst, then fell into bed and slept the good sleep of the unutterably weary.

Our new home was as small as the others had been with just four rooms, each about 10 feet square. It had a front living room and a back scullery, from where steps went up to the rear bedroom where we boys slept. My parents slept in the front bedroom, overlooking the Row.

We learned that No 7 Robinson's Row was one of many such cottages owned by my father's new master. Major Bennett was a very rich man, and something of a dilettante. He was also slightly eccentric and since he did not have to be concerned about earning a living, vetted any person who had the temerity to ask to stay at the new hotel. He ran things in a military fashion, but it was said that so long as you kept on the right side of him he was a good master.

Robinson's Row was a thrilling place to be. It was really in the centre of things with the constant bustle of shops and traders and people moving in the street. It seemed to Frank and me that there was always something happening, and we haunted the quays watching the ships and local boats loading and unloading and the passengers embarking and disembarking, trailing about them the magic of unknown places and experiences that we could only dream of. Even though the harbour was much emptier now, there was still the excitement of seeing the ships entering and leaving port. Seamen with sunburnt faces, tattoos and silver earrings in their ears, drank in the pubs and spilled noisily out onto the streets.

When I asked Aaron why they wore the earring he said it was to pay Father Nepture for their passage if they were drown-ded at sea.

Then, at the end of the day, there was the trip back home, through the arch and up the long, rolling cobbled steps between the cottages and the privies that was like another quiet, private world away from the bustle.

At the rear of the house was a back passageway which led past all the cottages. All the wash houses and store rooms were situated here.

The fishermen living in the cottages often spread out their wet sails and nets here; most families kept chickens or livestock. In the winter months there was usually at least one small dinghy dry docked for repairs.

One family had a very bad tempered goat which was given to head butting anyone who came close. The goat existed on the sparse grass and small bits of hedge topped up by occasional scraps given to it by various households. In return for this we were sometimes given a small cup of goat milk, which I didn't like because it tasted strong, but which my mother used in baking.

For a while a cow was kept here, but the slope was so steep that her owner moved her somewhere else. There were other hutches of rabbits

Page 65. Barges and Steamer at Customs House Quay. J Fairweather.

Newly enlarged and converted "Marine Hotel". J Fairweather

besides our own, once more reared for food and for the value of their skins and one man who was a mole catcher by trade, who kept ferrets which lived in the cottage with him.

He used sometimes to keep live moles he had caught before he slaughtered them. There was a great demand for mole skins for making waistcoats at this time, and we grew used to seeing the tiny skinned carcases pinned up on a board to dry with their little paws with huge curved claws stretched out stiffly beside them

Frank longed to have one of the claws, and in a daring raid after dark one evening, we seized one. We tied it onto a piece of cotton and Frank wore it around his neck, but when Aaron saw it he was angry and told us both off, saying that what we had done was stealing as well as being disrespectful to the animal.

We took the claw back to its owner who seemed to think the whole thing was a big joke and told us we could keep the claw, but strangely enough neither Frank nor I wanted it after that. To have upset Aaron was punishment enough.

There was enough land for each cottage to have its own garden. After

"Robinson's Row" c 1889. J Fairweather.

my father had set up the rabbit and chicken hutches, he immediately set to work to dig over an area for vegetables, making sure that we boys each had a patch which we could cultivate ourselves as always.

Right up at the top of the land was a tall oak and Frank and I together with several other local boys made this our headquarters. From here we could see clear over the rooftops to the sea, and it was a splendid place to sit and make plans. It was also an excellent spot to consume the toffee I was given by Mrs Cranch from Cranch's Sweetshop. She was a relative of my mother's and having a sweet tooth, I had immediately seen the possibilities there and on our second day in the cottage, had just happened to drop by and ask her if she needed any errands run. She was no fool and she immediately saw through my guileless expression and so we had entered into an agreement that was based on her need and my greed. I ran up and down the street for her before school, delivering supplies, collecting packages and making the occasional small purchase of something that she needed, and in return I received a supply of my favourite sweets – usually toffees. It was like all the best business arrangements, and both of us found it agreeable. Having realised that shopkeepers – who by and large had few if any staff - could not just shut their doors and go out whenever they wanted, I found my small business idea had several takers, and I repeated the magic formula with several other shops after school. For a five year old I had quite a flourishing business! There was an added bonus in that I got to explore Salcombe, walking up the street and out as far as North Sands.

We were all pleased to be in the new cottage. My father had less distance to walk to work. Mother could sell her eggs more easily, and could meet up with friends and relatives she had not seen when we were living in Batson. As for we boys, we were in seventh heaven. Whitestrand was our second home. Fred who was mad on boats soon discovered the Quay for himself and seemed to spend all his waking hours there. He was only little, but he was never happier than when he was climbing in and out of boats and being around fishermen. At first my mother used constantly to run and find him, but she soon realised that he was safe with the fishermen and the apprentices at Coves Boatyard to the side of the quay. While the sun still shone, he swam off the quay with us, continuing his strange practise of preferring to swim underwater rather than on the surface. It was only when a visitor dropped her purse into the water and Fred retrieved it and was given a whole threepenny piece as a reward, that I realised we had another potential business. This one however was immediately stopped by our mother who very firmly refused to let her youngest child hang around the quay in his under drawers in chilly weather on the off chance that someone might drop something in the water. She didn't say anything about the summer though, so I decided to wait until the warm days came and then re-start the enterprise.

Hanging around on the quay after school Frank and I learned to row a dinghy and to scull with one oar, standing up in the stern as the fishermen did. By this time we were big enough to be of some use, and we ran errands for the fishermen when they brought in their catch, often taking still living fish or crab to cooks in the big houses in town. Sometimes we were paid in kind. Helping out in town resulted in other small winnings such as stale bread or cakes, and bruised or un-saleable fruit or vegetables to add to our pot. Thanks to this we had never eaten better.

Several of our relatives also lived in Robinson's Row. Since like most of the other inhabitants, our front door was scarcely ever closed except at night or when it was very cold, it was sometimes the case that we found cousins asleep on our floor when we woke up. In common with almost everyone else we owned nothing that anyone would want to steal anyway and often some of the older boys returning home late and finding themselves with no space left to sleep in their own homes, made their way to us.

The best thing about the house though was that we had discovered that if we were very quiet, Frank and I could creep out of bed, down the stairs and outside without my parents hearing. Luckily Fred also in our room still slept deeply. If he did wake, he had to be encouraged to stay silent since he was too young to come with us, and at almost three, old enough to feel that he should. The means we used to facilitate this varied I am ashamed to say from bribes to outright physical threats!

The weather continued unseasonably fine for several weeks after we moved, giving us all time to get things as we wanted them. My mother's chickens had a new coop, and the rabbits a larger run. My father dug over his garden thoroughly. The garden was not as big as the one at "The Nook", but it was sunnier, and he had big plans for it. As he riddled and raked over the earth, he took out the stones and began a little path for my mother to use to walk to the chicken house. When that was done he brought a cart load of manure round from his brother William's farm in Batson and dug that in. We took the cart to the foreshore afterwards and scrubbed it out with seawater, but it took a long time before we had cleaned all the muck out of it and could return it in the state it was in when we borrowed it.

The barometer outside the Fisherman's Mission kept dropping and everyone said that a big change was coming in the weather. Then abruptly it was as if Nature herself had turned against the town with a violence that few had ever seen before.

The winds began first, growing steadily in intensity. They whistled down the chimneys, putting out the fires and sending clouds of smoke into the rooms. It began to rain and the rain grew heavier, slaking down from a deep grey sky, battering the town and sending the townspeople scurrying for shelter. Abruptly the rain turned to a bitter sleet, driven on a howling, freezing wind. Boats which usually bumped gently against wharfs and quays now thumped and crashed into them, sustaining damage which entailed extricating them from amongst the crush, and beaching or tying them fore and aft on running moorings.

The blizzard intensified. Fierce winds screamed through the street, tearing vessels from their moorings and driving them ashore. On one night alone five ships were wrecked in mountainous seas off Start. The fog was so thick that the light from the lighthouse was invisible. The thermometer continued to drop. Then, without warning, the snow started.

It just kept on snowing. Each new day we looked out onto deeper and deeper pillows of it, muffling street noise and camouflaging the shapes of everyday things. The snow banked up in the town and teams of men set to work to dig it away so that people could walk about, but it just came back. The freezing temperatures continued and the estuary began to ice up below Snapes. Men said that if it continued it might be possible to walk from the town across to Snapes. Certainly we were able to walk on the ice over the shallow water on the Salcombe side of the estuary.

We sent Fred out to test the ice to see if it would carry him before we ventured out far ourselves, but had to stop this practise after someone told our mother. The indignant and furious blows she administered to our behinds with the back of her hairbrush was enough to give us an idea of the general disfavour in which she viewed this latest perilous risking of the life of her youngest child.

The snow continued even into the second week in March with no let up. Then finally it stopped, leaving the townspeople to count the cost of what soon became known to all as "The Great Blizzard".

The weather had been so extreme that a great deal of livestock around the area was lost. But my mother's chickens thrived. She had brought them into the kitchen in front of the Lidstone range during the early hours of the Great Blizzard, and they had enjoyed it so much that they were quite bad tempered when they were finally moved back outside. One was unfortunately eaten by one of the Mole man's ferrets but the others survived.

Our cockerel escaped once and Frank and I and our father, with Frederik bringing up the rear, had to chase it half way up Fore Street before we caught it. By the time father had it in his arms with its head tucked under his armpit to quieten it, we reckoned half the street had been involved in its capture, with William Wood, the Shipping Agent, sprightly Mrs Sheriff from Myrtle Villa, Lieutenant Bridger, R.N, half a dozen assorted shop keepers and assistants, several children, about ten passers-by and Constable Grant all at one time or another hot in pursuit.

My mother kept our cottage in Robinson's Row as spotless as the others. There was never a need in our home to worry when the Master's Agent came round as they did periodically to inspect the tenants' premises and report back to the owner. My mother was house proud and she attacked dirt and the never ending layer of dust and mud that entered the house from the street and the back as if it was a personal affront. She had been brought up as most of the properly raised women were in those days, to do everything for her family. Ellen was always washing and cleaning, but there were times too, when she played games with us and we saw her lighter side.

I think Ellen had had a harder life than my father. My grandfather James had worn himself out physically trying to provide for his family. Jane, my grandmother still occasionally helped the local washerwomen in Batson, plucked chickens for Butcher Hannaford, or did whatever else she could to earn money, but the family had always existed close to destitution. I know that my father did what he could to help them, and he and Ellen often took them vegetables or some meat for the cooking pot, though we had little enough to spare ourselves. I think it was the grinding poverty the family endured, and the fact that she had been taken from her mother so young that had encouraged Ellen to be self-sufficient and to fight her own battles. She was tough and there was a fierce, determination in her that my father did not possess.

From very early on we boys had been taught to make ourselves useful, and as we grew older and stronger, we were able to help with more household tasks. We carried wood and we ran errands for those who were less able. "Wear out the young legs first", was a saying we heard often as we were charged with yet another trip up or down the Street, our arms laden with things to be sold, or delivered, or generally just moved from one place to another. Yet I remember that our lives were filled with laughter and love.

Aaron and Ellen loved each other very much. You'd never think it

Snow piled up in Fore Street, Salcombe during the
Great Blizzard of 1890. J Fairweather

though sometimes, to hear mother. She'd tell her husband off as if he was one of us boys, while Aaron just bent his head and listened, with his kindly blue eyes momentarily clouded as he waited patiently for the storm to climax and to pass.

Aaron was everyone's darling. He was sunny and kind, and he loved all of us, and we knew it. He was never much good at making money, but somehow that didn't matter. All our neighbours were poor too, except for one or two. Parson wasn't poor – well not as poor as us. The people in the big houses weren't poor. But we didn't really count them. They lived in a different world from us, a world of privilege and ease. We boys learned early on that these men paid our parents' wages – and by and large the whole town's – and just as we wouldn't dare take the Lord's name in vain, neither did we venture to speak ill of our masters... Mother said Aaron would have taken his belt to us if we had. But even from an early age that made us giggle. My father never took a belt to any one of us. He barely even threatened. He knew that we knew him too well. We didn't know for sure, but we guessed that he was one of the sweetest and kindest men who ever walked on God's earth.

My mother though, was another kettle of fish altogether. Just as Aaron never even raised his voice to us, Ellen our black haired, buxom and vibrant mother tolerated no nonsense from any of us. Ellen would pick up anything to hand if her temper was roused - didn't matter what 'twas, a broom, a blacking brush, a dish cloth. She'd hit us with it. I'd even seen her snatch off her apron and belabour us with it in impotent fury if she had nothing else to hand. She never hurt any one of us. What was worse was seeing Ellen's anger. She was a powerful sight when she was in a temper.

But we all knew that she loved us too, in her own way. And in her own fashion, her heart was as big as Aaron's. It was just that somebody had to rule the roost. She was like a lioness with her pride, and Ellen's pride was her strong, good looking husband and her three healthy sons. She looked after us so well. Our clothes were always clean and neatly mended – at least when we set out in the morning! We even had underclothes, which was unusual at a time when most working people owned only their top clothes. My mother made ours out of the same flour sacks from which she had made my christening robe. They were soft from constant washing and comfortable to wear. The only problem was the positioning of the miller's name. Both my pairs of shorts read "Trant's Flour" in big letters centred in a big blue circle across my bottom, though in time the letters faded until they were nearly invisible.

Frank, as the eldest always had new boots. Ellen's sons would not have to avail themselves of the Boot Club. Clever housekeeping and thrift meant that she almost always had funds in the little tin she kept on the kitchen mantel shelf. I knew too that she kept a small stash of money hidden under her mattress for "a rainy day". But so many hardships had gone into the building up of that pitifully small nest egg. One of the things my mother had always to force herself to forego was flowers...

My father had always grown flowers alongside his vegetables. They were a good cash crop, and when they were in season my mother would sell them in the town. They were seeds that he had raised in his work, and his expertise meant that his flowers were particularly prized in Salcombe. My mother admired them greatly, and was often to be seen weeding or hoeing and generally tending them. Ellen even talked to them sometimes as if they were people. Rarely, very rarely, my mother would keep one of the flowers for herself, or my father would give her one. But they were too valuable to be kept. They had to be sold. When they were sold they meant extra meat or something for the family. You couldn't eat flowers, my mother used to say. But her eyes went soft when we picked bunches of wild daffodils, bluebells and pink campions in the fields above Shadycombe in the spring and brought them home for her. When the cuttings my father took from her prized geranium grew, she was delighted, and found containers for them so that her windowsill now looked a picture with its bright pink and red flowers.

As well as the flowers Ellen packed up the chickens eggs and twice a week walked up through the town with her basket to sell them. She was quite a character, with her thick, glossy black hair and flashing eyes, always dressed in bright colours and flouncing skirts and quite a number of households in Salcombe brought her eggs. Years later I heard that she also had had quite a following amongst the gentlemen of the town, for she was a strikingly good looking woman, but I know for a fact that she never had eyes for anyone except my father, just as I am certain that he never looked at another woman. They were in love. And they remained that way all their lives...though you'd never think it sometimes to hear Ellen in a temper. She'd grab her broom and shoo Aaron out of the house, just like us boys if he irritated her. At times like that he would retreat to the steps on Council Quay, sitting there just above the sea, smoking his clay pipe, watching what was going on, or sometimes talking with a passer-by. We always knew where to find him. When we asked him what he was doing, he used to say: "Jest thinkin'". Then he would shift along a bit to make room for us beside him on the step. Sometimes he would start to tell a story, and before long there'd be people gathered around him. Grown-ups they wuz too, some of them big, important people in the world. They'd stay there listening to him, just like they was children. There was a sort of magic about Aaron that drew people to him.

Most locals were like us too many kids, too little money, but for the most part if not happy, at least fairly contented with their lot. We laughed a lot in our family, and we took care of one another and the people around us. And I suppose, because they were relatives, or neighbours, or friends, which pretty much covered everyone we met, we were kind. Kindness was a basic rule of life. It wasn't taught us, we just absorbed it. I've seen my mother give the shawl around her shoulders to a woman who was in need. And when someone was injured, when a seaman drown-ded, or a child died, mother was there. She'd find practical ways to help the family that other people hadn't thought of. She was the one who saw that old Harry Cook who lived a few doors down from us couldn't manage any more but was too proud to ask for help, and so she made sure that we boys helped him. Aaron chopped his logs and we moved them and stacked them by his fire, collecting kindling from the big beeches and sycamores over at Shadycombe and piling the dry twigs by his fire together with the paper twists that mother had made to light his candles. Mother gave him jams and preserves from the summer fruits and she and several other women baked him bread or an extra pie if they had the means. Milk and eggs were brought to him by people who had little enough themselves. We ran errands for him, bringing him a bit of bacon from Butcher Hannaford, or fish from the quay when the boats came in. When he became ill it was my mother who made him the milk puddings that were the only thing he could eat. When he died, it was Ellen who washed him, dressed him in his Sunday clothes, and laid pennies on his eyes. He had a pauper's funeral, but the whole street followed the coffin. He was a local man and he was one of us.

It was Ellen too who took care of Sam Putt when his arm got mangled in the winch on his fishing boat. We boys helped him sort the fish, carried things for him and tried to be useful, but it was Ellen who hitched up her skirts and sat down on the quay mending his nets just as competently and neatly as she darned our socks or mended our torn trousers.

She could turn her hand to anything. Ellen nursed the sick, and doctored them with her herb medicines. She could birth babies if needed and splint up bones. She was the one people called when little Joey Crispin fell out of the tree and cracked his skull, and when Elizabeth, a young Cranch cousin fell into the icy sea. And all the time behind Ellen was Aaron. It was a long time before I realised that it was Aaron who was the strong one, That without Aaron, Ellen could not have existed.

I used to watch them sometimes in the evening. They would walk down to the Quay together and stand and look out at the sea. Sometimes Aaron would put his arm around her, and we boys, who had crept out of the house and were watching when we were supposed to be in bed, would see her smile coyly and put her dark head against his shoulder like a young bride and we would giggle and pretend to retch because we were boys and we thought such things were soppy.. But I think secretly each of us was moved by the sight. My parents love for each other seemed to make everything in our world safe and secure. The heavens could move and the big tides rip in the November gales, but our little cottage with its yellow lamplight, was always full of warmth and love. It was a place of safety such as all homes should be.

CHAPTER THREE

It was at this time that the young men of several local families left Salcombe to seek their fortunes in countries such as America, Canada and Australia. They travelled in the footsteps of fathers and grandfathers who had sailed in the big sailing ships. In several instances, particularly with the fishermen who had followed the cod to Newfoundland and the North Eastern United States, they already had relatives there. Others, despairing of finding work at home, were lured by newspaper advertisements offering cheap land in the colonies. Sometimes it was just one son, the most adventurous, who left, but often they travelled with brothers or relatives, so that several Salcombe families were stripped of their sons in this way. The Burners family, relatives by marriage, lost four sons and one daughter in a single generation. Whether for good or bad, the emigrants seldom returned and when the adventurer was illiterate as was often the case, the family all too soon lost contact with him.

There were now few jobs left in the town. When work was available there were always too many applicants and employers reduced wages accordingly, so that even amongst the households whose menfolk had work, there was acute distress.

But there were good men in Salcombe who saw the hardship around them and tried their best to alleviate it. One of these benefactors was the Earl of Devon, who then lived for part of the year at "The Moult". He hired labourers and some Salcombe and Hope Cove fishermen who had fallen on hard times and set them to work cutting a road through to Bolt Head, which became known as Courtney Walk. The men were paid 1/- a day for the work, and they were grateful for it. My father was able to play a small part in this project which delighted him. His master, Major Bennett had bought "Woodcot" for his family home and Aaron had been given the task of re-designing its extensive formal and kitchen gardens. Though he was still

Head Gardener at "The Marine Hotel", he spent most of his time at "Woodcot".

Eastern view of "Woodville", later "Woodcot" from early engraving by Letitia Byrne.

A feature of "Woodcot"'s sweeping front lawn at that time was a massive Californian Monterey Pine which dominated the landscape. It was a tree which Aaron grew very fond of. He loved the giant twisted majesty of the branches and he had grown quite a number of saplings from its fir cones. Some of these saplings were now over six feet tall, and he ventured to speak to his master and to the Earl of Devon's head gardener, to put forward his idea that the trees would be ideal for planting around the newly cleared area of South Sands.

The suggestion was agreed on condition that the two gardeners use their expertise to train the workforce in their own time. Both threw themselves into the challenge and it was not long before labourers and fishermen had learnt how to plant and nurture the saplings and were keeping a knowledgeable weather eye on them as they grew. Though he had never seen the Monterey trees in their native habitat, Aaron instinctively understood their affinity with the rocks and wild places of a shoreline and he felt that they would look perfectly at home on the cliffs above our own harbour. And he was right, for the trees thrived, as did the others that he planted later on the East Portlemouth side of the harbour. They are still there as is their parent tree at "Woodcot", and years later I was able to point them out to my grandchildren.

But the men who had been helped in this way were only a small fraction of the town's workforce. As times grew harder, more and more working men were forced to leave. One after the other they made the agonising decision to abandon their elderly and infirm to the care of the Workhouse. Carrying bundles and pushing handcarts families began to move along the roads towards Plymouth or Exeter, heading anywhere where there were rumours of work. They walked stolidly, like cattle, day after day, hungry, filthy and exhausted. At night they slept in fields or ditches huddled together for warmth. There were men amongst them who felt such shame at the hardship they had brought upon their families, that they deserted them never to return.

The town was emptying, and the once bustling harbour was quiet. There were few topsail ships now in the Haven. Some boats with good skippers lasted longer than the rest, even now returning high profits, but as always there was the element of luck. Ultimately the boats were at the mercy of the seas. An overdue ship brought townspeople out onto the street, desperate for news. We boys had learned to recognise the local ships and often ran out to the cliffs to try and be the first to spot them returning, each wanting to be the one to bring the good news of its safe arrival to the town. Then there was relief and jubilation and the taverns did a fine trade, but there were other times when there was no safe return.

When a ship was feared lost you would see women waiting on the cliffs, wrapped in their shawls, staring out to sea. Sometimes they would have a baby in their arms, or little children at their skirts, and that broke your heart to see.

Little by little the character of the town had begun to change. Plots of land were auctioned in London and strangers came. Building work began, and the first wealthy incomers arrived to take possession of the homes they had had built. Others followed, and they in their turn bought land, and their presence made work for masons and carpenters.

The builders needed sand in their construction work, so building sand for Kingsbridge and Salcombe was collected from the lower part of Millbay beach and was delivered to the town quays. On Spring tides when the town flooded, three, four or more such barges were engaged in this trade, the boats grounding at low water to enable gangs of men to shovel the sand aboard. The noisy shipbuilding yards on the waterfront were mostly gone by now except Patey's Yard, which continued in these years by building sailing barges for use in the Estuary. It was said openly however that Mr Bennett who had other building projects going on in the town at the time, had designs on this yard too, to further enlarge "The Marine Hotel".

At the age of seven we were moved to the Higher School which was also a church school. We boys gained a new headmaster, a bearded Cornishman

New houses at"The Park", Salcombe. P Marshman

called Mr Coad who we gradually came to appreciate as a wonderful character. He knew boys and he knew how to teach. Once again he was assisted in the classroom by pupil teachers, former scholars who would be going on to teacher training college. There was one paid assistant, a tall, thin, rather dour looking man who was given to brandishing a large black ruler menacingly at us for any misdemeanour. However all corporal punishment was administered by our headmaster, which was a mixed blessing as although he was fair, he was an artist with the thin cane which he used liberally on our hands and sometimes our posteriors.

Summoned by the tolling of the school bell, we lined up for assembly at nine o' clock. We had prayers and a hymn – often "Non Nobis Domine", which we bellowed out lustily to the tinny accompaniment of our rather battered piano played usually by Mr Coad, before heading off to our classrooms. Our lessons consisted of a continued relentless grounding in the three "R's", again rigorously instilled in us by means of rote learning. We recited our times tables, and did maths, and we read and then laboriously transcribed words written on the blackboard in the neat, legible copper plate script that we were being taught. At about 11 a.m. we had a ten minute break before continuing our lessons until 12.30 when we had the food we had brought with us, usually thick slices of bread and dripping.

School started again at 2 p.m and continued until 4.30. No organised games were ever attempted. We were there to learn, not to play.

It was taken for granted that as Englishmen in the making we possessed a sense of fair play: it was assumed that we would naturally be good sports who fought by the Marquis of Queensbury's rules. All these worthy precepts would have been instantly dispelled at the sight of the rough and tumble we participated in when school let out and we turned back into little savages!

I was in the choir for most of my school life and had to stay behind for half an hour's practise twice a week. The practise was conducted by Mr Coad, who was both the organist and the choir master. He always detailed a full complement of eighteen boys with six substitutes to allow for absences. At harvest times especially when every last pair of hands was needed on the farms, there were always gaps. Now that money was scarce, many boys had to work rather than go to school and in such cases teachers often turned a blind eye to absences.

I was a reasonably attentive scholar and came top of the VII Standard for a few months before I left. Seated next to me in class was the head master's only son, Will, who was a little older than me. We were both addicted to a magazine called "Boy's Friend", and used to read it together under the desk.

When he caught us at it, Mr Coad used to snatch it up, wave it triumphantly above his head and bellow "Boy's Friend – Boy's Enemy, more like" before hauling each of us forward by the ear to receive a double dose of his cane. Will, when I last heard of him had become a Church of England Canon, and Vicar of Macclesfield.

Along with the "Boy's Friend" we devoured "penny dreadfuls" illustrated with lurid pictures of highwaymen, bandits and cloaked villains liberally endowed with curling black moustaches. Our favourites were always the pirates, sailing under the skull and crossbones flag, wearing tri-corner hats, possessed of fearsome names; the doers of blood curdling deeds. With our slates tipped to provide cover we pored over pictures of these anti-heroes poised on the gunwales of gale tossed ships, cutlass in teeth, and a wicked, devil-may-care expression on their faces, but there was a curious ambivalence about our attitude to them. We were Salcombe's sons, and we too felt the blood pound in our veins when the storm winds howled, and knew within us the primitive lure of the wrecked and helpless ship floundering on the rocks, ripe for the plucking. A great number of the very homes we lived in had been built from shipwreck timber. Many of us were descended from the pirates who had once terrorised the harbour. Years later I discovered that at least two others of my immediate ancestors had been found guilty of piratical acts besides the ubiquitous William and Lizzie.

We lived with this hidden side of village life, with what we, with good Devon common sense, called self-sufficiency but what the Crown still chose to call "Acts of Piracy" and "Smuggling". There were few Estuary families who had not been directly involved.

When my brothers and I got home from school we were given something to eat before we started our chores. We all had our tasks to perform, even my younger brother Frederik who had not yet graduated to the Higher School. Children's labour was essential in order for the family to live respectably and hold its head up in the community, to save a little where possible, and to maintain membership subscriptions to the Sick Club, vital in those days before the National Health Service. Any extra money that came into the household coffers, controlled always by the women, was saved if it could be.

Every possible way was found to stretch the family budget. Each extra penny tucked away beneath the ticking of the horsehair or straw mattress or in the old cracked tea pot on the mantelshelf above the range, was a little more defence against debt.

Debt was the bogeyman which haunted us all. My mother Ellen lived with the fear of poverty all her life and she passed this on to us.

The Kingsbridge Poor House set in extensive grounds back from Fore Street and visible everywhere around the town was the Bogeyman incarnate.

I had not been there, but my brother Frank had been taken there one day by my father who had been told by his master to deliver some old blankets from the hotel. They had set off in the horse and cart early in the morning and made the delivery, but a cart wheel had split just as they were pulling away from the Workhouse and made it impossible to leave. While father went off to get help, Frank stayed with the horse. After a while it began to rain heavily, and he took shelter under the building's eaves. As he was standing there, a man came out of a room leaving the hall door ajar, and through the gap my brother had a view of a vast, vaulted room. There was a big table running the length of the room and seated on benches on either side of it were grey clad women, he told me later. The table was piled high with a tangle of tarred rope and the women were picking at the oakum and unravelling it under the supervision of a fat, stern looking woman. Most of the women were elderly, but some were young and one or two had small children with them Frank told me. He said that several of the older women were agitated and appeared unable to settle, but it was the rest, bent dull eyed over their endless task with such an air of defeat about them that he said he preferred to stand out in the rain with the horse rather than spend a moment longer looking at them.

Ending up in the Workhouse was considered a disgrace. But such an end sometimes happened almost without anyone knowing how. Aaron told us

Page 85: Salcombe from Onslow Road. P Marshman

gravely that we should not judge others. My father taught us compassion by his own gentle, kindly example. Ellen, being Temperance, tended towards a more militant approach. If a man preferred drink or gambling to saving money for his family, he would always come to a bad end, she declared darkly. But Ellen was only too well aware that for each man who chose that path there was a woman and innocent children who were dragged down it with him, and Ellen was always a champion of the oppressed. People in need seemed to gravitate towards my mother, and she always did whatever she could to help them.

She was in Fore Street one day and came across an elderly couple sitting on the wall in front of Council Quay. Their names were Bill and Betsy Dozmay, and they were itinerant crop pickers from Cornwall. They had walked from Ivybridge where they had been digging potatoes. Both had terrible arthritis due to sleeping out in all weathers. Betsy's hands were so swollen that her fingers looked shapeless and knobbly like the vegetables she garnered. Bill walked so bent over that he could only look at your face if you spoke to him by twisting his head sideways.

They had nothing and nowhere to go and they were in despair. Betsy was too weak to carry on walking, and so mother took them to sleep in our shed and sit by our fire at night. She gave them a blanket from her own bed and did her best to take care of them. She fed them and looked after them for as long as she could, but that year was a hard one and my parents themselves could barely make ends meet. So Betsy and Bill were taken to the Workhouse. They were sent to different areas, he to the Men's Ward, she to the Women's. They were perhaps in their mid-seventies, and they had never been apart before. It broke their hearts. Bill died first.. He was too proud to accept that he could no longer take care of his wife. Betsy did not die, but it would perhaps have been better if she had, because her mind went, and she wept constantly for her husband, wailing and clutching at anyone who came near her, demanding to know where he was and when he would be coming for her.

It was the only time I ever saw my indomitable mother weep.

I had begun to get a sense of things happening outside my own world. Events in the world at large affected us, Mr Coad taught us. The blackboard in the schoolroom became our information sheet. As was proper for young men, it was important that we should know about world events, he declared. He began to pin up articles cut from his newspaper, making sure that we read them. He based his lessons around the more interesting stories. In that he was well ahead of his times. Thus information about Gladstone's resignation as our Prime Minister after 62 years in 1894, gave him the chance to teach us about the English parliamentary system.

Later that same year the announcement that the government had passed a law called the Local Government Act, to create 6880 parish and rural district councils which would each oversee its own immediate area, gave him the impetus to declaim for almost an hour about the way villages and towns like Salcombe had developed through the ages. He said nothing about the newspaper article telling of Oscar Wilde's imprisonment in Reading Gaol and the reason for it. That sort of thing did not go on. If he had told us, we would not have had the vaguest idea what he was talking about anyway.

Some of the items of information that permeated from the greater world were tremendously interesting. They came to us sometimes not from the newspapers, but from some of the still very few visitors who came to the town, whose presence in Salcombe was advised in the local newspaper. I was turning the corner into Onslow Road early one morning on an errand, and was nearly mown down by a young woman careering down the hill on a bicycle. The method of her passage was so intriguing, as it was the first bicycle I had ever seen, that I almost forgot to tell my family the other fascinating fact which was this wonderful machine was being driven by a woman, and a woman who, astonishingly, was wearing trousers!

My mother had a full time job looking after us and the house, although she still did occasional dressmaking work, but both my parents were thrifty and they influenced us in this regard. My mother was particularly inventive in the ways in which she stretched the housekeeping money. She made her own lye soap and candles, and whenever she had any surplus fruit or vegetables, she bottled them and added them to the storage shelf in the outside shed, against the time when they might be needed. Everything was saved. String and brown paper was carefully re-used. Sacking was re-sewn and made into small storage sacks, or used as an apron for rough work such as scrubbing the step or the entrance way at the back. She made her own brooms with twigs tied firmly around a straight hazel stick, and her own vinegar which she mixed with sea water for cleaning. She even saved the ashes from the fire, using them to scrub the yard, to keep her brass flower pot gleaming, and to spread around my father's two precious apple trees that he had grown from seed.

In addition to his gardening work, my father, who was well known locally for the quality of the vegetables and fruit that he grew in his garden plot was part of the barter system which was widespread in Salcombe. We boys often carried baskets of his produce around the town. His first choice for exchange was always one of the butchers, usually John Vivian's or Hannafords in Island Street, but he also dealt with the grocers, Sarah Shepherd in Union Street, or Hardens in Church Street   In return we received offcuts of meat and offal, sometimes even a few sausages, an ounce or two of tea or some broken biscuits. The system benefitted all. My father handed out his surplus from the goodness of his heart and because he hated to see waste, but he was a family man and he needed to feed his family, and thus he chose his recipients carefully.   When Frank or I appeared in a shop with a basket of Aaron's produce it was very seldom that we did not return with a basket bearing goods of at least equal value. It was how the town worked.

Sometimes household need dictated Aaron's gifts.   Mother's enamel washing bowl rusted through soon after we moved to Robinson's Row, and only weeks later the handle came off her saucepan so Frank and I lugged our baskets of garden produce to Fred Trute in Union Street, and came back with a new washing bowl and the promise that her saucepan would soon be returned as good as new.   That was a good trade and everyone was happy. We were definitely less than pleased at the number of baskets we had to carry to William Murch the boot maker in Island Street to get new boots for father.   Considering he was family – although not close – we thought the price in vegetables to be quite high.

Father said nothing except that he wished he had trained as a boot maker

---

Page 85: Salcombe from Bonaventure Road. C 1900.P. Marshman.

rather than a gardener.

One of the best trades was for newspapers. Newspapers were our entertainment. Father usually took them first, looking at the pictures and painstakingly making out the words of some of the articles that interested him most. When we were older we would read to him, none of us caring that sometimes by then the news was several days old. After they had been thoroughly absorbed the newspapers were used in a variety of ways. The pages of the biggest were used for getting the stove to draw and for putting on the floor in wet weather. My mother used other pages to polish windows, to wrap vegetable and eggs to keep them fresh, and to tie around the cloth that covered my father's pasty to keep it warm for his dinner. It then came to us boys for cutting up into neat squares and threading on string for use in the privy. Finally when all other uses had been exhausted, my father chopped up the remainder to add to his compost heap, which was one of the secrets of his fine vegetables.

As well as the eggs from the chickens my mother kept and the flowers in season from my father's garden, we boys contributed by combing the fences of the fields above Shadycombe where sheep were kept, and sold these gleanings. We gathered mushrooms and wild garlic, and blackberries and countless leaves that we knew were good to eat. But one of our best scavengings was for sloes. We knew the areas where they grew, and we would set out with our baskets, returning home scratched and sore, sometimes with bruises from fighting off rival sloe gatherers, but always with our baskets full. My father would see to it that our pickings were sold to the pubs which made their own sloe gin. Everything had some value, particularly we found, when it was something that rich people would not bother to garner for themselves.

And rich people there were in Salcombe, living in the same town, but enjoying a completely separate existence from us. Their antics and conduct proved endlessly interesting. Just at this time a group of eight gentlemen met to form what they originally called the "Salcombe Sailing Club" but which two years later became the "Salcombe Yacht Club". It was a club for gentlemen only, and had little to do with the town itself. Most of the originators came from outside the area, though we knew some by sight. My father's master, Major Bennett was a founder member, as were Charles Roddick, E Hopkins, Dr. Arthur Pearce, W J Shaw, T W Latham, the Rev. Edmunson and Cyril Turner. Mr Froude was on the committee. The Honorary Secretary was Cyril Turner who went on to serve in that capacity for twenty five years. The Honorary Treasurer was Commander Herbert. The Vice Commodore was a man called Andrew McIlwraith. I had seen him around town a few times and I knew he was Scottish and the owner of a shipping line. He was a big, bluff man. He must have been in his late fifties then and his red hair and beard were shot with white. If I had known then

Holy Trinity Church and old cottage. C 1899. J Fairweather.

what an impact this man would have on the lives of all my family, I would have been astonished. As it was at that time, the most important thing I knew about him was that he had a sailing dinghy called "Foam" which was reckoned to be one of the fastest boats around.

But it was as if Fate had been waiting for these signs that we had taken our eyes momentarily off the struggle for daily survival, for it was at this time that my father lost his job. By now in the early 1890's there was a great deal of building in Salcombe. A new hotel, to be called the "York Hotel" was under construction. It was the first purpose built hotel in the town. This was owned by the magnificently dashing Mr Ryder, the man who had sailed in Russia and recently been the subject of a cartoon in Punch for his exploits. He had just returned from Paris, where he had moved to escape the attention of the press, and he was now again to be seen about town.

The work on this rival hotel brought more alterations and extensions to"The Marine Hotel" and for a while this meant that the gardeners were laid off. It was at this time that Major Bennett moved with his family from "Woodcot". Perhaps if anyone had given any thought to the fate of the man who had once rejoiced in the title of Head Gardener, some work might have been found for him, but suddenly there was none. The cottage in Robinson's Row was a tied cottage that went with my father's work, and we were summarily given a week's notice to leave by Mr Bennett's agent. Everything that had seemed secure about our existence disappeared overnight and our little world came crashing down around us. We had nowhere to go and we were only too aware that if my father did not find a job quickly we would soon have nothing to eat.

Aaron immediately began looking for work and searching for somewhere for us to live as my mother started to pack our belongings.

My father had a reputation in town as a hard worker, but that did not help him now. There was simply no work for him. Zealously guarding her small teapot of savings, my mother became more frugal with our food rations. To make matters worse it was winter and my father's vegetable garden yielded little.

Every morning brought the day of our eviction closer, and still we had found nowhere to live and no work for my father to do.

Frighteningly quickly my mother had to dip into her reserve savings and use the money to buy food for us. As if they sensed the trouble in the household, the hens chose this time to stop laying. We conferred, and then began killing them off one by one, eating well for a time, but acutely aware that when the last of them was gone there was no money to buy more.

We found a cottage to rent at 16 Island Street, and used the last of our savings to pay the deposit. The building was in a bad state of repair, but Aaron talked to the landlady and they agreed between them that he would attend to the renovations in return for a reduction in rent.

We had somewhere to live but we had still had to find money to pay the rent, something we had never had to do before as all our homes had been tied cottages. We were living on a knife edge and things rapidly went from bad to worse. My boots began to leak and I patched them with cardboard without telling anyone so as not to worry my parents. But then my brother Fred tore his trousers beyond repair...

My father got a few days piece work shovelling sand on Millbay and then was employed to clear an overgrown garden for newcomers at the top of town. Two weeks went by with nothing, then he was hired to travel up the estuary on one of the barges to help load slate from Frogmore Quarry. Then that work too, dried up.

A few weeks later Aaron found piece work loading stone on the road to Plymouth. He was used to hard work, but the overseer on the job worked the men like pack mules. Though he tried to be cheerful for our sakes, my father came home at night exhausted. The limestone cracked his hands and made them bleed. My mother rubbed them with lard which helped a little. Lacking gloves, he bound them with rags. But in the house things were bad. The cooking pot on the stove now seemed to be always half empty, its contents bulked out with suet pudding and hedgerow leaves. The love in our family now worked against us because both Aaron and Ellen insisted that we boys had the pick of whatever food there was, and would not listen to our refusals. The food tasted like ashes in our mouths as we saw our

dear parents grow thin and gaunt from lack of food. My mother mended clothes and took in laundry to earn a little extra and the kitchen dripped with steam from the big pan boiling on the stove. There were times when we were so hungry that the bubbling laundry looked appetising.

We boys did what we could, and there were several times when we were employed by new comers to do tasks that should properly have been done by men. It seemed that wealthy people did not like to pay proper wages. They wanted work done on the cheap. Still our labour meant a few extra coppers coming into the household and we were glad to do it.

One morning my mother told us quietly that the rent had not been paid. Aaron said little these days. We knew he blamed himself for our situation, but it was not his fault. He and my mother talked things over and agreed that it was better to be honest and admit to the landlady that we could not pay her rather than have our non-payment drift on into acrimony and possible eviction. My father, dressed in his Sunday clothes and with his cap in his hand, his shoulders tense with worry, went to see her to explain our situation.

We waited anxiously at home, but when he returned we saw by his face that we had been reprieved at least for the moment. "'Er said 'er would allow us time to pay, s'long as us pay what us owe as soon as able," Aaron reported. We learned later that our landlady had agreed because she said that we had been good tenants even though we had been there for such a short time, and had fully kept our side of the agreement by working hard on the house and garden.

At least it gave us a little breathing space, but I knew my mother barely slept for worrying in those days. We had a roof over our heads, but our main concern was still finding money for food. Locals helped. William Hannaford the butcher, gave us bones to make broth from his shop; the Pepperells in the grocer's shop nearby, proved themselves good neighbours and gave us a regular supply of household basics such as flour, salt and tinned peas on credit. We gave them what vegetables from the garden we could spare, but as yet our garden was not producing much. Baker Yeomans gave us left over bread, and once their niece, Sara Gillard who had trained as a confectioner, brought over a cake with icing on top which had been ordered by the cook in one of the big houses, but had not been called for. Now and then we also received a sack of potatoes or vegetables from Aaron's family. Though he hated doing it Aaron had been forced to call on his brothers and sisters for help. Friends and neighbours did what they could, but they mostly had little enough for themselves. The pittance Aaron was earning from occasional work at least kept us from starving, but our subscriptions to the Sick Club had to be allowed to lapse. I think this frightened Ellen more than almost anything.

We were surviving but only just. We boys each had small jobs outside the house but we were earning very little. We made sure however that we did what we could to make Aaron's load lighter when he was at home. We had largely taken over clearing the cottage's overgrown garden; we had cleared the rubbish that our landlady's previous tenant had accumulated in the store that adjoined the house and had cleaned and tidied up around the outside. We had even attempted to mend some of the broken woodwork, but had not made a good job of it since although we had painstakingly straightened and re-used old nails, we could not afford to buy the necessary paint.

I was in the old store next to the house, sitting with my legs dangling over the top floor on a bright March morning when Frank came to find me. I had been sweeping up, clearing what seemed to me like a hundred years accumulation of cobwebs and filthy bits of straw, all morning, and I was taking a breather.

I could see immediately from my brother's face that he was upset, but it was a while before I could get the story out of him. When he did tell me how poorly my father had been treated I was horrified, almost unable to believe what I was hearing.

The weather had been unseasonably warm and breaking stones was thirsty work so father took a bottle of water to work with him each day. The day before his water bottle had fallen over and smashed. There was a stream thirty or forty yards down the road and my father asked permission to leave his post to drink from it, but the overseer refused to allow him to do so. Another man offered him water from his own bottle but Aaron refused it in case it ran the other short.

He tried to reason with the overseer, saying that he would make up the few minutes he would lose by going to the stream, but the overseer became angry, and threatened him with his whip. To keep the peace Aaron was forced to continue working, thirsty.

I don't know how Frank came by this information, because my father certainly wouldn't have told us, but my first reaction was a desire to go and find the overseer and hit him. I grabbed my jacket and swung down to the floor, and took off through the house followed by a worried Frank. But in the passageway I collided with my mother. She guessed instantly what had happened, and she grabbed hold of me.

I was strong but I was a child, and she swung me against the wall and pinned me there, forcing me to listen as she told me bluntly that we simply could not afford to upset the overseer and risk father losing his job.

I could barely see for the fury that was in me. The fact that someone

Unloading bricks on Millbay, Salcombe. c 1900

could treat my decent, hardworking father in this way made me angrier than I had ever been in my life, but gradually Ellen's quiet, insistent voice penetrated the red mist of anger that half blinded me. "Quiet now, quiet", she murmured over and over again, and though I think no-one else could have calmed me, Ellen did. We were so alike. Both of us had an anger in us, a hard toughness that none of the others possessed.

She let go of me, but she stared into my eyes, holding me now by the force of her will rather than by any physical restraint, and slowly the anger drained out of me, leaving an eight year old boy shaking with an impotence he had never experienced before. Then that emotion too left me, and in its place came a coldness, a hatred for men who could treat others so, that lay like a piece of ice in my soul.

I had no words to put into speech what I was feeling. "I won't let it 'appen agen" I said fiercely. I didn't have to explain: through all the years of her own childhood suffering, my mother understood.

"I know, boy," she said. "I know…"

They say that it is always darkest before the dawn, and I believe that.

Abruptly in the next few weeks, things changed for the better. As spring approached, Aaron began to pick up the occasional day of gardening work. He was employed at both the big new hotels, though they now kept only a small staff of gardeners, as these workers had been replaced by hotel staff. But my father packed in as much as he could each day, starting early and working until it was too dark to see, and with the money he brought in, gradually, infinitely slowly, our family drew back from the abyss. Bit by bit we repaid the overdue rent. We paid up the Sick Club which I know made both my parents relieved. Then we made sure we returned the kindnesses we had received, bringing food to replace food that had been given to us and money where that too had been forthcoming. We bought some fertile eggs and mother hatched eight chicks which pleased her no end. She successfully reared seven of them, and we put them in a pen in the garden which we boys had made from oddments scavenged from the town refuse dump. Our father met up with some gardening friends and came home in high delight with a pocket full of seeds and some dried beans in tiny paper packets which William Lapthorne and James Putt had given him. He later swopped some for other seed with two of his brothers, and then did a further swop for parsnip seeds from Bill Lapthorne, who gardened for one of the incomers. Meantime, we boys dug and weeded to increase the size of our vegetable garden. We built a rabbit hutch and a few days later Aaron brought home a box containing baby rabbits for us to rear and sell to the town's butchers where there was always a ready market. We all hoped that there would also be enough to give us some for our pot. Want had sharpened our appetites.

Then one evening my father managed to replace the first shilling in my mother's savings tea pot. That night we had a small piece of broiling beef for our meal and we all ate our fill for the first time in a very long time. Cautiously optimistic our family began to get back on an even keel, but this episode had shaken us all. It taught us boys as perhaps nothing else could have the necessity of a hedge against disaster. I understood now the connection between my mother's thrift and her savings, and the lack of money which had made people like Bill and Betsy Dozmay so vulnerable and helpless in their later days.

My brothers and I continued tidying gardens and running errands around the town In season we picked blackcurrants and other soft fruits from our own garden and several allotments. This was a job we hated. We had to pick each berry singly, being very careful not to crush or bruise them. Then we had to deliver them to Patey's shop in Union Street. Mrs Patey would scrutinise our offerings minutely. If she noticed a single stem, a stray leaf or a damaged berry, she would glare at us and scold us until sometimes Frederik was in tears. I would never cry. I refused to give her the satisfaction of seeing that she had upset me. I repaid her by carefully picking the required number of perfect berries, but putting them in as many separate containers as I could find, and delivering them one by one, so that with an air of complete innocence I could claim I was doing exactly what she had instructed. By the time I had invaded her shop for the sixth time taking up her time and preventing her from conducting her trade, Mary Patey couldn't have cared less how many bruised berries I presented.

We boys all hated her at the time, but I wonder now if she was just exhausted. In common with most shop keepers then, she would have worked what was probably at least a fourteen hour day, six days a week, only opening shorter hours on Sunday. Mary Patey in addition was a widow with four children at school and a dependent mother, brother and sister in her home, so she must have had her hands full.

On Saturdays my work took me to the churchyard where I was responsible for the care and cleaning of the gravestones, for weeding the paths, removing the dead flowers mourners had left at the graves, and generally looking after the churchyard and keeping it tidy. I also cleaned the memorial brasses inside the church, dusted the pews, tidied the hymn books and made sure the kneeling cushions were all hanging properly on their hooks.

Before I was ten I would also go up to the Vicarage after school to do odd jobs. The Wesleyan Minister, Mr Green, had let out the vicarage to enable him to afford a curate to help him in his work. He lived in the house next to the girls' school, but at this time a family from London were living in the "Old Vicarage". I had been working for them for a year. My duties in their household were to clean boots and household knives; to carry up coal and lay fires; to sweep down the front steps, polish the door knocker and letter plate and overall to run errands and make myself useful wherever I could.

My education continued until I was eleven years old, when my elder brother, who worked in Doctor Twining's household, crushed his finger while helping their maid feed wet laundry through the mangle. Though the injury was quite severe and had been sustained in the course of his work, Frank received no compensation and so, as was normal in those days, the next child in line in the family was taken out of school in order to keep his job open. There was no question of regret at my missed schooling, or discussion as to whether or not I was strong enough for these duties. Frank had been employed to do odd jobs, including washing the bloodied bandages and emptying medicine bottles as well as delivering medicines and potions to the sick, and so this work now devolved upon me.

At the end of seven weeks, when my brother's finger had healed sufficiently for him to go back to work, I returned to school. Now I was bigger the number of jobs I had to do in my spare time increased. My parents had always taught us to look out for others, and it seemed to me that

Fore Street, Salcombe. c 1894. Fairweather. Note dirt road. Beneath the gas lamp is the entrance to Robinsons Row.

there were at this time quite a number of older people in the town who needed help. I hauled coal, cleaned boots and swept paths, as well as chopping wood for several households. I was a dab hand with an axe though it was almost as tall as I was.

Frank was now fourteen, at the age when he would be apprenticed. Thanks to their thrift, my parents had put aside enough money to pay for this. My father managed to indenture him to a carpenter and joiner, one of the most respected and best paid of all the apprenticeships, so my parents were justly proud.

That left the thorny question of Frank's job with the doctor which would now become vacant. I wanted that job, but more to the point we needed it. Frank had been told that in his apprenticeship he would receive no pay for two years, so the family had somehow to make up that missing income. My younger brother was still at school, and though he too had several jobs, he was not earning very much. It meant that after my father, I would become the main breadwinner. It was very important to us all that I secured that job.

I talked to Frank at length while he was working his notice and together we made a plan. I hoped that I would benefit from the fact that I had already covered for my elder brother while he was injured without major incident but I wanted to make sure of the position.

I got Frank to make a copy of the new timetable of his duties that the doctor's wife had recently pinned up in the little back eaves room where the medicine bottles were stored. I learned this rota by heart so that I knew exactly what I would have to do, and when. I realised that the doctor and his wife were busy people, and my plan was to show them that I could seamlessly follow on from my brother, performing the same duties just as well – if not better, for I was competitive! – so that they did not have the bother of teaching a new boy. Frank's part in this was to talk up my skills, passing over to his employers the handwritten list of my previous employments, together with a note from the vicar and two other employers praising my industry, which I had given him. Just in case they had forgotten, he would remind them that I had already worked in their household and been deemed satisfactory.

I thought that I had covered everything and confidently expected the summons to attend for an interview, after all both the doctor and his wife had professed themselves pleased with my brother's work, and sorry to see him leave. But in the meantime I discovered to my dismay that Mrs Twining had already advertised the position in the "Salcombe Times".

I knew that this was considered a plumb job amongst the boys in the town, and I was aware that there would be much competition for it. I discovered that one of my Cranch cousins, a bigger, stronger boy than I, had been telling his friends that he was applying and confidently boasting that he would get the post, and this made me even more determined.

All was now in hand, and I persuaded Frank to let me go to work with him on his last day. I knew that the interviews were set for that afternoon, and that meant as I saw it, that I had the morning to prove my worth…

I was nervous as we walked up the street. I was neatly dressed and with my hair freshly slicked down. I had a cowlick which always stood up, and despite my having plastered it down before I left home, standing at the pump holding the small piece of cracked mirror which I had taken from the shelf in the kitchen, by the time I got into the street, I could see by my reflection in the shop windows that it was sticking up again.

We walked up towards "The Knoll". Several of the shopkeepers putting out their wares saw us passing and guessing where we were going, called out to me, smiling and wishing me luck.

My plan worked as well as I had hoped it would, and I got the job.

Dr. Twining laughed and told me I was a clever fellow who would go far, though I had to fight my cousin later to defend my position, wrestling him down into the mud of the estuary until he surrendered.

I was cock-a-hoop. I walked like a man as I strode back through the town that evening with my brother. I was not allowed regret at the fact that I was barely 12 ½ and my schooling was over. I think anyway I was rather proud of having a real all day working job and to be earning what seemed to me then to be the vast sum of 3/6d per week.

I gave all my wages to my mother of course. It was expected. But she always managed to give me back a little, sometimes even as much as 6d for myself. I saved it carefully. I saw this money as a passport to a better life.

My tasks in my new job were to clean and dust the waiting room, the consulting room and the surgery, taking away any dirty medicine bottles and replacing them with clean. I shook the mats, cleaned the steps, fed the doctor's wife's chickens and collected their eggs. At 8.30 I went home to breakfast, but I had to be back again at the surgery by nine to answer the door to patients.

Between times I cleaned boots and knives, swept the paths and general areas, washed down the iron railings at the front, wiped the paintwork on windows and doors, swept the front steps and the stairs, cleaned the boot scraper and polished the front door knocker and the rest of the brass, which thanks to my church work I had had a lot of practise in.

At about ten o'clock, the doctor's wife used to ask me to see what vegetables I could pick in the garden for what they called "lunch" but which to me was "dinner". Sometimes I had to kill and pluck a chicken for their meal. But though this was a task I did not enjoy, and, I am ashamed to say, botched the first couple of times I tried it, I was pleased to do as it meant that my family got the bones later. There were two cooks in the doctor's household, Mary and Grace, both in their early twenties. They were sometimes too lazy to use up the chicken bones and the skin for making stock, something my mother always did. So this was another way we gained.

There were always errands for me to run, letters to take to the post office or last minute jobs to do. My duties included assisting Ellen Youlden, the maid, who was the only one who lived in, though two others came in from the town every day. I would fetch the step ladder and climb up to dust the tops of the bookcases and the tall cupboards; wipe the skirting boards and picture tops and take down the delicate gas mantles for cleaning every week. I hated doing the gas mantles as I knew that if I broke one of them the cost of a replacement would be a large chunk of my wages. On Monday wash days I had to help Mrs Putt the laundress who came in, to squeeze the washing through the old mangle wringer. It was a cumbersome, unwieldy thing and knowing that this was how my brother's finger had been crushed, I was always very careful when I used it. I knew I could not afford to lose this job.

I still maintained the schedule of duties that Frank had worked to, with each day of the week listed together with the tasks that should be completed on that day. Like Frank before me, I spent a lot of my time in the little eaves bottle store. The room was perhaps seven feet long and between three and a half and five feet wide, with a sloping roof. It was over the wash room, and the smell of bleach which Mrs Putt used on Mondays permeated the whole place. It was a smell I quickly grew to dislike intensely.

The clean medicine bottles were lined up on the shelves. There were clear ones as well as blue, green and brown ones depending on what they were needed for. Nearby were containers holding different sized stoppers and rubber topped droppers. The dirty bottles were piled in boxes scattered haphazardly on the floor. Some of the bottles such as the big ones for "Kaolin cum Morph" used for stomach conditions, the calamine used for calming chicken pox spots, the much smaller bottles in which sedatives such as laudanum or morphine were dispensed and the two sizes of ointment jars, large and small, were used often. Other sizes for the more obscure conditions such as fevers and congenital illnesses as well as problems which were not mentioned in front of the ladies, were less frequently employed, while a few sizes were almost never used at all. Instead of organising the bottles by size as Frank had done, which meant that I often had to clamber over several boxes of unwashed containers to find what I wanted, I decided to arrange them by popularity so that the sizes most often used were closest to the door. I stayed late and spent most of one evening sorting them out, and found that it saved me a great deal of time on a daily basis. After discovering how successful that was, I turned my attention to the dirty containers which seemed to take an inordinate amount of time to clean since the stoppers sometimes stuck fast and slowed down the whole operation considerably. All I could do with these was soak those with stuck stoppers and put the others aside for cleaning later.

In fact a seemingly never ending spare time job was washing the dirty bottles, wiping them dry and returning them to the shelf ready for re-use. They had to be spotless and with only cold water to wash them in, it was a long task. Some bottles had very greasy contents, and I could not get them clean no matter what I did. These I secretly took into the garden and buried. Some years later when I was chatting to my brothers and another boy who had taken the job after Fred, we discovered amidst gales of laughter that all four of us had resorted to exactly the same technique. Even now, all these years afterwards, I believe that I could still locate my bottle burial place. The collectors of old bottles would find a veritable treasure trove!

What with washing bottles, peeling potatoes and vegetables, cleaning grates, scrubbing the slate floors, and black-leading the range, in short doing all the rough chores that no-one else was employed to do, my chapped, red and blistered hands gradually become covered in half healed scars. Even now, when I am what the world choses to call a man of means, I can still see these scars on my hands. It is how poverty marks us.

My days at the doctor's house were fully occupied from early until late. One day I had to clean the windows, on another it was the turn of the brass fenders, the stair rods, the front door knocker and the bells. On the next I had to scrub the surgery and another two rooms thoroughly. The day following my tasks were to meticulously clean the kitchen, the scullery and the larder, and so on and on. I was also charged with bath bricking the pots and pans, helping the gardener with the digging and clearing the weeds from the vegetable bed. The fact that I was small and skinny for my age made no difference. I was expected to lift and move things that were often too heavy for me.

At one o'clock I went home for a meal, returning again at two to begin delivering the medicines which Doctor Twining had prescribed during his morning rounds. The bottles for the private patients were sealed in white paper, but those of the club patients were unwrapped. When I delivered these unwrapped bottles, always to the home of someone who was desperately ill, because otherwise the family would never have countenanced the expense of calling the doctor, I felt badly. These people had paid even more in proportion to their meagre earnings than the rich patients. I felt they deserved the same consideration. If it had been left to me I would have wrapped all the bottles the same.

Then it was back to work until 5 p.m, when I had a break for food at home. At 6 p.m. I was on duty once more at the surgery door to answer the bell. On occasions I also had to hold horses and watch carts, since there were those callers whose animals were nervous and disliked the noise of the street.

After the last patients had gone, I had to wait while more medicines were dispensed, then I went on my delivery rounds. Medicines were taken to the Coastguard Watch Room for those patients who lived out of town to collect, while others were passed around by the night patrols. Sometimes in the winter I had to walk back in the dark from Bolt Head or further around the coast, towards Hope Cove, steeling myself to pass by the black shapes of the wind twisted trees and bushes on the track, which in my imagination looked like robbers and bandits. Once in almost complete blackness I took the wrong track and nearly walked over the cliff edge.

With the completion of this task, sometimes as late as ten o'clock at night my day's work was finished, and I could go home, tired out and hungry. My only time off during the week was a few hours on Saturday afternoon, though I still had to report for deliveries as usual on Saturday evening.

Sunday was our day of rest, and it was a day we all looked forward to eagerly. Sunday was the day when the older boys tried to woo whatever girls were available, but we younger ones were not interested in that. I was still in the church choir, and even though it was my day off, my Sundays were busy since I attended Sunday School as well as three church services during the course of the day.

But to my huge delight that year my voice broke, and suddenly I was free. I think that not one of God's creatures had ever greeted this unexpected leisure time so gratefully. I still had nominally to attend at least one service on Sunday, but since I was no longer needed in the choir, I could go swimming or fishing instead. Catching fish was just something we boys always did. We never went anywhere near the sea without at least taking a crab line with us. We spent a lot of time discussing the best baits to use, and each family had its own special fishing spots which they guarded jealously. By this time I had a half dozen of my own places, and my father, brothers and I spent a lot of time trying to predict where the fish would be at various times of the day and trying a variety of ways of attracting them.

The Doctor expressed himself pleased with my work, and after a while my pay went up. I was now earning the princely sum of 5/- a week.

My family was fortunate in that they had not had to pay a premium to my brother's master, as all other apprentices' parents had to do – I don't know the reason for this, but I think it was because of the high regard my father was held in locally. In addition to this bonus had come another. Frank's master was a fair man and had promised initially to give my brother three pence a week if he behaved himself well. Pleased with him, his master kept his word. Once more our little family seemed to be making way.

But then came news from the world outside that shook us all to the core.

In 1899 war broke out between the British and the Boers in South Africa.

CHAPTER FOUR

The declaration of war by the Dutch settlers of Cape Colony, South Africa in October 1899 seemed to take the British government largely by surprise. Few people were even aware that a state of simmering discontent had existed in the country ever since the British Expeditionary Force had seized the Cape from the Boers during the Napoleonic War. Fewer still had taken notice that our British Colonial Secretary, Joseph Chamberlain, had issued an ultimatum to the Boers demanding full equality for British settlers in the Transvaal, or that Paul Kruger, the President of the Republic had retaliated by issuing his own ultimatum, giving Britain 48 hours to withdraw her troops. It was the failure to comply with this that had led to the Transvaal and the Orange Free State declaring war on the United Kingdom.

Something of the shock with which the news was received was evident by the growing crowd of Salcombe people which followed in the wake of the rotund figure of the Town Crier, Eli Drew, as he strode majestically through the town towards South Sands, ringing his hand bell and shouting: "Oyez, oyez, Boers declare war ... South Africa at war with England..."

Over the following days as the newspapers reported that fierce fighting had followed the pronouncement, we learned how anger against British rule and our policy of encouraging immigration to South Africa, had led the Boers to leave the colony and trek north along the eastern coasts towards Natal where they had established a new Dutch colony. In 1843, as Britain annexed Natal in turn, tens of thousands of Boer men, women and children had walked north towards the interior, in an historic "Great Trek" to establish two independent Boer republics, the Transvaal and the Orange Free State.

Expansionist ideas notably propagated by Cecil Rhodes who sought to incorporate even these republics into a federation under British rule, were bitterly resented by the Boers and tensions escalated from local to national level. There were political manoeuvrings and drawn out negotiations over the rights of Uitlanders or outsiders within the white community and the rights of the original non-white Aftrican populations.

According to the "Western Morning News" things had come to a head in 1871 with the discovery of diamonds at Kimberley, which prompted a diamond rush and subsequently a massive influx of foreigners to the Orange Free State. Then gold had been discovered in the South African Republic in 1886. Lacking the manpower and the industrial base to develop the resource by itself, the Transvaal had reluctantly agreed to a fresh wave of immigrants who flocked to South Africa intent on making their fortunes.

Given that the more recent arrivals, mostly of British origin, already represented the majority of the white community in Johannesburg, and that more were arriving all the time, our own government demanded at the very least the full voting rights that the Boers denied the Uitlanders. Recognising that if they did this they would be outnumbered and would eventually lose control of the South African Republic, the Boers refused.

Talk of the fighting was now on everyone's lips. Anyone who knew anything about South Africa or had been to the country was in demand for his opinion. A sailor who had been in the fleet which took the British Expeditionary force to the Cape during what was now being referred to as the First Boer War in 1880-1881, when our troops had first attempted to annex the Transvaal, appeared opportunely in town. He was a grizzled old man with washed out blue eyes sunk deeply into a patchwork of wrinkles. We never knew his name. He was known locally just as "Towhead" for his mop of sun-bleached hair. Like so many before and after him, Towhead had just appeared one day, walking up from Plymouth to pastures new, or mebbe just to revisit ports he had sailed out of, nobody knew. But Towhead or "To'ed" as we said his name, had been to South Africa and knew the land. Holding court at "The King's Arms" he gave his opinion of the Boers, telling anyone who would listen that they were a hardy race, and skilful, determined fighters. They had caused a series of British defeats in the past, he said, including the annihilation of the British Expeditionary force of 359 men, with the shooting of its commander, Sir George Colley, with a single bullet through the forehead. He described the browns and yellows of the endless veldt, and told stories of the strength and bravery of the native Zulu race to eager listeners. The information winged its way around the town.

Though Gladstone, our then Prime Minister, had in the past signed a peace treaty with the Transvaal President, Paul Kruger, public opinion had it that it had been only because he had reckoned that a show of strength in the country would have required considerable troop numbers and cost a great deal for what was seemingly little in return. "To'ed"'s opinion, echoed by my father, who had a strong streak of the political debunker in him, was that the reason the British government were now reneging on that deal, was that the worthless veldt the Boers had seized no longer looked so worthless now that it had been found to be rich in diamonds, and, at a place called Witwatersrand some sixty kilometres south of the Boer capital of Pretoria, the world's largest deposits of gold ore.

After a class discussion which included the outbreak of this war, our headmaster Mr Coad pinned up a "Daily Record" cutting featuring a correspondent's sketch of black, muscled, half naked Zulu warriors wearing feather plumes and lions teeth necklaces. The picture fired our imaginations. We disliked the Boers for no other reason than that they were pitting themselves against the British Empire which we all knew to be the most marvellous institution in the world. The Zulus with their hide shields and spears seemed to us to be the underdogs, and that was enough for us to give them our support.

There was universal outrage at the Boer's behaviour. To seize someone else's land and slaughter the inhabitants, then have the temerity to challenge Britannia herself, was thought the most terrible outrage. Everyone was united in his desire to teach these upstarts a lesson. To'ed had moved on, and people now dismissed his opinions. The Boers were just farmers, it could surely not take very long to whip them into shape and teach them some manners, was the common viewpoint. But there were still others, including old Tom Friend who did odd jobs around the school, who had been a soldier back in the '70's who spoke admiringly of the Boer's grit and determination on their long trek to freedom, venturing that the Boers were a force to be reckoned with and that our soldiers would have their hands full when they took them on.

Our teacher echoed this view in a classroom debate, though I think he was really just trying to encourage us to think things out for ourselves. But it was enough for us boys to know that the Boers obviously thought they could govern the country better than our British sovereign. Everyone knew that ours was the Empire on which the sun never set, ruled by the wisest, most benevolent queen in history. The globe in our classroom showed us the vast swathes of pink that denoted British colonies. All these countries could not be wrong, we maintained indignantly. If you had the good fortune to come under British rule, you should consider yourself lucky.

On street corners and outside pubs little knots of men gathered to discuss the news. They said that the British settlers in the gold and diamond fields had been treated so badly by the Boers that they had been driven to petition Queen Victoria herself to redress their numerous grievances. But talks held in a place called Bloomfontein between the British High Commissioner and President Kruger had broken down. And now war!

Most people seemed to think that it would soon all be over. The nerve of these Boers! was the general attitude of the patients I overheard discussing it in the Doctor's waiting room. Our British troops would soon sort them out. Show them what was what!

But it did not happen like that. Rather than hearing reports of a resounding victory after British redcoats had marched into the Transvaal, we learned to our astonishment in mid-October that Boer forces had surrounded the British at a small town of no particular importance named Mafeking. Two days later they had laid siege to the town of Kimberley. By 2nd November, a Boer force led by a Piet Joubert had laid siege to a town called Ladysmith.

On 11th December the news was that the Boers under a commander named Piet Cronje, had defeated our troops at a place called Magersfontein. A few days later British forces under their Commander-in-Chief Sir Redvers Buller, who had arrived in the country with reinforcements from England, had been defeated by the Boers during a battle in the town of Collense. By 16th December at the end of what the newspapers had unanimously described as a "black week" for Britain, almost 2,000 men and 12 heavy guns had been lost. From the newspapers we learned to our disbelief that a despondent Sir Redvers Buller had actually cabled the British cabinet asking permission to surrender! The whole country was horrified. When he was swiftly recalled to London and replaced as Commander-in-Chief by Lord Roberts, the hero of the Afghanistan campaigns, we gave vent to our anger calling Buller a lily-livered coward.

In Salcombe as elsewhere throughout England, we tried to make sense of it all. We knew that our British troops had been heavily outnumbered when the war had begun with the Boers invasion of the Cape Colony in October. We had barely 15,000 troops in South Africa – though up to 10,000 more were expected almost daily to be sent from India – against the Boers 50,000 mounted infantry. But the rag tag Boer army was up against the best trained army in the world. True the Boers were used to the terrain and to living off the land, and a retired army officer who visited the town from Exeter echoed To'ed's words when he declared that the Boers were superior in field tactics and the gathering of intelligence. But despite this opinion people just refused to believe that such an untrained army could ever defeat our men. You had only to look at the pictures of them, dressed sometimes in little more than rags, some of them even barefoot, compared to our troops' spic and span scarlet uniforms to see that it was not possible, we declared.

But within weeks the newspapers were reporting that the Boers had the British forces besieged at Ladysmith, Kimberley and Mafeking.

The Boers had ten thousand troops around Mafeking alone, the "Western Morning News" leader thundered, outraged. Old timers declared bleakly that the enemy had only to contain the British troops in the three towns and push their main force into the Cape, and they would deprive our troops of their supply port and naval base and have virtually the whole country under their control. Faces in town were glum. No-one could believe it had come to this.

Harrowing accounts now started coming from the Front. Our soldiers were encountering situations they had not expected. The war had culled many thousands of British lives, leaving widows and grieving families. What Christmas would be like in those bereft households was not to be imagined, the "Western Morning News" declared sorrowfully. The newspaper announced that it was setting up a fund to help soldiers, sailors and their stricken families. Other collections had started up in Salcombe and the doctor suggested that we might do the same.

There were moments though when news coming back from the Front still made us proud. The man leading the troops besieged in Mafeking was a cavalry officer called Colonel Robert Baden-Powell (we learned to pronounce his name to rhyme with Maiden-Pole).

Fore Street, Salcombe. C 1900. J Fairweather.

Surrounded by a force of 10,000 Boers, he had organised teams of sappers to dig trenches and throw up earthworks, keeping outposts in touch with his HQ by utilising the town's schoolboys whom he christened "Boy Scouts", as runners. Messages from him via the newspaper correspondents assured the readers that morale was high amongst the soldiers and townsfolk.

We thought he was marvellous: a true British hero. We boys all longed to become Boy Scouts. We poured scorn on newspaper reports of the comments made by the colonel commanding the Rhodesian detachment, who was reported as saying sourly, "It's an odd sort of cavalry officer, who, at the first whiff of battle, begins digging trenches and eating horses."

I set up a box in the waiting room decorated with an image of a soldier cut from a copy of the "London Illustrated News" that a wealthy patient had donated to the surgery. It was a splendid picture of a strong looking soldier with big black moustaches that reminded me of the pictures of the heroes in "Boy's Friend". The brass buttons on his scarlet uniform gleamed, and he looked very dashing. As I glued it on with the doctor's glue pot, I thought it would be just the thing to attract people's attention. We did not achieve anywhere near the staggering £10,000 total the "Western Morning News" fund reached by January, but with the doctor's help, we were still able to send £55 to the fund, almost all of it raised from pennies, threepenny bits and sixpences donated by some of the poorest of the town. Hearing tales of the bitter cold our troops were enduring on the veldt, Salcombe ladies turned to and began to knit scarves, socks and shawls for the besieged troops. A collection point was opened in the Town Hall to collect blankets for sick and wounded soldiers Some of these were stored at the surgery until they could be packaged up and taken to the Post Office and because we were running short of room, some found their way into my cubby hole. I fought them daily as I tried to get to my bottles. But I was glad of the slight inconvenience, as it seemed to me and many others that when our brave soldiers returned injured or sick, or worse when their bodies were repatriated or known to have been buried on foreign soil, no-one seemed to care about them or their families much anymore.

But I had other things to think about now, in that bitter cold winter with its booming winter gales which for so many years flooded the town, for on 19th December 1899, I would turn fourteen and I, in my turn, would be apprenticed. I would be a man.

The subject of my future apprenticeship had come up often at home over the last year. Though my first choice had been for mason, because I was becoming increasingly interested in building construction, both my father and elder brother convinced me that masons were not only poorly paid, but were at the bottom of the social ladder, being generally regarded as little more than labourers. Carpentry and joinery was the apprenticeship to have, both assured me. That was the most highly regarded of all trades. Partly influenced by the extra money on offer in this apprenticeship I agreed, and my father set himself to sounding out the various carpentry and joinery establishments in the town, until finally he had settled on what he considered to be the best for me which was with Mr James Cranch who had his workshops and funeral parlour on Customs Quay. It was a good apprenticeship and Aaron and my mother were justly proud to think that they had done so well for their two elder sons. My parents had a serious talk with me on the day that I was accepted, engendering me always to work hard and do my best, impressing upon me that I was now set on my life's course and should always endeavour to make the most of my advantages.

My status as apprentice marked a new chapter for me which I welcomed, though initially it proved to be a great financial strain for our family as I would now be earning only 1/- a week, rising annually by one shilling to eight shillings a week at the end of my seven year apprenticeship.

I was on trial for a month, but Mr Cranch professed himself satisfied with my progress during that time, and I was indentured. My master (whom we all called "Sir") endorsed this document and ceremoniously handed it to me. The contract imposed very strict conditions on my master, my father and myself, and was legally binding.

I was put to learn on the other side of a bench where a taciturn joiner called Bill Pert worked. Though he said little, Bill was a good teacher, being patient and good at explaining things, and in time he came to mean much to me. Our relationship developed as good apprenticeships should. Bill stood no nonsense from me. I was impatient and I wanted to learn everything at once, but he taught me to take more time and to do a thorough job of whatever task I undertook. For the vast majority of the day he worked in silence but when he did speak it was usually after he had been mulling over a subject for a while, and what he said invariably made good sense. He had the gift of really listening to people, which I liked and tried to emulate.

Most people think they listen, but in reality they don't, he once said to me. When you are standing in front of a customer, you need to concentrate on him, and only him. Don't think about your own problems, or how you want to handle the job. Listen, and try and find out what he wants. If he doesn't know, help him to decide. If he wants something which you know with your experience won't work, make him understand this tactfully. He impressed upon me that if I learned to handle customers this way it would save a great deal of time and misunderstanding, and would be more likely to result in referrals.

But these little pearls of wisdom were passed on sparingly. "Most people don't know where they are going in life," he said out of the blue one day, as he was showing me how to drop a plumb line down a window reveal. "They don't know what they want, so they never get it... and then they spend their time complaining and envying others. The important thing is to know what you want in life."

Where a simple carpenter learned something like that, I will never know. I often wonder if he knew how much he was putting into my impressionable young head. He taught me to believe in my dreams. I owe you Bill Pert.

My brother Frank was 16 and two years into his indenture. He now

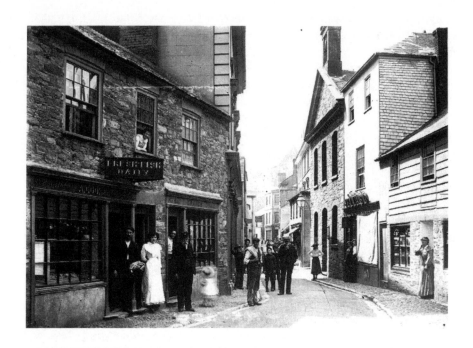

Cranch's Dairy, Fore Street, Salcombe. c 1900. Fairweather.

received three shillings a week. Frederik a year younger than me had now inherited the Doctor's job thanks to a repeat of the performance I had instigated when I took over from Frank. This was a hat-trick with all three of us brothers having been employed there, though privately both Frank and I each thought that Fred was not as good at it as we had been. Really all Fred wanted was to go into the Merchant Navy. It was all he had ever wanted. He was crazy about ships. In that he shared an ambition with my elder brother. Frank wanted to leave his apprenticeship and join the Royal Navy. My parents were worried for him and were against it. It was a subject that seemed to be endlessly discussed at home now. Despite his amiable nature, Frank was stubbornly determined. He was nearly at an age when the navy would take him, and he did not want to waste any time. Eventually Aaron spoke to Frank's master, and it was agreed that my father would pay a sum of £5 to have him released from his apprenticeship. Since my father did not have such a large sum, he sold the small rowing boat that we had acquired a few years earlier for fishing. I know that Frank felt bad that the boat had to go, but the money paid for his clearance.

The siege in South Africa was still continuing. It had become a tangible though now largely unspoken of thing, a source of national shame and embarrassment, and deep, simmering anger. In spite of the politician's rhetoric the country was very much aware that with every week that passed, our soldiers were still captives in a foreign land. The very names of the towns where they endured, now as familiar to us as the names of our own Devon towns, were spoken with raw emotion: Ladysmith; Kimberley; and Mafeking. And still it went on...

North Sands and Bolt Head. Valentine

Then on a glorious May day in 1900, after a siege lasting 217 days, Mafeking was relieved. The country went crazy. In Salcombe people danced in the street, and hugged perfect strangers. A band marched up Fore Street and young children dressed in red, white and blue costumes, processed through the town. Flags and bunting hung from shops and buildings, and the pubs threw open their doors. "The Union Inn" served beer and cider from a table out on the street, and the Council voted on a grandiose gesture by renaming the long steps, " Spion Kop Steps". People dared to hope that now the Boers would get the drubbing they richly deserved.

As for me I was enjoying my new life hugely. There were four other apprentices besides myself, and now and again when we were busier than usual, our master hired a journeyman to help out. I was inclined to be left handed, but aware that it would make life more difficult for me in future, Bill Pert had from the outset made it his business to correct this habit. He was a fit and athletic footballer with a heavy hand which he did not hesitate to use on me if I so much as reached out for a tool with my left hand, and so gradually I became more comfortable using my right.

Our master himself was a splendid craftsman. He was a giant of a man, physically very strong and very hard working. He taught us for some period every day. Although a Salcombe man he had worked in London and held a City and Guilds Certificate. He was a hard taskmaster, and would never accept less than our best from any of us, and that attitude, coupled with Bill's teaching, was what later enabled me to get on in life. Despite the differences that occurred later in our lives, I will always be grateful to Jim Cranch for the thorough training he gave me.

At about this time I met a man with whom my father had gone to sea years before. I never knew his surname. We all just called him, "Jock".

Jock was an old seaman who had sailed years before the mast. Some said he had been press-ganged when he was just a boy. I remember him as a cheerful man, with a Glaswegian accent that was difficult to understand. He came into town one day on the steamer from Plymouth and my parents allowed him to sling his hammock in our outhouse. With barely a word he joined my father in his allotment, bending his back with a will to digging potatoes, though he was probably in his eighties even then. He disappeared as suddenly as he came. What happened to him, nobody ever knew. Men like him and To'ed drifted into town and then out again. Once they would have shipped out somewhere. Now they just existed on the fringes of the only world they had ever known. Flotsam and jetsam, Bill Pert called them.

But Jock had one tremendous talent which I envied greatly: he could play the mandolin. In his gnarled hands, that instrument sang. He taught us boys old folk songs and once again we sang the sea shanties with rollicking movements, that we had sung with our father in the vegetable patch as young children.

For a while Jock became a well-known figure in the local bars where he was plied with pints of scrumpy in return for his playing. He had drunk so much over the years that he had bright purple veins on his nose and cheeks and was nearly blind. Farm scrumpy did that to people, my father used to say in one of his lectures against the demon drink. Father was not Temperance like so many, but he never drank except for a glass at Christmas, and on occasional high celebrations. In the old days the scrumpy was so thick and cloudy you could stand a spoon up in it. It had a kick like a mule. They used to put everything in it: straw, manure, dead rats, everything you could think of... Still it was like nectar... Cut a Devon man and you'd find cider in his veins instead of blood, they used to say.

'Tennyrate, old Jock fired me up to want to learn the mandolin myself. Fred was working in a house in Kingsbridge at the time and I asked him to go and look in the town to find one. He came back and told me that he had seen one in a shop window.

I saved hard and eventually managed to get the necessary 4/6d, then hitched a lift on a cart going to Kingsbridge and purchased my mandolin.

I walked back along the old road as pleased as Punch, my boots kicking up the dust as I passed. It was high summer and the overhanging trees made the lanes shady and cool. When I got to Hanger Mill, I took off my boots and cooled my hot feet in the water. Sitting on the little bridge in the still green wood, I began to pluck the strings of my mandolin, sending the notes soaring into the trees. I was so happy sitting there, my head filled with dreams. I hummed sea shanties and old folk songs and pictured myself surprising my family with my talent.

Jock disappeared just when I needed him most, but there was a small instruction book with my instrument, and I practised hard, eventually becoming good enough to play in a local band. But in time I was forced to the recognition that I had little ear for music, even though I had been a choir boy for seven years, and I sold my mandolin to the Cranch cousin I had wrestled into the mud during my job application with the doctor. I charged him less than I would have done anyone else, in a tacit agreement that this transaction cancelled out any lingering resentment he might have felt for his beating.

Though I missed my mandolin I preferred to use my time in other ways. By now I was skilled enough to do odd carpentry jobs for friends and neighbours of our parents. Frank had already been pressured by Ellen to work his way through our rented house, doing all the small jobs that Ellen had decided needed doing, for to tell the truth my father was not handy at such things, so at least I got away with that. But there always seemed to be someone needing some work doing. I put up shelves, mended creaky doors and window sashes, and even built an allotment shed, all of which were within my newly acquired range of skills, and for this my family received favours in kind, or food. Occasionally I did a small job for a member of the gentry, because it seemed to me that they were often very careful with their money and liked to have an apprentice to work for them so that they could get the job done more cheaply. But the benefit of working for them was that they actually paid for the work, usually in cash, which, always being in short supply, came in handy. My mother, who held the family purse strings tightly, now allowed me 1/- a week for clothes, which I saved until I had enough to buy a shirt, a new pair of trousers, boots, or a jacket for best, whatever I needed. Meanwhile, Ellen patched and re-patched our working clothes, turning the cuffs of our shirts and using the tails to repair the necks, reinforcing the knees and seats of our trousers, until there was often little left of the original. During our apprenticeship the tools we used were supplied by our master, but my parents agreed that in the last two years of my training they would allow me 1/- a week extra to enable me to save up for the set of tools that I would need to start my career.

With my work and all my odd jobs and errands, I had little time to myself. When I could in the summer I went swimming which I enjoyed very much. I often swam with Fred when he was around. He had continued his strange practise of preferring to swim underwater and several times had saved the day by diving down to free an anchor that was stuck fast, or helping to repair a boat damaged beneath the water line to save it from being taken out of the water. He had made a primitive breathing apparatus and used an old glass jar to look through to see beneath the waves, and he had constructed a fishing spear from a broken kitchen knife that a neighbour threw out.

Ferry across to Higher Passage.c 1900. Fairweather.

For my part I dug lug worms in the harbour mud at low tide, which I sold to the fishermen usually one of the Cove or Distin brothers. Father and I often fished together, and sometimes one or both of my brothers would join us. We caught dab, bream and bass. We set a 50 hook spiller near the bar once and we caught a lot of fish on that. At times we landed a good haul of plaice which we sold at the kitchen doors of the big houses, always saving some for our own pot at home. Ellen made a wonderful thick fish soup with potatoes and herbs, which we ate with chunks of fresh baked bread and thick, golden butter. It was delicious.

Looking back these were England's glory days. We had finally beaten the Boers, after what were admittedly a few worrying months, and now the whole country was riding high on a tide of optimism.

But waiting just around the corner was an event that would change all of our lives forever.

Our Queen, Victoria, was 81 years old now, and she was said to be in increasingly poor health. It was reported that she suffered greatly from insomnia, that her eyesight was failing, and that she was becoming more and more frail

They said that the news from South Africa during the war had filled her with sorrow, and perhaps had even led to the undermining of her health. But there was more bad news now. Her son, Prince Alfred, named after her departed husband, had recently died; the King of Italy had been assassinated, and a grandson, Prince Christian of Schleswig-Holstein had died of fever in South Africa. Her 63 years on the throne had seen times of danger and hardship but nothing quite like the Boer War where a puny foe had been able to humiliate the greatest power on earth. Victoria, the daughter of the impoverished Duke of Kent, had seen her island people carry her power to the far corners of the world. They had made new countries, drawn new frontiers, and enjoyed wealth beyond the dreams of avarice. But now there were other runners in the race, and they were bigger and potentially more powerful. It could not help but diminish her at the end of her life. We all knew that it was only to be a matter of time before she died, but we collectively closed our minds to it. It was too awful a thought to contemplate.

Then on January 22nd 1901, the event that all had dreaded, occurred. The newspapers reported that soon after 6 p.m. the woman who had become known as "the grandmother of Europe" had drawn her last breath at her home at Osborne House on the Isle of Wight. At her bedside, together with her grandson the German Kaiser, were the nine children and many grandchildren who now formed part of an alliance of royal houses which had spread across Europe.

The shock of the loss was immense and it hit everyone. None except the very elderly had ever known any other monarch. Whereas only months before gay bunting had hung from the houses and shops and public buildings in celebration for the relief of Mafeking, now there was only sombre black wherever you looked. Shops closed out of respect. Churches held special services. People wore black armbands and were silent in the streets. Straw was laid in Fore Street to quieten the noise of the carts just as was done if someone was very sick. It was as if life itself had stopped.

"She was only eighteen when she came to the throne. Just a maid..." Bill Pert said. He wore a black tie and a black mourning band on his sleeve as we all did. Master had shut the shop on the day she died, but there were orders to be filled, and we were back to work, though the atmosphere in the workshop was subdued. It was on our morning break, and one of the joiners had a newspaper.

"From earth's shining circle a gem has dropped away," he read haltingly. "The longest reign…" he hesitated. There were too many big words all in one sentence. He passed the newspaper to me. I had always read a lot and even in my working clothes carried the small dictionary that I had bought with my first week's wages. I was proud that both my reading and writing skills were very good.

"The longest reign on record has come to an end," I read, "and into the realms of eternal bliss has passed the Mother Queen of a people who have grown up under her rule of gentleness and love." We went back to work with solemn faces, each of us musing on those words, wondering what life would be like under the new monarch, who we had learned was to take the crown as King Edward VII.

A few days later came the account of the Queen's funeral which I read to my parents in a dusk darkened front room. We had gas in the cottage, but like most locals my father always insisted that we didn't light the mantle until you couldn't see a hand in front of you. "All pomp was observed for "the mistress of the sea", as her body was borne to the sound of minute guns, by a ship which carried her aboard 'The Alberta', beneath a purple canopy…" I read. "Thirty battleships and cruisers allied to gunboats and torpedo boat destroyers formed a line from Portsmouth Harbour, with the knell of a canon sounding across the water." In silence we each created our own image of the event in our mind's eye.

Services were held across the West Country, and wreaths were sent in from even the tiniest parishes. People started collections, and all threw whatever they could afford into the collection tins. It was reported that one Devon woman, too poor to give any money, reverently placed a single flower in the collecting box, saying that it was to be used for the poor queen's wreath. Shops were closed, and all business was suspended. Everybody in the street wore some form of mourning. Mother made us all black cockades for our caps. For herself she wore her best black bombazine dress, though it had needed letting out at the seams, for she was plumper than she had been. Her hat though, which she had made herself to match her dress looked magnificent. My brother said that she looked like a "galleon in full sail" and got a clip around the ear from mother for it, though I think she was actually rather pleased, for I heard her repeating his words to Jane Thurston the wife of the Tea Dealer from Buckley Street, later.

We had terrible storms in March of that year and two boats were damaged in the harbour. The news was all of the increased national debt which they said now stood at £59 million, largely due to the cost of the Boer War. To help pay for this the tax was raised on sugar, molasses, glucose and exported coal. I didn't really register the other things, but I loved sugar and often spent some of my money on sweets, or the sugar cane sticks that Mrs Yeoman from Yeoman's the grocers made after she had boiled the raw cane sugar up for the shop, and was furious when this went up. Soon afterwards the miners went on strike for higher wages, which meant that coal prices also went up again.

But even as the country mourned, the dastardly Boers attacked once more. It was impossible to believe their effrontery. But then, as one old timer said, what else could you expect from men who dressed themselves in the muddy green brown camouflage clothes they called "khaki" which rendered them almost invisible on the veldt, rather than the smart uniforms our troops wore so proudly.

As a country we were incensed by the Boers' actions, declaring that they were not playing the game properly. More men were called up to join the fight. We boys all longed to enlist. We heard patriotic stories from across the West Country. All were moved almost to tears of pride by the front page picture of a man identified as a PC Hambley from Cornwall, who set off to re-join his corps in the Transvaal, head held high and carrying a silver headed walking stick.

Our new king was due to be crowned in June, but he developed appendicitis and the coronation had to be delayed. "It's a bad sign you mark my words," Bill said, dourly, shaking his head. We had a rush job on and we had all been working extra time. I had spent days planing long planks of Oregon pine which was hard work. Bill hated rushing things. It always made him grumpy.

King Edward VII was finally sworn in that August with great pomp and ceremony. We grew to know his face and that of Queen Alexandra from the newspapers, but even so it was strange to sing "God Save the King", instead of "God Save the Queen" as we had always done. People celebrated the event with flags and bunting, and dressed in their Sunday clothes.

Charles Weymouth a distant relative died that September. He had consumption, which caused many deaths in those days. I had visited him a few days before his death. He was thin and frail, and his face was as white as paper. He coughed continually and spat up blood. Afterwards people said it seemed almost a kindness that his life was snuffed out to end such suffering. But he was only fifteen, and so should have had many years ahead of him. My whole family attended his funeral, and the Holy Trinity church was packed. When his coffin was put into the ground the grave diggers scattered quick lime around to prevent infection as was normal when death was caused by disease of that sort.

At the opening of Parliament, Mr Chamberlain spoke at length of new legislation he was campaigning for which would set up an old age pension to take care of working people at the end of their lives. It was a very good thing and it would help a great many people my parents said wonderingly. But the Liberals squabbled amongst themselves and nothing more was heard of it.

That summer was boiling hot, and we boys spent as much of our free time as possible down by the water. We usually swam off the quays. If we had the money and time to spare, we took the ferry and if the tide was right walked or waded round either to Fishermans Cove, or Smalls. My favourite beach was always Sunny Cove, but I did not often have the time to go there. Sometimes, just for the fun of it, we swam across the estuary, because there were always girls around to see us, though it was difficult getting into the water and out again without them seeing us in our drawers. Fred was practising staying under water for as long as he could, and was getting better and better at it. He still spoke of little but ships and longed for the day when he could go to sea.

We sorely missed the small fishing boat that our father had been forced to sell, but that summer he was offered another one. It was a 16' clinker built dinghy, a good, sturdy boat that would be ideal for us. We discussed it as a family and agreed that we would all chip in to buy it. We overhauled it and painted it, and mother mended some of the stitching on the mainsail which had come adrift, and we all went out in it often in the evenings, even my mother, who enjoyed it hugely. It opened up the way to going out beyond the Bar where we fished for shoaling mackerel off Jones' Wall.

This was the year that W G Grace was playing at the Oval in the Gentlemen v Players match, and we boys or young men as we now considered ourselves, were greatly inspired by Mr Grace's cricketing exploits. Our games, which featured hand-made bats and stumps, were held on the beach and they were rowdy but great fun, tending to degenerate into mock brawls which usually culminated in the losers being thrown into the sea.

It was at this time that something even more exciting happened, as we heard that a Mr Lipton who had made a fortune from tea, was entering a marvellous new boat in the America's Cup. My brothers and I learned that a model of this boat was to be set up on Plymouth Hoe for all to inspect, and we burned with the desire to see it. But the cost of getting to Plymouth was prohibitive, not to mention the time it would take, and try as I might I could not work out how to do it and still get in to work. And work was the most important thing, my father reminded us severely. Work should always come first. Having fun came no-where in the great scheme of things. It was not to be considered. Any chance we might still have had to get down to Plymouth was squashed by my mother who had been told that the city was a den of iniquity, with a great number of licensed premises putting temptation in the way of innocent young boys, and with women of easy virtue to be found on the streets at all hours of the day and night. Ellen therefore determined that her boys would go to Plymouth over her dead body. It all sadly came to nothing anyway, as Mr Lipton's boat, "Shamrock III" lost to the United States contender.

Though I had longed for that brief respite from work, I was at heart a sensible boy. I had my share of fun, but I was always determined to do what I could to better myself. I had saved my money, and now enrolled for extra schooling in Kingsbridge in the winter from 7 to 9 p.m. three evenings a week. I was to study technical drawing and building techniques. The total fee for the term was 3/- and I paid for it myself. I also studied Pitman's shorthand which I thought would enable me to take notes more easily, and I obtained an elementary certificate in this, though I failed the correspondence certificate which we took in the classroom of my old school, supervised by the very bored looking curate.

A cousin of ours, John Murch, an Army Sergeant then stationed at Carrickfergus had also learned shorthand, and in a letter to him I rather rashly suggested that we should correspond in this way. He agreed and we dutifully struck up an exchange of letters, but I was glad when he eventually suggested we should discontinue this. Years later, after John had been killed in the war, I found one of his old letters, and read through the strange squiggles with a lump in my throat. After the war memorial to the Salcombe dead had been raised, I never failed to look for his name amongst the others whenever I passed.

Amongst the work that came into our workshops were commissions from the council. Generally speaking the work consisted of making gates, fences and sign boards. Sometimes the council men came to the workshop. The Local Urban Council as it was then employed two part time and one full time man. The clerk, so Bill said, had a salary of about £20 a year. There was a surveyor, who was generally a local tradesman, and one workman, John Wood – or "Janood" as we all knew him because of his particularly strong accent. There was also a part time Gate Collector, who worked on commission, and when the water pumping station at Hangar Chase came into use there was a part time man there as well.

The administrative staff of the council remained the same until the 1914-18 war, but grew rapidly afterwards, as did the number of workmen it employed.

The Council provided almost nothing in the way of services then. Each family looked after its own waste. Scavenging, a sort of precursor of re-cycling, was carried out by a hired man with a horse and cart. He collected only very occasionally, as we used almost no tinned or packaged goods.

The Scavenging Man. c 1900. J Fairweather

Amything that could be burnt went on the fire. Bottles were re-used many times then were buried when they broke. Our pottery nearly all had cracks or chips in it from constant use, and when it finally was damaged beyond repair, we usually smashed it into pieces and used it to construct garden paths. Any rags we had went through several rebirths. If it was for instance, a shirt that had finally got to a stage where it was no longer wearable my mother would first cut off all the buttons, saving those and any part of it that she could against future re-use, then cut it into different sized pieces. Something like a shirt was most useful since it yielded soft, fine material, which had generally been washed so many times that it was nearly transparent. My mother used this to wrap around the starchy suet puddings that we ate to dull our appetites before a meat meal; or else it was used to drain home-made jelly, such as coltsfoot, blackberry, rose hip or crab apple which were needed when someone was ill; other pieces were cut into lengths for bandages in case of need; a bigger piece might make a particularly fine pressing cloth, carefully hand stitched around its edges; or it might be cut up to make the tiny bags which Ellen filled with lavender or other herbs grown in our own garden, and sold in the town at Christmas time. If the piece of cloth was big enough my mother might use it to renew or patch a window covering, or perhaps it would be used to make a fine garment for someone's new born baby. Only then was the rest cut into different sized rags for cleaning, graded carefully into differing materials depending on whether it was needed for rough work such as mopping the floor, or finer work such as polishing or dusting.

The Scavenging Man would also take bones, though he gained few enough of those from our kitchen. Our meat bones were boiled and boiled again for their goodness in making stock. Only then did the remains go to the dogs who roamed the town. Our diet was mainly potatoes, vegetables and bread supplemented by dairy produce from the nearby farms, and of course whatever fish we could catch. Once in a while, particularly at harvest time, we would have a rabbit or a hare. Some of my friends went lamping at night with a slingshot, but I didn't like the sight of the helpless creatures frozen in the glare of the lamp. Once I tried pheasant which Fred had killed with a well-aimed stone, but I didn't like it much. I had always had trouble with my teeth and that bird was tough. I think it had walked halfway across the South Hams before it reached Fred. We teased him by saying that if he had just waited a bit longer it would have lain down and died of old age, and saved him the trouble of killing it.

Sometimes there was an animal such as a badger or fox that had been killed on the road and these were always picked up and put in the pot. But there were few enough of these. Horses and carts were the main form of transport, and they generally did not move fast enough to be a danger to any creature.

The roads in those days were not tarmacadamed but simply beaten earth. In the spring when the rains came the roads and lanes became quagmires, and the cart wheels cut deep grooves in the mud so that passage became increasingly difficult. The result of this was that passengers often had to lend a hand to extricate their transport so that they could continue their journey.

The holes and ruts were filled with limestone that was delivered by smacks from Plymouth or brought down from the quarry up past Bowcombe Bridge. Many men augmented their wages by travelling down the estuary on barges in the evenings, and helping to pitch the stones overboard at places where they could be collected and taken on.

The stones were rough and of all shapes and sizes. They were collected by horse and cart and dropped off beside the road wherever they were needed. Men from the Workhouse broke them into smaller lumps with hammers and shovelled them into the ruts. Rollers were not used then, so the limestone was pushed gradually into the mud with the help of passing traffic. Occasionally when the ruts were particularly deep the heavy filled water cart was driven over the surface to help compact it. Though the Workhouse inmates broke most of it, the John Collins we had known as children was perhaps the best known breaker. By this time he had bought himself a donkey which he rode about on with his wooden leg sticking out stiffly to one side.

Early summer or autumn before the rains came was the best time to travel, though the limestone dust mingled with the dust from the red earth and the piles of dried animal dung rose in great clouds whenever a traveller passed. But even that was preferable to the months after the autumn rains had come and the mud was so churned up that it was sometimes a foot deep. Owing to our southerly latitude we seldom had snow or frost in the winter, but in some years when the lanes froze onto rain, horses, carts and pedestrians slipped all over the place.

But road repairs were nothing to do with us. An apprenticeship meant that a boy would get on in life. We carpentry and joinery apprentices knew that we were regarded as the cream of the apprentices. There were about sixteen of us in the town, all of whom I knew well – in point of fact I was probably related to most of them! As well as us there were perhaps ten or twenty boat building and shipwright apprentices, their number including Fred who was now apprenticed to Aaron Dornam at Dornams Boatyard and perhaps three or four plumbing apprentices.

Then there were the general masons, poorly regarded because their trade had developed from the unskilled general labourer of the previous centuries, as my father and brother had impressed upon me. If they possibly could, parents sought to apprentice their sons to trades, but not that many families could afford the expense. Even then the cost of the tools that had to be purchased at the end of the apprenticeship was prohibitive and most families could not do without a son's proper wage for seven years. I was grateful that my parents, with their thrift and careful husbandry, had been able to provide for my future, and also that their provision of an additional one shilling a week was enabling me to save for the tools that would one day help me to earn my living.

As well as trade apprentices, many boys joined the Royal Navy; some were apprenticed in the Merchant Navy, while others worked as boys in ships. The age for entry now was sixteen, which was what Fred was waiting for. The Army was another route for boys, however this was not at all popular in Salcombe, being generally considered as being just for the down and outs. My father had talked with Aaron Dornam and both had agreed that

Fred could follow his dream and transfer to the Navy when the time came. I knew my brother was just counting the days.

For girls, there was dressmaking, employment as a nurse maid, farm work, teaching or domestic service, with much the largest numbers of girls employed in the latter, as most big houses at this time employed at least one or two servants. "The Moult" and "Woodcot" each had eight or nine staff. Other girls followed the trade that their mothers worked at and stayed at home. These girls might be laundresses, dress makers, or children's nurses who worked in the big houses. Or they might set up on their own as washerwomen, daily cleaners, or any of several other similar lowly paid jobs.

Group of young apprentices watching regatta c 1920. A Fairweather

There were almost no positions as shop assistants to be had in Salcombe. Many shops were owned by the widows of skippers and mates of lost ships, and they ran the business themselves with just family help. To make a living meant everyone in the family even to the youngest had to play a part, for there was seldom money to employ an outsider. Quite often you would go into a shop and find some tiny four or five year old standing on a box behind the counter barely able to reach the produce on the shelves, but already a sharp business man.

After our experience with our relation Murch and his expensive boots, my father insisted that we boycott his premises and travel to Kingsbridge to buy our boots. No factory made footwear was on sale in those days and each boot and shoe maker had his own following. Mr Jarvis in Kingsbridge now made our boots. Only Frank had new boots and even that was only until his feet were big enough to inherit my father's boots. Fred and I usually went along to the fitting as an outing, and watched enviously as Mr Jarvis drew around our brother's foot on a sheet of paper. Since Frank had very ticklish feet the experience always earned him Ellen's wrath as he curled his toes up and giggled the minute the pencil touched him, so that sometimes it needed several attempts before Mr Jarvis could finish his drawing. Ellen always swore that if the boots came out the wrong shape because of his silliness, she would still make sure that he wore them.

But owing to Mr Jarvis's skill they always fitted, though my penny conscious mother insisted that they were made with so much room for growth that sometimes Frank had to spend several months with his boots packed out with newspaper. It was soon after the arrival of this last new pair of boots that my mother realised that Frank's feet had stopped developing and would always be quite small, whereas my own were growing fast. It meant that before long, our positions were reversed, and I became the favoured son who now stood on the paper to allow Mr Jarvis to draw around my feet, and clumped down the street in over large, creaking new boots.

At least with new boots you did not have to go through the performance of re-breaking them in. The problem with wearing passed down boots was that by the time they were handed on they had assumed the foot shape of the original wearer. At night, when they were removed, you could tell whose boots they were by the shape of them. It took a long time before they were comfortable. Often it was only when they began to pinch that they had adopted their new owner's foot shape.

The first new footwear I had as a boy that was not working boots, was a pair of patent leather dancing shoes which I had saved hard a whole year for. I was a king in those dancing shoes, but this was no frivolous purchase as will be shown, but a seriously thought out career move, so though I was not usually a spender, I considered the purchase to be money well spent.

In those years there were quite a lot of amusements to be had in the town. In the early spring before Lent, the schools each had a week of theatrical performances. Boys and girls separately put on a play with one night's rehearsal and two night's performance. When I was younger I had formed part of a group of five small boys who had been coerced into becoming fairies in a pantomime production put on by Miss Andrews, the girls' school teacher. Since we were each dressed in little dresses complete with a full set of petticoats and pantaloons, it took a long time to live this down. Many years later I met up with another of the former fairies in Australia and recalling the occasion, we both roared with laughter.

The main winter amusement for some of us older boys, was the weekly dancing lesson held in the Town Hall, which was the reason why I had invested in the patent leather dancing pumps.

This entertainment was conducted by the two spinster ladies who ran the kindergarten school. They were both tall and thin. One of them wore her hair in two plaited buns, one over each ear, a style which had been the height of fashion some years before.

These dances were very strictly controlled. No domestic servants, labourers or mason apprentices were allowed within the hallowed sanctum, and other apprentices were very carefully supervised. Dressmakers were allowed. I suppose because they so frequently consorted with ladies of quality, it was assumed that they knew how to behave properly.

The dance evenings were very snobbish affairs. At the end of the season, a "Winding Up Ball" was held. All the gentlemen who attended wore white gloves, two and a half inch stiff collars and white bow ties. The ladies wore long skirts to which were attached loops which they slipped over their wrists to enable them elegantly to hold up their skirts so that they would not trip on them. All the ladies had dance programmes complete with tiny pencils often with a silk tassel on the end, which they used to note down the names of their prospective partners in the small space allowed beside the dances. I know that several of these dances resulted in the partners' names being later linked in matrimony, though it was considered not quite the thing to dance too often with one person.

Three musicians were especially brought in from Kingsbridge to provide music for these festivities, which we all looked forward to with great excitement. School teachers of each sex were generally amongst the stars of these evenings, as were the few young women of independent means who lived locally.

In those days, the 1900's, we had a good Town Band that was always available for gala occasions and of course there were also concerts – both good and bad – at intervals.

One highlight in the summer was the Teacher's Picnic held at Millbay which was given by all the school teachers, and which was usually attended by upwards of fifty or sixty young people. It was an event which was eagerly anticipated. There was no sand in Millbay then owing to the beach being over used for building, and we crossed the estuary in a flotilla of small craft, tied up the boats to the quay wall, and then after an hour or so of games and sports in the flower decked meadows beyond, partook of tea. On the way home across the estuary, the sound of our singing and laugher reverberated across the water. In the dusk I glimpsed more than one stolen kiss as the oars dipped and fell in the water.

There was a paddle steamer running to and from Kingsbridge in those days. Travel cost 4d each way, with a saloon ticket at 6d. This steamer, called the "Reindeer", towed cargo boats at times though if the wind was favourable, the boats were sailed. There was also a horse drawn bus which went via Marlborough, a journey which took one and a half hours.

Steam ferry at Customs House Quay. c 1910. J Fairweather.

The "Kingsbridge Packet" which was a screw steamer, made two or three trips a week to Plymouth, berthing at the Kings Arms Quay. There was a wooden paddle steamer, the "Express" which covered the same route, but extended the run to Dartmouth. She berthed at Custom House Quay. Both boats carried passengers and cargo, and often the fine ladies on board would have to put up with the bellowing of a heifer being taken to another farm, or would be forced to touch their lace handkerchiefs to their noses in mute protest, as a pig was loaded.

The "Express" was later converted to a three masted topsail schooner. I occasionally saw her when she brought coal cargoes to Salcome. All coal came by sea in those days and there were five coal merchants in the town selling best coal at 1/- a cwt.

The morning mail was delivered from Kingsbridge by pony and trap, with the outgoing mail transported the same way every evening.

The Post Office was now at the west end of the new "York Hotel".It was staffed by the Post Master and his wife and one Telegraphist. The telegraph boy had to deliver from Salcombe to Hope Cove and Prawle on foot, so delivery was not always prompt. There were no telephones but grams were delivered on Sundays, as was one delivery of mail. William Murch, the son of the bootmaker our family had feuded with, was the postman responsible for the rural post rounds.

At the top of the Ferry Steps, "York Hotel" and the Post Office.
c 1910 J Fairweather

The outgoing mail was carried by a post man in the mornings, and he brought back mail for a second delivery in the afternoon. A man named J Ash did this for years. My father remembered that when he was a boy a widow called Sarah Stone delivered the mail on foot for many years, walking from Kingsbridge through Salcombe with a heavy sack on her back. She charged a penny a letter for delivery. Her lot was such that she was always known as "Poor Sally Stone". But Sally had a business head on her shoulders. She saved for years until she managed to buy a boat which she rowed up and down the estuary every day. The mail delivery flourished and Sally became a well to do woman.

Mail delivery. J Fairweather

There were quite a number of working craft moving about the harbour at this time. Sailing schooners and coastal ketches brought coal and other bulky cargoes, and limestone barges came up from Plymouth. At times there were bound craft, and in the summer usually quite a number of large yachts, whose crew manned four-oared galleys which seemed to be constantly on the move, as their wealthy employers enjoyed trips ashore or to the beach. The crews for these boats were recruited mainly from experienced, deep water seamen who in the winter sailed in the large sailing ships mainly on the Australia run. These ships, sailing up the Channel in April and May and outward bound in September and October were quite a familiar sight. Whenever we saw them, we boys stopped to watch their passage. They were magnificent! Running before a South-Westerly wind their sails billowing, catching the sunlight, they were the emperors of the

Channel run. I wanted to be on board one of them, but common sense as well as the knowledge that I could not afford to buy myself out, told me that I must first finish my apprenticeship.

Though the ships that passed through the harbour were undoubtedly a stirring sight, there were many wrecks around the coast. Whenever a ship foundered the whole town flocked to the scene – it seemed that the old pirate spirit was still very much alive.

One of the wrecks at about this time was a Russian oil tanker named the "Blesk". Her cargo was crude oil and it spewed into the water and ruined the crab fishing for a summer.

The earliest wreck I remember was the "Hallow'een" a China tea clipper which had made a record run from China, and hit the rocks off Soar Mill. When she broke up, the tea chests in her holds smashed and tea spilled out and was piled up three or four feet high right around the cove. Word got around quickly, and it was a race to get as many containers as possible down on the beach to salvage the tea. It was said that no tea was bought in the district for many years afterwards. A whole generation of Salcombe children grew up knowing nothing but salt tea.

My father's work seemed now once again secure and we looked forward to a comfortable future

Then Major Bennett died, and his passing brought up the old insecurities. My parents stayed up late in front of the range in the kitchen talking. We boys could hear their anxious voices as they endlessly debated what to do. Jobs were scarce in Salcombe and there was little chance of my father finding another easily. It was not nearly as bad as the previous time that he had been out of work, as Aaron still had regular work around town, but he had nothing secure, and that was what he wanted. There was not much money coming into the household now that all three of us boys were apprenticed, and both my parents were very aware that our little family had no security net. Added to this was the unspoken fear that this time around my father was older, and everyone knew that employers wanted younger men.

But then came such astonishing news that we could none of us believe it. Major Bennett's estate was placed in the hands of executors in Exeter, and this firm wrote to my father. We were all in the house when the letter arrived, and everyone waited as I opened it and scanned the contents. I have to admit that I read it twice before I passed on its contents, and even then I could barely keep the smile from my face though I tried to keep them all guessing for as long as possible, for the executors had asked my father to caretake "Woodcot" as well as continuing to look after the garden for as long as it would take to find a buyer for the property. When that happened the executors wrote that they would do all they could to make sure that my father's job was secured by the new owner. To facilitate my father's new responsibilities, our family was to move to "The Lodge" at "Woodcot".

It was the best of all outcomes, and it was a situation that was eventually to continue for three years. In the meantime, after a small family celebration, we prepared to pack our belongings and move home, all of us happy and greatly relieved, my father's face wreathed in smiles.

CHAPTER FIVE

I now returned from work in the evenings to the Lodge at "Woodcot".
We had the whole beautiful estate to ourselves, and a warm dry cottage
where we were all comfortable. In the evenings when we gathered after our
day's work, it was impossible not to stop at a window and stare out at the
view. We picked grapes and peaches, nectarines, strawberries and other
fruits from the glasshouses and sold them in the town as we had been
instructed, carefully keeping account of the money we sent to the solicitors.
But there was always so much fruit left over for us to enjoy and to give to
others. Aaron had such a steady stream of youngsters coming to the gate for
fruit that he began to put out a small basket each day in the season so that
locals could help themselves. Often there would be small items left there in
thanks, a slice of fruit tart or a piece of apple pie made with "Woodcot"
apples. Several of the children used to come to help our father pick in the
season. Edith Harnden of a Salcombe ship building family, was one of the
girls drawn to "Woodcot" by the big plump juicy peaches Aaron put in the
basket. She later went on to become Frank's wife. Fred always swore the
marriage was all Aaron's doing.
    We watched the sun go down over the sea, and the fishing boats come
in. We saw the winter gales crash and roar and the dark clouds gather over
the harbour entrance but we were safe and secure in our cottage at the
entrance to the estate. We boys all clubbed together and bought our father a
telescope which he delighted in. He spent a lot of time looking through it,
and it was only when he reluctantly put it aside to go to work that we could
look through it at the estuary with its empty sands and the green rolling hills
above, at any boat that happened past, and the big ships far out to sea. We
had all this without any master looking over us, and I think my parents had
never been happier.

Of course my father probably worked even harder than he had ever done. He was meticulous in this, and we boys helped wherever we could. There was a tremendous amount of upkeep to do even in an empty property we soon found out. We did a lot of odd jobs around the place, repainting and repairing, pruning and cutting down overgrown bushes as well as keeping the beds neat and the kitchen gardens thriving. My father had a free hand with the gardens, and he enjoyed himself hugely enlarging and re-siting flower beds as he wanted. He had a long term plan for the estate and worked the land as if it were his own. And with all this his pay came in regularly, sent by the executors in Exeter. We were living like wealthy people, my mother said wonderingly.

These were perhaps the best days of all our lives. I was happy in my work, and I was learning so much. Bill Pert continued to be my mentor, and every day I could see my skill developing. I loved woodworking. But I was still true to my first love, construction in all its aspects. My master, Mr Cranch, had seen that I favoured house building rather than furniture making, staircases or windows, and he tried to use me on building sites where he could. He had the sense to try to employ his workforce where their interests lay whenever it was possible. He used to say that a man worked better when he was interested in his task. Now that I had completed my evening courses I was of more use to him, and seeing that I was keen to learn, he allowed me to draw up simple construction plans and workshop drawings. He let me put in my pennyworth occasionally when there was a potential problem with a house build, and praised me more than once for suggesting ideas that saved him money. I thought privately that he lacked imagination in his designs, but it was not my place to say anything.

There were a few houses being built around Salcombe now, and several building sites which had been sold by the South Devon Land Co., and were awaiting house construction. Increasingly outsiders had begun to come into the area. These people had made their money in the big cities, and now wanted to live somewhere quiet and beautiful. You heard their accents in the town, brash sometimes, and harsh. Their voices were different from ours. They were louder and more forceful. They thought they were important men – and maybe they were by their standards. But their ways were not ours. Their presence was just another sign of the changing times.

And times were bad in Salcombe then. By the turn of the century the one remaining industry left in the town was fishing, mainly for crab and lobster. It was a very hard life conducted from rowing and sailing boats, sometimes with two men to a boat, more often than not only one.

The boats were mainly sprit sail fixed keel craft. Some had drop keels and were yawl rigged. Twenty or more men from Salcombe and East Portlemouth were engaged in this work. They set trammels and long lines baited with lug worms. If they were short of bait they sometimes hailed passing Brixham trawlers on their way up Channel, and bought bait fish from them. They also bought coarse fish, mostly gurnards, for this purpose from the fish quays in Plymouth, double banking their oars and rowing their boats all the way there and back. Gurnards made good bait, though they were not much good for anything else, and so the fishermen were glad to be rid of them for whatever they could get. The strange thing about gurnards with their armoured heads and spiky fins, is that they grunt like a stuck pig when caught, a characteristic which set the hair on the back of my neck on end when I first heard it one evening about sunset off the Bar. I thought I had caught an angry merman!

Bream caught well out in the Channel were one of the choicest fish, and most of these were sold in the town. A large bream – delicious stuffed and baked – which was enough for four people, cost 6d. The shell fish catch was stored in large wicker pots moored in the cleanest parts of the harbour. Some of the crabs and lobsters were sold locally. The fishermen would each have their own following of the gentry's cooks who would usually advise them in advance when company was expected or when they would require specific seafood. Fishermen's wives traditionally gathered in two or three different places, in the main Council Quay, off to the side of Customs House Quay or on the quays around Island Street but the wives of the crab fishers lived in the cottages by the ferry steps. You could hang over the stable doors of the little houses and watch them hard at work on the crabs scraping out the shell, stripping out the dead men's fingers and breaking and picking out the legs so as not to miss any of the flesh. They would dress and deliver a hen crab to one's door for 3d.

A great deal of the shell fish was sold on to other places outside the town. This catch was stored in large wicker pots moored closer to the bar. In the summer fast sailing craft from the Hamble called almost weekly for it. The collection craft I remember best was the "Stella", a fore and aft rigged schooner, which had probably once been a gentleman's leisure boat, but which when I knew it, had had large tanks fitted to keep the catch alive for the return journey.

Many of the tougher fishermen laid their pots at shoal grounds four or five miles outside the Bar, others and those who were fishing single handedly, chose closer spots. Each fisherman had his own favourite place and these were jealously guarded.

One Whit Monday when we apprentices had a rare day off, Jim Cove asked me if I wanted to go fishing with him. I agreed and we met up before dawn to get the boat ready. Jim usually fished alone so we both looked forward to an enjoyable day together.

We left about 4 a.m. There was no wind and we rowed almost to Prawle Point, a distance of nearly two miles, in a choppy sea. We hauled in single pots at intervals, rowing between them to about a mile below the Mewstone, then returned to harbour just before 2 p.m., having rowed or hauled pots continuously the whole time. With no mechanised equipment, all pots were hauled individually and it was hard and heavy work. This was in the days long before mechanical winches were fitted and pots were laid in strings (rows) in deeper water to be hauled in under power.

We had only covered a few miles, but it was some day. We later went out and set a trammel, but even though I was used to hard work, I had had enough for one day.

In the winter months, when it was often too rough to go out to the traditional fishing grounds, some of the Salcombe men fished for conger eel which had a good London market. They said it was served in the capital as jellied eel, but it was not eaten in our town. Sometimes our fishermen chopped up the eels to catch squid. You could see the boats at twilight rigging and baiting long lines. They stayed outside the harbour all night, returning early in the morning often with a very large catch.

No fishermen went to sea on a Sunday, neither was a boat seen in the harbour and nearly all the men attended church or chapel. Belief was strong in those days, and superstition stronger. No-body ever whistled around fishing boats, and strangely, even though most of the boats were named for women, no women ever set foot on them, as both actions were thought to bring bad luck.

The crab fishing industry dwindled and revived again with the coming of the outsiders. There was some market locally, but by now crab fishermen had begun to send their catch to the big towns inland where it fetched higher prices.

Salcombe had by now become once more almost a feudal village, dependent largely on the owners of the few large houses for its existence. These houses all kept staff and servants, as did the owners of the lesser houses right down to the small business owners who might perhaps have a maid of all work, a washerwoman or a nurse maid for their children. Snobbery, especially from the bottom up, was rife. But there were still not enough jobs to go around, and with jobs scarce quite a few of the servants employed in these houses were poorly treated.

It was not all work however, and in those days national events were the cause of great celebrations. The first I can remember was the Duke of York's wedding when there was an alfresco dinner and tea held in the field at the junction of St. Dunstans and Onslow Roads. Sports were held in the afternoon and a torch light procession followed in the evening in which we all processed down into the town to the accompaniment of cheers from the onlookers. It was great fun, and only a few burns were reported. One boy who carried his flaming torch too close to his head, managed to set his hair alight.

For any celebration arches were erected in Fore Street and at "Woodcot" which we helped Aaron to dress with flowers and vines. A procession formed, headed by two marshals, which was an hereditary post traditionally held by members of the Hannaford family. They were followed by the town band in their best uniforms and with their brass instruments polished especially for the day and gleaming brightly; the Coast Guards wearing their straw boaters; up to fifty Volunteers forces in uniform, who formed a stirring crowd; representatives of the various Friendly Societies; the life boat crew all wearing their life jackets; the Foresters; Oddfellows and National Branch employees all with ceremonial sashes draped over their shoulders, their officers sporting neck bands and medals. These were followed by parties of excited school children dressed in their Sunday best clothes, and, last of all, horse drawn traps for the aged, who were kept warm with rugs tucked over their knees.

Then there was the annual one day Regatta in the harbour, a great, eagerly anticipated event with sailing, rowing, swimming and sports, including the often hilarious wrestling on the greasy pole which was my favourite. The Coast Guards from all the nearby stations took a very prominent part, rowing their galleys and usually participating in some sporting event, conscious that all female eyes were upon them. The craft in the harbour were dressed overall and altogether it was a gala day. The money prizes were subscribed to by all, but the main contribution came of course from the wealthier residents of the town.

Salcombe Regatta, 1908. Fairweather

There were sharp, un-breachable divisions amongst the classes in those days. Titled people and landed gentry were on the top of the heap, followed by religious men – particularly those of a higher calling. Next were army and naval officers, and retired persons. Anyone engaged in trade was very second rate and not included in society. People generally knew their class and stuck rigidly to it. On occasion a man who had made money in trade tried to rise above his station, but was quickly ostracised by his "betters". The value of money was such that the rich were very well off indeed. The poor, as ever, just grew poorer; most of the time, even if they worked hard, they existed just on the poverty line. Any small mishap was enough to topple most working people over into the abyss.

Wages were low. Farm labourers were paid 10/- week, artisans 4 1/2d to 5d an hour, and unskilled labourers 3d to 4d. an hour. These men lost money if it was wet and they could not work. They had no holiday pay for bank or other holidays. A hymn we often sang in church services, "All things bright and beautiful", reflected this sentiment exactly, in its verse -

"The rich man in his castle,
The poor man at his gate,
God made them high or lowly,
And ordered their estate."

This state of affairs carried on until well into the Edwardian era. Change began with a change of government. After ten years in opposition, David Lloyd George the Welsh leader of the Liberal Party, gained an overwhelming election victory over the Conservatives. The growing strength of the six year old Labour Party was shown in the 54 seats they gained. They said that Liberals and Labour made an electoral pact which is what enabled the Liberals to gain their seats.

Lloyd George was the first politician who seemed actually to care about working people. He ended the hated Workhouse system, and introduced the National Insurance Act which provided a safety net for the vulnerable. The Act created terrific feeling on all sides. The rich were loud in their condemnation of it, probably because they understood that it marked the beginning of a sea change in society. But the poor were overjoyed, though they could scarcely bring themselves to believe that in exchange for a small payment each week they would no longer have to worry about losing their jobs or having no money to feed their families. There were some who for a long time remained convinced that it was just another way for the government to take money from them, and refused to accept that they would ever actually pay out when needed. I remember hearing of a domestic servant in a big house in Malborough who adamantly refused to stick a stamp on a card for "that Lloyd George". Despite her employer's patient explanation that it was for her own good, she continued in her refusal and in the end her employer stamped her card for her every week and kept it safely without telling her.

My elder brother Frank signed on to H.M.S "Hyacinth" bound for the East Indies station for three years. He had leave before sailing and I asked my master for a week off to spend with him, which of course was unpaid. We had a wonderful time, enjoying the first holiday either of us had ever had. Although we still managed our household duties, and the occasional odd jobs, we spent most of the days on the beach, swimming, fishing and joking around, generally enjoying ourselves hugely. Frank and I had always been particularly close, and we resolutely put our pending separation out of our minds so as to make the most of these last few days together.

On the day of Frank's departure my father borrowed his brother William's horse and cart and we all went to Kingsbridge railway station to see him off. We drove the back way into Kingsbridge, through Batson up the lane past Ilton Castle Farm and Blanksmill, twisting and turning up and down the small hills which offered the occasional tantalising view of the estuary beyond, and for some reason we sang all the way. I think it was just the pleasure of the sunny day, the dancing new leaves overhead, and the fact that we were all together, despite the nearness of a parting that would take one of us away from the family table for so long. By the time we'd reached Tacket Wood, and down the Ropewalk to the station, we had got onto hymns. Anyone hearing us must have thought we were a band of travelling preachers!

When I went back to work my master berated me for wasting time, saying that he had heard I was only larking about on Sunny Cove, and could just as easily have been at work. His attitude epitomised the usual attitude towards recreation for such as us. Work was all that mattered for ordinary people. Idleness was the prerogative of the rich. But I knew we had made the most of that last week, and had given Frank a send-off that would stay with him in times of loneliness and trouble ahead, and I wouldn't have missed it for the world.

It was soon after Frank left that some members of an up-country Canoe Association visited Salcombe and set up camp in the meadows above Millbay. They held a Sports Day there, and performed acrobatics and complicated manoeuvres off the shore in their canoes, turning the boats in and out of markers and capsizing and righting them again. Word of these strange craft spread like wildfire, and all of this was watched with great attention by the youth of the town, many of whom, including me, just happened by with an eye to examining these hitherto unknown boats.

The members of the Canoe Association departed after less than a week, but they left behind them a group of young Salcombe men and boys who were fired up with enthusiasm to possess such craft. Not wishing to appear as unsophisticated country bumpkins next to these townies, and well aware that the only way we could procure similar boats was to build them ourselves, we had used subterfuge. Comparing notes we discovered that as well as the surreptitious drawings that I and another boy had made, one apprentice had even under some pretext or another, taken measurements. We were as well prepared as we could be to begin.

Several of us set ourselves to save up what we estimated was the necessary 5/- for materials, and then, by a process of trial and error which involved much discussion, much scratching of heads and not a few heated debates, we set to work in the evenings to build our craft.

Finally they were finished, complete with shiny, varnished top sides and double bladed paddles just as the originals had been, and we were as pleased as punch as we launched them off Council Quay with due ceremony and the help of a bottle of ginger beer.

The craze swept through the town, and before long everybody was building canoes. There must have been up to twenty of these craft on the water eventually, and, despite one drowning fatality, they were the ultimate object of desire. We developed sailing canoes with centre boards and hand-made sails and began racing them. I built one of these for my own two boys in the Thirties.

As proud owners of these new craft, but with dire warnings about breaking the Sabbath echoing in our ears, we gradually started to gather on Sunny Cove on Sundays. There was almost virgin solitude on that beach then, and we young, rebelling against the conventions of the first decade of the 20th century, enjoyed ourselves hugely, racing, practising our turns and rolling our vessels, and driving the boats through the breaking waves of an incoming tide. There was a lot of head shaking from the older generations, but the introduction of a one hour bible class by a very popular Curate, allowed us to pay lip service to religion as well as having our fun. Later, when the Curate had the idea of a canoeing picnic on Mill Bay exactly as the original club had done, we were delighted. We felt now that we had showed those townies that we could do just as well as they had done, but with the difference that having built our own boats, we knew them inside and out and they meant infinitely more to us than if we had just gone to a shop and bought them.

We were all very patriotic in those days. The South African war and momentous events such as the ascension of the new king made us want to play our part. We boys all shared a strong sense of wanting to be able to contribute something to our country. I cast around for what I could do personally, and made up my mind that I would join the Volunteers. The decision was helped in no small part by the discovery that the Volunteers attended a fourteen day camp once a year for which they received pay of £2 – riches galore!

The lowest age for entry was supposed to be 17, except for buglers who could be younger, and a minimum height of 5'6" was set, though during the

South African war this was relaxed. I was not yet 16 in 1902 when I was enlisted and duly sworn in.

The local force was about fifty strong. Its full title was No 2 Company of the Devon Artillery Volunteers. Our erstwhile headmaster, the bearded "Skipper" Coad, who held the rank of Sergeant Major, was our instructor.

We were equipped with stiff blue serge uniforms and helmets and little pill box caps like those of the Church Army, though later these were replaced by forage caps. We wore our uniform, complete with spotless white gloves and with the jacket buttoned tightly up to the neck for all drills, parades and meetings, and thought ourselves incredibly smart with our Lee Enfield carbines over our shoulders. Our employers did not dare interfere with our military duties and camps for fear of being thought unpatriotic, and so, though they grumbled when we had to miss work, they were in the main supportive.

We did musketry practise on Saturday afternoons, firing from the Crofts to a target under the cliffs at Snapes – the farmer wisely kept no sheep in the field above on the Saturdays when we held our firing practise, as much of our shooting was wild, to say the least. Then we practised gun drill at the Battery, now the site of Castle Point. There were two 64 pounder muzzle loading guns there. Together with other small fry, I had several times as a youngster been in the woods behind the Battery with my fingers in my ears, when these guns were fired at a target barrel moored outside the Harbour entrance. Whether the sights were deflected to avoid hitting it, or whether the troop were just poor shots, I'll never know, but not once did we see the barrel hit, though we did see some mighty big splashes.

Our guns were mounted on wooden carriages with iron wheels, and when loaded were levered out with handspikes to the mouth of the embrasure. The drill was to sponge out the muzzle, insert the firing charge, then the projectile, take the handspike out and then put the firing pin into the touch hole. The gun was fired on pulling a lanyard. We drilled all movements including inserting the firing pin but we did not charge the guns. We did however on one occasion have a real firing practise on similar guns at Dartmouth Castle. We discovered then to our chagrin that the gun recoil was almost the same length as the gun, a fact which, embarrassingly, bowled a couple of us clean off our feet.

Our annual camp was held on Maker Heights above Mount Edgecombe across the Hamoaze from Plymouth. Thrilled by the crowds who gathered to cheer our passage, we marched smartly behind our band to Fort Picklecombe which commanded the western entrance to Plymouth Sound, where we drilled on and occasionally fired 6 and 12 pounder general field guns. During a special Saturday afternoon trip to Bovisand Fort at the eastern entrance of the Sound, I qualified as a Gun Layer, afterwards proudly wearing a G.L badge on my uniform. My rank was now Bombadier

The Battery, looking across to South Sands and Bolt Head.
c 1907. J Fairweather.

or Lance Corporal.

At this camp our full regiment was assembled, No. 1 Company Dartmouth; No. 2 Company Salcombe; Nos. 3 and 4 Companies from Lynmouth and Ilfracombe and the rest from Plymouth and Devonport. There was also a North Country militia regiment which pitched its tents near us.

We considered ourselves vastly superior to the troops, and, conveniently overlooking the part the £2 pay had played in our own enlistment, joked amongst ourselves that they were merely "Bounty Men". But on one occasion during the celebrations for a royal birthday, we both lined up for three rounds of Feu-de-Joie, and they were much less ragged than us. Firing a Feu-de-Joie, consists of each man in a line firing consecutively after his right hand neighbour, with the minimum of delay. If carried out properly it should sound like a slow machine gun in action, but our display sounding rather more like an elderly dog with a coughing fit. Discussing it afterwards, we had shamefacedly to admit that it had not been the finest hour for No. 2 Company Devon Artillery Volunteers.

When in camp we slept eight to a tent. We were under the command of a Lieutenant, and besides Sergeant Major Coad, had a regular army Sergeant Major as our instructor at camp. He was responsible for records, arms and uniforms as well as for drill instruction.

The first big event of my service was when we of No. 2 Company joined with the Dartmouth Company to form a guard of honour one hundred strong, in Dartmouth for King Edward's visit to lay a foundation stone for the opening of the imposing new Dartmouth Naval College on the top of the hill overlooking the town.

We were lined up at the railway pontoon and I guess as we marched smartly to our station. caused considerable amusement to the regular troops positioned along the route. Tremendous preparation had gone on beforehand to ensure we looked our best. We had been told that our trousers must be taken to "Tailor Jack" in the town to be properly pressed with the required "knife edge" crease – an instruction with which my mother took umbrage, complaining loudly to whoever would listen that she considered herself just as competent at pressing trousers as "Tailor Jack" whomever he might be - and we all wore spotless white gloves. I remember the whole troop walking around with their hands held rigidly at their sides, scared stiff to touch anything which might get their gloves dirty.

Preparations at innumerable dummy run parades held in advance of the day, had included stern instructions that if it should happen that we were to have the unmentionable honour of being addressed by the king, we should reply "Yes, or No, Your Majesty" as the case might be, and we all practised hard at doing this. On the day, the king did actually speak to our very diminutive bugler, who was almost invisible as he wore a trumpet over one shoulder and a bugle over the other. Though no-one heard what he squeaked, we all agreed that having been drilled so often, he would have managed the right reply, and not brought shame to the company.

When it was all over we entrained to Brent, tired, but pleased with ourselves and with the feeling that we had made a good showing. Arriving at the station our Sergeant Major, "Skipper" Coad, discovered that we were to have a long wait for our transport back to Salcombe and so he led us all into a nearby pub. There, as we packed into the saloon bar, he thrilled us all by singing not just one, but several renditions of the currently popular song "Comrades", to much applause. After all this time we were astonished to discover that he really was human after all.

A decree was passed to form a Special Service Section of Volunteers so as to have a way of retaining the services of some key personnel should they be needed in a national emergency. This was necessary because mobilisation of the Volunteers generally required either an order in council or parliamentary approval, both of which took some time. Eight men from each company were to be retained, and as one of those chosen I was paid a retainer of £1 a year for my services.

We S.S.S were allocated war stations; mine was G.L of No. 2 Gun Eastern Kings Redoubt, Plymouth. This was the fort covering the Hamoaze entrance but I never saw my gun or even the Redoubt. Still as my father kindly said, it was comforting to know that if the country was threatened, he was at least confident that G.L of No.2 Gun Eastern Kings Redoubt, Plymouth was up to his task!

I had three periods of fourteen days at Shoeburyness on G.F. courses. I was fortunate to be picked as the usual quota was only sixteen men from

Devon Artillery Volunteer Brigade c 1903

the whole regiment. The highlights were the weekends during which we had leave in London, though this only happened three times in total.

At Shoeburyness we were housed in barracks and for once had no fatigues. For the first few days we had intense instruction and many drills, and then spent two days firing through one inch aiming tubes.

On the third morning we were marched down to the guns which were set on the shoreline. The guns were 4 ½ and 6 pounders mounted on gantries about 20-30 feet above the sea. The shells were not live but were filled with rock salt and were fired over the water. The targets, set at varying ranges, ran on rails controlled by wires. Each man had to take turns to captain the gun and all members of the crew changed positions with each firing, so that eventually every one of us was competent in all aspects of gun drill. After the shells had been fired horse-drawn wagons went out at low tide and collected them for refilling.

During the second week of manoeuvres there was a full scale shooting exercise which made the gantries rock. One night there was a simulated alarm. We were all assembled on the beach, a siren sounded and we all dashed up the iron staircases in the dark to our guns, loaded and fired about one dozen rounds per gun at each run of an illuminated searchlight which represented the target. It was exciting stuff.

When we were not training we were free to spend the evenings in Southend, which for us was almost as thrilling. There was a dance hall at the rear of the "Ship Inn" on the front where we used to go. Shy and inexperienced but conspicuous in our smart uniforms, we vied to be the first one to ask a girl to dance – almost always without success.

I qualified as a Sergeant soon after this but as promotion was strictly on availability of position and there were then no vacancies, I could not take up my new rank. However even this partial promotion brought me preferential treatment as I was afterwards excused fatigues and guard patrol duties.

In all I served seven years and seventy days with the Volunteers before they were disbanded and replaced by the newly named Territorial Army. I served only a few months in the Territorials.

My life was full and generally happy, but I was keen to learn as much as I could. I had always loved working out how to overcome problems, and my apprenticeship had made me aware that it was possible to use the same techniques in both joinery and building work. My master, Mr Cranch had noticed this trait and the fact that I loved a challenge and had begun encouraging me to work out problems on difficult sites. Our firm worked closely with masons on building projects and I took whatever opportunity presented itself to learn as much as I could from them. Many times when a particularly difficult site was involved, I would arrive early and watch things happening. I realised about this time that I wanted to be involved in building houses.

Soon after we came to "Woodcot" I had made a discovery which thrilled me. My father had the keys to the big house and I had gone with him on his first visit and came across a library filled with books. I had never seen so many books before, and I went from shelf to shelf pulling out those that interested me most, and leafing through them. The majority of the Major's books were of historical subjects, most of these concerned with warfare, which given his army career was not surprising. But there was also a fairly extensive section on civil engineering and construction including several books which dealt with the subject of constructions in difficult sites, such as building bridge supports in silt, which fascinated me.

My father followed me into the room and I asked him if I could borrow one of the books. Giving me permission was a hard decision for Aaron, as he was very much in awe of books and book learning and he took his responsibilities for the house very seriously, but after some hesitation he agreed. I sped home that afternoon with my prize clutched tightly in my hand in the first of what would become over the years, extensive borrowings. I had begun to take the next steps in my chosen work. Lacking facilities or money for further education, I had begun to educate myself.

It was my ambition to be my own boss. It was a huge dream for a poor boy from a poor family, but living as we were gave rein to my imagination.

I spent quite a lot of time in the big house at "Woodcot", ostensibly

"Woodcot"

helping my father as he polished floors and generally maintained the building, but I used these visits to explore the building from top to bottom, studying how it had been constructed, running my hands over wood joints and plaster techniques and trying to work out for myself how they had been constructed. I have to admit there was more though. As I walked from room to room the desire to one day own a house like "Woodcot" grew in me. I wanted to be able to see the sea from my window. I wanted to look across smooth green lawns dotted with immaculate flower beds, or take my relaxation in the shade of a majestic tree. I wanted richly patterned oriental rugs on the floor, a long polished table with chairs arranged around it, a big chair for myself and one at the other end for the unknown lady who would one day become my wife. But most of all I longed for a room with shelves full of books just as there were in "Woodcot".

It was not long before we all grew so familiar with the house and the grounds that it was almost as if they belonged to us. We had the run of them. I had grown used to sitting on the window seat in the library leafing through several volumes before choosing one to take home to read by the light of my candle after the household had gone to bed; grown used to taking a peach from the greenhouse as I fancied, or helping myself to a handful of strawberries from the big beds. All "Woodcot" was ours to enjoy. We had no-one to oversee us. My father took what decisions were necessary for the smooth running of the estate, and if this entailed additional expenditure he just informed the agent, and the money was sent to him with his wages. These halcyon days were to continue in the end for almost three years.

Then one day in 1903 we had news from the Executor that shocked us all. "Woodcot" had finally been sold.

My parents were openly frightened. We were no longer children, and so they included Fred and me in their discussions, but we did not know how to reassure them. Easy living had softened us all. Cushioned by our idyllic lives, we had all but forgotten that we were not rich people but nobodies, and our proper step on the precarious ladder of life was on the rung just above the gutter. In the early days we always had in our minds that our position here was temporary. By now we had just accepted it and shut out all thought of it one day coming to an end. I think it was harder for all of us than if we had never enjoyed this respite.

We were informed by the agent that the arrival of the new owner was imminent. In the meantime gossip doing the rounds of the town was that he was Andrew McIlwraith, the owner of the McIlwraith McEacharn Shipping Line whose ships sailed the Australian route... the heavy set Scot we had occasionally seen around town who had been one of the founders of the Salcombe Yacht Club.

We waited anxiously, unable to settle to anything properly. Then, one Saturday afternoon, when by chance both Fred and I were at home, Mr McIllwraith arrived, driven by a chauffeur in a big, black motor car, one of the first seen in Salcombe.

We were all in the kitchen. The arrival of the motor car set my parents in a tizzy, and they scurried to get ready to receive him. My mother whisked off her apron, and tidied her hair. My father, who had just come in from digging the potato bed, washed his hands hurriedly, rolled down his shirt sleeves and put on his jacket. Nervously, they walked outside together, shoulder to shoulder, while Fred and I waited in the cottage, watching from the kitchen window.

The chauffeur, wearing a shiny black peaked cap got out of the car and moved to open the rear door for the vehicle's sole occupant, but the man was already out. Bill Pert had taught me to people watch, and I concentrated on the man as he strode around the car and stood staring up at the house

I had not had cause to pay him much attention before, now I tried to make a quick assessment of his character. He was a big, stocky man in late middle age, with thick hair, once red, now mostly white, and a bushy white beard. He was energetic and strongly built and he moved quickly.

My judgement of him was that he was a man who knew what he wanted and would make sure that he got it. Not a man to tolerate fools lightly.

My parents walked towards the car. My father had his cap in his hand. The man glanced across at them, and my mother dropped a curtsey. Fred and I exchanged looks. We had never seen Ellen curtsey before and it shocked us. Holding tightly to his cap, my father introduced himself and my mother, and I saw the man nod curtly. I noticed that he gave them only a cursory glance, that his attention was with the estate, and I guessed that business was all for him, and that people were only important for what they could do or procure for him. It was the first time I had been close to such a powerful man.

That night we discussed the situation around the kitchen table. The executors had promised our father that they would do their best to ensure that his employment continued, but none of us had any faith that this would be the case. People in our position all too often learned to their cost that the promises of rich men were easily broken. Any idea my mother had had of appealing to such a man on a personal level to secure my father's job went out of the window. She was as good a judge of people as my father was a poor one, and she recognised that this was a man who would appoint whomever he wanted for the position of Head Gardener. We could only wait and see what Andrew McIlwraith decided.

So in the days that followed we stayed on uneasily at the Lodge, going about our normal business, not sure what else to do, not knowing who would pay my father's wages, or even if he would be paid at all.

A few days later a removal van from Pickfords arrived, and behind it the motor car containing the family. I was out at the time so all I learned was that an elegant woman, presumably Mrs McIllwraith had arrived together with two boys and a young woman.

Our insecurity was increased when we learned that Mr McIlwraith had been seen around the town asking about gardeners. Two days later he called my father to the house. We saw them soon after walking the grounds together. We saw my father pointing out the improvements we had made, the greenhouses that we had repaired and the ponds and the grape vines in the old proving houses that were his particular favourite project. Then they disappeared from view, presumably to visit the gardens below.

They were gone some time, and we waited on tenterhooks. When our father finally returned across the lawn, his face was wreathed in smiles. "'Er wants me to stay…" he said. "We'm to stay on at "The Lodge". "'Er likes what us have done in the grounds and 'er wants things to carry on as 'twas afore."

It was a tremendous relief for all of us. My mother had taken the uncertainty hard. It had brought up all her old worries about money. She was convinced her brood would all starve. That fear was with her all her life.

Filled with a new enthusiasm we all turned to and helped. For the moment my mother did the laundry for the house, and also cooked for the family in the days before they appointed a cook, while Fred and I helped father when we could. I think we all wanted to do our best to prove that we were a good business expense! We met Mr McIllwraith and his wife and their sons. I had taught myself to repair basic garden machinery such as was found in the sheds at "Woodcot". I had also watched a stone mason working through the course of a couple of months during a construction, and had learned the principals of building both dry stone and cemented stone walls. Mr McIllwraith wanted some additional walls built in the gardens and I volunteered to do this for him. It was the first building project I had done all by myself, and I must say that I was pleased with it when it was finished.

I helped my father repair one of the big greenhouses that was damaged during a winter storm the following year, working out how to replace and remake the wooden stringer bars and cut the glass in my spare time, for which I received McIllwraith's grunt of thanks and a shilling. But it was the expression in his eyes, a fleeting recognition of a job well done, that was my real reward, as well as knowing that I was helping my father. McIlwraith was a man of few words. His way of rewarding you was to come back to you maybe years later with some favour or help, I later learned. I think it was then that my father's employer first took notice of me.

I had considered myself comparatively well off with the money I had earned at the doctor's surgery, but I had learned enough of life to understand that you needed large sums of money in the bank before you could do very much at all. Thanks to my mother's teaching, I was no spendthrift. Now of course, because of my apprenticeship my earnings were considerably reduced, but even so almost all the money my mother allowed me went into the savings account I had opened in the Post Office in town. But beyond knowing that I wanted to be my own boss, I had no idea how this money could be converted for use in my future plans.

I observed Mr McIlwraith covertly as he moved about his property. He was perhaps 58 or 59 in those days. He was a Calvinist at least by birth and he was a hard man. They said he was teetotal, but I saw him the worse for wear on the brandy which he said he drank for his health. He was a rich man undoubtedly, but what fascinated me most was the aura of power that hung about him. This was a man who made things happen, who was at the centre of events, and I wanted to be like him.

I was curious to know how he had made his money, but when I questioned my father, he did not know. It was not the sort of question that would have occurred to my sweet natured father. Aaron was content the way he was. It was not our place to know such things, he told me firmly one Sunday afternoon as we walked together out towards Bolt Head. They were the masters, and we were the workers. He believed that I think. But I did not. Perhaps he was old fashioned even then. They were our masters only because they had more money I told myself...But they were not necessarily our betters.

I set myself to finding out how Andrew McIlwraith had earned the sort of money that had enabled him to buy "Woodcot". He was I learned, the fourth son of a John McIlwraith, a plumber and small ship owner based in Ayr, Scotland. He had been educated at Ayr Academy and then joined his father's business in the burgeoning shipping line that was colloquially known as "the Scottish Line" in 1858, establishing close commercial relations with his brothers John and Thomas (later Sir Thomas) who were based in Melbourne and Brisbane. In 1875 he had combined with Sir Malcolm McEacharn to set up the London based shipping and mercantile firm of McIlwraith, McEacharn and Co. When he visited Queensland soon afterwards, his connection with his brother Sir Thomas McIlwraith, by then premier of Australia, had resulted in a royal commission to transport settlers to the colony.

It was the gardener of the tenants in one of the houses in Egremont Terrace who told me that there had been allegations – finally deemed unfounded – that the McIlwraith family had conspired to obtain lucrative government contracts and, after they speculated in steel rails, had been charged with making undue profits at the expense of the colony.

It was this gardener, during a two day stint when we were working at the house, who explained how McIlwraith had made himself a rich man.
He told me that in 1871 Mr McIlwraith had married the daughter of the engineer James Campbell, which had proved to be a very good business move, for in 1878 after studying freezing plant and the freezer ship "Northam", based in Australia, he had capitalised on his own business acumen and his father-in-law's mechanical aptitude, and organised the chartering and fitting out with a freezing plant of a steamer called the "Strathleven". It was very soon after that this ship had earned the company a great deal of money by becoming the first to successfully transport a cargo of frozen meat from Australia to England.

As I realised Andrew McIlwraith had used his brains as well as his connections to make his own way in life, I admired him more. But as I got to know him better I realised that dogged persistence was another quality he possessed in abundance. This pleased me particularly because I knew that it was a trait I shared. Within the family they knew that I would continue worrying at a problem until I had found a way around it. When we were growing up Frank had sometimes teased me by calling me "Terrier", or sometimes just barking.

I continued the practise that our headmaster had enjoined in us, and I

Andrew
McIlwraith Esq.

now regularly read "The Times" newspaper, which Mr McIlwraith took and which made its way to me after it had been read, via the scullery maid who was a distant relation of my mother's. I was sitting on the small grassy hillock next to my father's vegetable patch one warm summer's evening when I opened it to find an article that described the first manned flight.

I read it to Aaron as he raked around his cabbage patch, as I often did things that I thought would interest him.

"... With Orville lying face down in a cradle beneath the wings and Wilbur, the elder brother running alongside, 'Flyer I' powered by a 12 m.p.h. engine, moved along the runners that supported it, and then, as the wind caught it, the flying machine rose upwards into the wind" I read.

My father lent on his rake, his mouth open. "They flew...?" he asked, shaking his head in astonishment.

I nodded. "They started with gliders...they spent years studying all the flying machines that had not worked, and came to believe that the secret lay in fixed wing aeroplanes," I summarised.

My father shook his head, dumfounded. "To think that this has happened in my lifetime," he said. He put down his rake. "I must tell your mother," he said, and set off back to the house.

I cut out the article and pinned it up in the bedroom I shared with Fred. If man could fly, what else could he not do? I thought. If two bicycle mechanics could do such a thing, I could eventually build houses. I walked into town that morning as if I were already a big business man.

That was the morning I saw the Suffragettes in town. I had read about the campaigning women but these were the first ones I had seen.

There was a group of three. Two of them were holding banners in what I later came to recognise as the Suffragette's colours of white, green and purple. One of the women was standing on a soapbox. She was quite tall and fairly young and she was wearing a green and purple sash across her body.

A small crowd of curious onlookers was gathering around the group who were handing out leaflets. As I approached I heard the woman on the soapbox appealing to the crowd.

"… And I say to you, that now is the time for action…. Women have been patient for too long…the politicians do not listen to us…It's been over 36 years since parliament first debated women's rights…". She had to raise her voice above the sound of seagulls squabbling on the nearby rooftops. "…And that has achieved little except to gain us the right to participate in local elections…"

One of the women pressed a leaflet into my hand. It bore a picture of a middle aged woman on the front. Underneath was a caption reading: "Mrs Pankhurst calls for action".

More people joined the growing crowd. Ordinary life was suspended around the campaigners as shoppers and shop keepers alike crowded onto the street,

"…I tell you now it is time for militant action…" the speaker continued shrilly. "We women have to cast aside our principles, our ladylike voice, and fight for what we believe in…"

Quite a few children had wriggled their way through the crowd and had taken up a ringside place, staring up in astonishment at the sight of the woman on the soapbox, but the general mood amongst the bystanders seemed to be negative and restive. Some people began drifting away. Others laughed. A couple of fishermen coming down the street yelled at her to go back home to her husband and children, and stop making a spectacle of herself.

"She ain't got no husband or babies," old Mrs Chant hooted. "That's why she's got the time to stand here in the street…"

There was general laughter and more drifting away. I saw a couple of apprentices coming down the road and knew that I was in danger of being late, so I shoved the leaflet into my jacket pocket and fell in with them. I didn't give what the woman had said much thought – Salcombe women were mostly like my mother, tough and hardy, used to fighting their corner to protect their families. I didn't think a vote would do much for them. But maybe ladies were different.

I read the leaflet briefly in the dinner break. I was glad of the short rest as I tucked into the pasty my mother had given me. I had spent several hours dove tailing joints and my arms ached. I passed the leaflet to Bill and he glanced through it. He said he had seen the lady too, and had also stopped to listen for a while.

"What do you think?" I asked him. "

" I think that women have no views worth expressing," Bill said dourly, and we all laughed. It was later in the day that I had a chance to discuss the really interesting information about the flight with him.

Then even the flight was forgotten when news that long standing Russian and Japanese rivalry over Manchuria had erupted in a Japanese attack on the Russian fleet lying at anchor in the heavily fortified Russian naval stronghold in Manchuria.

It had echoes of the Boer War, though this time England was not directly involved, but we boys talked of nothing else, eagerly scanning the newspapers to learn more.

The workshop was busier than ever. I was now being tasked with more responsible work, set to planning, measuring and drawing out designs by myself which pleased me. I began to learn the actual business of designing a house. I spent some of my free hours wandering around Salcombe and the harbour and looking at the lie of the land, seeing how the designs of the houses worked to my newly educated eyes. The whole subject fascinated me. I longed to be someone who could construct a house from nothing.

I found that I instinctively disliked the houses that just sat like boxes in their surroundings. I valued the beauty of the Haven, and a part of me hated even the thought of changing its face with concrete and mortar. If you were going to build a house somewhere so magnificent, it had to be a house that complimented its surroundings I felt. But then again I supposed it had to do with the contract you were given. Lucky would be the man who could make his living designing and building only beautiful homes.

I looked at many houses as if I had never really seen them before, and came to see areas where other houses might be built. If I could only afford to buy some of that land I would be able to build there in years to come, I thought. But I knew that it would be some time – if at all – before I could afford even the smallest piece of land.

It was at this time that I really looked at the tower for the first time.

The tower was little more than a ruin at that date. It lay at the

junction of Newton and Devon Roads. It was a strange construction. Until you knew what its purpose had been you could not make sense of it. But once you knew that it had been put up during the Napoleonic Wars, and was a show of strength to deter feared invasion by the French, you understood it. Built to be viewed from the sea, it appeared to be a military fortification. As part of a chain of real and mock defences that extended across the southern coast of England, it was meant to show that the country was ready to repulse any French attack. In reality the tower comprised a pile of shabbily put together blocks, crenellated at the sea end to make it look like a fortress.

From where it was situated though, the views across the harbour and out to sea were some of the best in the estuary. It occurred to me that given the right treatment this ruin might be transformed into a splendid house.

But it was only a vague idea and I put it aside. There were other more immediate things to interest me.

In 1907 the "Jebba" a West African liner was wrecked near Bolt Tail. She had many passengers on board and these were hauled up the cliffs by breeches buoy. She carried a valuable cargo of fruit. There was fine weather for ten days after the wreck and many boats went out to her. Together with three others, I rowed down and returned with our boat loaded with pineapples, bananas - which were soon selling in Salcombe at twelve for a penny - and a quantity of other loot. After ten days the weather turned stormy and the ship broke up. Rubber and palm oil was retrieved as far away as Soar Mill as it was dispersed by the tide

Early picture of the "Jebba" wrecked near Bolt Tail.

So the seven years of my apprenticeship drew gradually to an end. My duties had increased year by year, until now I was doing a man's work.

Towards the end of my time, I bought a set of tools with the money I had saved from my allowance. I also bought some fine seasoned Oregon pine planks and made a sturdy trunk to house them. I determined that at some time I should do my best to paint a sailing ship onto it such as I had seen some seamen had. In the meantime I made interior compartments to fit my new tools as I bought them. I was as pleased as punch with my box. Soon I had all the tools needed for starting out in business by myself.

I was now ready to make my mark on the world.

CHAPTER SIX

My apprenticeship came to an end on my birthday in December 1907.
There was no work available locally at that time, but Mr Cranch promised
that he would employ me as soon as he had a contract. Several of the other
apprentices had moved away up country in search of work on construction
sites, but I was minded to stay in my home town even if it meant I had to
take whatever was going.

Then towards the middle of December, my former master was awarded
the contract to build a new Coastguard Station at Prawle Point, and he
offered me work on the team. Inevitably, knowing my circumstances, he
did not propose to pay the going rate for a carpenter, but it was all there
was, and I was grateful for any work.

Accordingly I joined a group of around twelve men and boys of various
trades who assembled at Whitestrand at 6.20 a.m. We loaded our tools into
Mr Cranch's working boat and rowed to Higher Passageway, then walked to
Prawle, getting there in time to start work at 7.30 a.m. while it was still
dark. There was a time keeper on the job so we had to be punctual
otherwise our wages were docked.

We left work at 5 p.m. and walked home in the dark, crossing the
harbour in the rowing boat which we had left tied up during the day. The
pay was 24/5d for a full week and I finished with the job at the end of
March, by which time my employer had a contract to build "The Pines".
The pay was 1/2d per hour less than I had been receiving, but Mr Cranch
assured me that there was every likelihood of a great deal more work
coming along, which made up for the reduced wages.

My father's employer, Mr McIlwraith, now proved to be a great
benefactor to Salcombe. He had bought "Cliff House", and now announced
his intention of converting it, and opening up the Lower Terraces which
would mean a lot of work for local men. He was also chiefly instrumental in

obtaining the protected National Trust status for land that he owned on both sides of the Harbour entrance. We had not understood exactly what this meant, but my family were amongst many locals who attended a meeting in "Cliff House" after the renovation work was completed, and we learned that McIlwraith had organised things so that our beautiful harbour would remain unspoilt forever. My father was amongst others who went up to shake his hand for this generosity. We owed so much to this outsider who also loved our Haven. He was a strange man, most generous in public ways, but very Scottish in his business dealings. My aunt Mary Ann was married to Samuel Farr, who was the builder who had done the reconstruction work on "Cliff House". Samuel went bankrupt over the job. The family's previously high standard of living suddenly came to an end and they moved to South Milton.

It was about this time that Fred was preparing to join the Merchant Navy. The rules had recently changed and he had to wait until he was 18 before he could sign on, but the minute his birthday came he went down to Plymouth and enlisted. No-one could have been happier. As with Frank when he had gone into the Royal Navy, I managed to spend some time with him before he left. We went fishing together and talked. I realised for the first time that Fred had always been somewhat in our shadow, and I tried now to even things up with him. He was not an outgoing boy, and I did not have the same easy relationship with him as I had with Frank. But in these days we enjoyed ourselves, making up slightly for lost time.

With both my brothers away, it seemed to me to be time to consider my own future. I was not content with the work I had. Perhaps because my younger brother had left to make his way in the world, I began to want something different, something with more prospects. Though I was loathe to leave Salcombe I realised that I would not achieve what I wanted where I was.

Hearing that Mr. McIlwraith's firm was building a new ship in Belfast which was to go into service on the Australian coastal trade run, I approached him to ask if he would consider signing me on. He agreed, and I was offered passage out as Carpenter's Mate and Crew. The law stated that a man signing articles for a voyage in a ship had to be paid even if it was a nominal amount, and so I was offered and accepted, a shilling a month wages.

In July 1909, with a reference in my pocket from Mr Cranch describing me as a "steady, honest, industrious and efficient workman" I travelled up to Glasgow by rail to join this ship, the SS "Karoola" to start my new life.

I was not to return to Salcombe for ten years. I had spent most of the 1914-19 war in the "Karoola" which after transporting A.N.Z.A.C soldiers to the front was converted to No. I Australian Hospital Ship, responsible for bringing injured men back to their homelands. During this time we traversed the world, taking patients to Australia, and to other ports as far afield as the U.K, India and Cyprus. Though we carried the Red Cross on our sides, we were in the thick of the fighting, bringing wounded men on board from the field theatres. The ship was off shore at Gallipoli for some weeks and we experienced first hand the horrors of warfare.

Letters from home and my brothers who were both away serving on ships kept me up to date with news from Salcombe. First Fred and then Frank married while I was away. Circumstances meant that we none of us could attend the weddings. I heard of the memorial march through the town on the death of King Edward in 1910, the devastation of Hallsands and the lifeboat disaster in 1917 through their letters.

Memorial march on death of King Edward VII. Salcombe. May 20th 1910. J Fairweather.

I managed three visits home. On each occasion after seeing my parents, I managed to escape to the solitude of Sunny Cove. I sat there, knowing that generations of my family before me had probably done the same thing and I tried for a while in that quiet solitude to forget that the world had gone mad.

I had brought with me the notepad and pencil I always carried, and after a while I began to draw, sketching in houses around the still largely empty hillside, losing myself totally in the idea of reconstruction after all the destruction and horror I had seen. I knew now that all I wanted to do was to build houses and come home to Salcombe.

On my last visit home I saw my boss Mr. McIlwraith in the grounds of "Woodcot", and I asked if I might speak to him.

He granted permission, and I informed him that I would be leaving the ship and the sea when I got back to Melbourne, and could sign off my contract.

Hallsands Village before its 1917 devastation.

Aware of food shortages and conditions in England during the war, I had brought him and his family a large parcel of provisions which I had bought in Australia and stored in the ship's freezer for him, just as I had done for my parents. When I had told my father what I had done, and he said dryly: "Rich men get hungry too". I had not expected thanks, but I had expected courtesy, but instead McIlwraith was blazingly angry.

He pulled no punches. He had a fiery, Scottish temper, and he called me a fool in very strong language. He told me that he had seen my record, and that I was in line for a good job in the company if I stayed. My future with the McIlwraith and McEacharn Line was secure, he added. I would be a bloody fool to compromise that. When he asked me what the hell I thought I could do on land anyway, I told him that I proposed starting a building business in Salcombe. He dismissed me summarily then with the caustic words, that in that case I should not expect any work from him.

I stared after him as he stomped away across the lawn. I was furious and deeply humiliated. He held all the cards. He controlled my family. I knew that if I angered him my parents would almost certainly lose their home and their livelihood. I was helpless and deeply frustrated.

I turned and walked swiftly away from him, needing to put as much distance between us as I could, because I knew that if I didn't I risked everything my father had worked for all his life. I was a sailor, and I had been in some rough places in my young life. Several times I had had to defend myself, and I knew I was handy with my fists. I longed to punch McIlwraith, but I could not. He had emasculated me with his words, and I hated him for it.

I kept walking, my fists clenched. I did not know, even less cared where I went, and I found myself down on the ferry steps. I was fully dressed and it was late November but I just took off my boots and jacket and dived into the icy water, and began to swim strongly up the harbour against an incoming tide. By the time I came ashore at the Old Fort, I was exhausted, but my anger had quieted. I realised that the best defence was to concentrate on making a success of my business. But the most important thing first of all was either to swim or walk back up through the town, and quickly, before I caught pneumonia!

I went back to sea for my last trip, knowing now what I planned for my future. I was under articles in Australia and I had to sign off there, so I would have one last trip there and back to England – to Salcombe – again. I could hardly wait to begin...

CHAPTER NINE

"Karoola" reached Southampton just before Easter having been held up by the influenza epidemic in Australia. As we neared the coast we learned that the port was congested with vessels returning to their home bases after war service and our ship was advised to go on to London. Before long this was changed again. This time our destination was to be Plymouth. With no idea where we would actually end up, I decided to take no chances and sent my luggage on ahead. We finally docked at Plymouth on Good Friday and I arranged to go home for the weekend and then come back to give my successor a chance for some leave. Returning on the train that Saturday I met a Salcombe man named Ern Lethbridge and we got chatting. He told me that he was the Carpenter of the Hain Line boat I had noticed in the Sound, and that he had been in her practically throughout the war. When he said he was going to Rotterdam in the ship and was then coming home to look for a job, I told him I was starting a business and suggested that he come to work with me back in Salcombe.

I rented a small workshop on the Kings Arms Quay and set about fitting it out. About a month afterwards, Ern Lethbridge turned up at the workshop and told me he was ready to start work. I said that I was still getting the workshop ready, and as yet had no work, but suggested that he help me make work benches for which I would pay him. The first job came in a few days after this, when we were asked to make some stepladders. We made these and finished the workshop benches, and suddenly work started to come in. Ern Lethbridge remained with me for just on thirty years and never missed a day. There was no paid holiday in those days but after twenty years I gave him a week on full pay, which delighted him.

After a fortnight during which we two did all kinds of odd jobs I received a message from Mr McIlwraith instructing me to call and see him.

We had not met since our conversation in the garden, and this peremptory message only served to rekindle my anger. However because my father wished it, I reluctantly went to meet him.

He opened the conversation by demanding to know why I had not been to see him. This was rather awkward as by now I had learned that despite his telling me in no uncertain terms the last time we had met that I could not expect any work from him, he had actually kept back some alterations to "Cliff House" for me as long as he could, until my delayed departure from Australia had forced him to get another firm in to do the work.

So I said nothing, but just waited for him to speak. We were in his study in "Woodcot". It was late afternoon, and the bright spring sunshine shone in through the window onto the deep, rich colours of the wood panelling. He turned over some papers on his desk while I waited.

Workshop on King's Arms Quay c 1919

"I'd like you to have a look at two old cottages at Walland, West Prawle," he said. I remembered something his son had told me many years before: You'll never get an apology from him, but he'll go out of his way to help you if he feels he has not treated you fairly"... he was one of the most complicated men I had ever known.

He stomped across the room to the door of his study, threw it open and called loudly for a Miss Symmons to come and take a letter. I guessed that this was the new secretary whom my father had mentioned to me some days before.

A young woman came into the room. She was dressed in a soft dress in a sort of mossy green colour, and she carried a notebook in her hand. She was tall and very slim, with dark hair cropped short like a boy's, and warm brown eyes with very dark eyelashes and she moved so gracefully that it made me think of wind going through corn. I was captivated. For all my experience and knowledge of the world, I felt like a gauche, awkward boy. My hands and feet seemed suddenly too big for me, and though I stood up politely when she entered, I immediately took my seat again after acknowledging her, for I felt clumsy, certain that I would knock something over. I had met my future wife.

She took McIlwraith's brief dictation, while I tried to look anywhere but at that shining bob bent over her notebook, or the slim hand that travelled apparently effortlessly across the page.

When she had left the room to type up the letter, McIllwraith questioned me about current conditions in Australia, asking my opinion of the resumption of the coastal trade, and I answered him as best I could. Then Miss Symmons came back with the letter, placing it on the desk before her employer for his signature. She glanced at me briefly as she left, and I thought I detected the faintest smile.

With McIlwraith's letter in my hand, and my head full of the girl I had just met, I went to West Prawle. I looked over the cottages and confirmed Mr McIlwraith's opinion that they should be torn down. I had been instructed to look around the farm for the best site for new cottages, and accordingly I walked the land with the farmer, Mr Oldridge. Between us we chose what we both considered to be the ideal site for future development.

I returned to Salcombe and reported back to Mr McIlwraith, and was told to draw up plans for the proposed new houses. There was no sign of Miss Symmons, though I looked for her. I remember I asked my father casually that evening about her, but I guessed by the broad grin he gave that my questions had perhaps not sounded as offhand as I had hoped.

I knew that with this building project, Mr McIlwraith had given me my big chance, and I determined to grasp it with both hands. I worked hard on the blueprints over the next two days, drawing and re-drawing, getting up in the middle of the night a couple of times to alter some angle or figures.

My heart was in my mouth when I showed the plans to Mr McIlwraith, but he seemed pleased with them. I took them to the Rural District Council office and got them passed: I had completed the first hurdle. My house building career had begun and I felt light headed with relief. I had not realised how important it was to me. Building houses would mean that I would become a man of substance. The sort of man that a graceful young woman in a mossy green dress might want to marry...

My little firm then set to work to build the new cottages. Mr McIlwraith came over to Prawle once to look them over, and inspected the ancient farm house close to the new site. Before the cottages were even finished, he had instructed me to begin rebuilding the farm house.

In a matter of weeks we had gained more work than we could handle. Ern and I needed to find more workers quickly.

Masons were very scarce in the area, and I went to talk to my old master Jim Camp, that evening. I explained my problem and we discussed it at length, eventually deciding to combine our small teams of builders and work together. We agreed that we should become a partnership and we each took shares in the company in which I allowed him name preference because we had agreed shares of 40 to 60 in my favour. I went home that night as majority owner of a building firm named "Camp and Murch"

I had been trained by Jim Camp and had worked with him for the best part of seven years. He was without doubt a splendid artisan, but I had always known him as my master, and now I was working with him as an equal. It took me a while to understand him as a man, and I admit when I did I was surprised to discover that he had no interest at all in business matters. I had insisted on having a partnership agreement drawn up giving him the power to sign cheques and control the day to day running of the business account, but in all the years we were in partnership, he never once signed a cheque or showed more than a rudimentary interest in the firm's affairs. He appeared to trust me absolutely. In fact I would say that he trusted me more than I would ever have trusted any man.

Right from the onset I gave him to understand that my intention was one day to buy out his share of the firm and he seemed content with that. We wanted different things from our business agreement. He was largely content to go on as he had always done. I wanted to give my ambition full reign. I wanted to build up our firm so that in time it would become a big business. Over the next years I gave him notice on several occasions. Each time I gave him money and increased my share of the ownership.

But for now we had at least the workmen that we needed for the contracts I was securing. Lots of work came along, and I was rather surprised but pleased when a Mrs Morton for whom I had done many small jobs asked me to design and build a £2,000 house which was to be given the name "Uppercot".

Starting a new business in June 1919 after the war was hard. Supplies of everything were short and the labour market was flat. To find timber for benches and other fixtures for the workshop I rowed the small family dinghy to Kingsbridge where I bought some of what was then a very small local stock. When we later needed more timber, I contacted Fox, Elliot and Co. Ltd., of Plymouth and bought about £80 worth, paying 50% before delivery as per their terms. The timber was delivered by rail to Kingsbridge.

I had it carted to the quayside then loaded it myself onto a barge heading down for Salcombe. I could unload directly from Kings Arms Quay into the workshop, which was one of the reasons I had chosen these premises.

For building work we were then contracted to at West Prawle, we used mostly larch from Gidley, delivered the same way, but it was taken to Horse Pool, East Portlemouth, then on to the farm site by wagon. Cement, lime and other building materials were brought in the same manner, but all building sand was collected from Millbay. For wood lintels we cut down oak trees in West Prawle wood, where we also hewed poles for scaffolding. Our plant was still very limited in those days and I remember Camp and I each wheeling a wheelbarrow containing practically our entire stock of tools and materials from the ferry to West Prawle

After a year I employed another carpenter and then one after the other took on two apprentices. I worked alongside them in the workshop. We built most of the interior joinery there, which made for easier conditions on site. When the window or door frames we were making were completed, we loaded them onto a barrow or a borrowed cart, and, often with several of us pushing and pulling on the slopes, moved it up through the town. If the pieces were smaller we would more often than not walk them to the site.   .

Site work around the estuary always entailed hard manual labour. More often than not the site was difficult and we grew used to hauling timber or stone up steep slopes or cliff faces to where it was needed. But I determined that in the workshop at least I would make things a little easier. I bought a circular saw bench with the master winch placed under an outer shed. As the winch had a driving wheel for a belt, I connected up a gravity tensioner to enable the saw blade to be lifted and lowered and we began to do all our rip sawing like this which saved us quite a considerable amount of time and energy.

When the winch was required out on jobs, I installed a 5 h.p petrol-paraffin motor engine. This was our sole machine until 1928, when, winning the contract for a new Methodist Church where there was going to be a lot of joinery, I installed a general joiner and a band sawing machine with all necessary shafting. I also acquired a large grindstone in a stand from Devonport Dockyard, and an emery wheel, all of which were still in daily use in 1961.

And all this time I used any excuse I could think of to visit Mr McIlwraith, on the off chance I might meet Miss Symmons. She had begun to see through some of my rather obvious excuses for visiting her office at the back of the house I think - certainly they made her smile. She told me later that whenever she turned around she seemed to see me, and when I was not there she expected me at any moment! Even Andrew McIlwraith was in on the act for a couple of times when he yelled for Miss Symmons, he added, "… and if your love-sick swain is in there, I'll have a word with him too!"

After a while she gave me permission to call her Elsie. Elsie Muriel. Elsie Muriel Symmons. I wanted her to be Elsie Muriel Murch.

We began walking out together and I took her to several entertainments in both Salcombe and Kingsbridge. We both loved to dance, and I took her to several dances. Years later she showed me the dance card with its tiny pencil attached on the finest silk cord, which she had kept as a remembrance of our first engagement at" Cliff House". Beside the Waltz she had pencilled in my name in her fine, sloping handwriting. But the other names she had pencilled in had been firmly overwritten in my chunkier handwriting, and my name had been put in their place. I had forgotten that I had committed what was in those days an unforgiveable social sin by marking her card for all dances. But I smiled as I remembered the evening, and the fact that I had secured my partner through the "Military Quickstep", the "Foxtrot" and the "Gay Gordons" right through to the "Goodnight Waltz".

The woman whom I was determined would be my wife, was artistic and sensitive, but she was also a girl with a keen sense of fun. I discovered to my amusement that she was as ambitious as I was. I knew that my parents liked her. My mother had already spoken to her several times before I met her, and as for my father… His guileless blue eyes just crinkled at the corners when I tasked him with it, but he did admit that he and Miss Symmons had once or twice eaten their lunch together in the garden in fine weather.

There seemed to me to be a conspiracy going on. My mother even went so far as to say to me in private that she thought we would be well matched. They knew I was a hard taskmaster and that I was driven to achieve as much as I could, but they said that they both felt that I had reached a stage in life when I needed to marry and start my own family. Up until now I would have paid no attention, but now everything had changed…

Elsie took me to meet her parents. Her father had had a bookbinding and publishing company in London, but had suffered a break down in health over the last few years, and had brought the family down to Salcombe where his father had had connections. He had at first leased "Torre View", which was a substantial semi-detached house in Devon Road, then later very much enjoying living there, had persuaded the owners to sell it to him.

He was the fifth generation to run the business which was an old established company started by his great-great-grandfather Edmund Symmons more than a century and a half before. The name had continued down through the years, so that the man I hoped would one day give me his permission to marry his daughter, was also called Edmund Symmons.

His wife, Annie Lucie, was a warm, charming and very good looking woman, whom I liked straight away. They were all Cockney born though an educated and cosmopolitan family with contacts in the Bloomsbury Group of artists. Annie Lucy had taught violin and piano in London. Like her husband and daughter she was refined and charming. Though they all spoke beautifully enunciated King's English, Annie had an amazing ear for accents, and could easily drop into Cockney rhyming slang if she wanted. Elsie too had picked it up, and the two of them, both accomplished comics, made me laugh heartily at their Marie Lloyd music hall act, sung in a language which to the uninitiated sounded like complete gibberish.

I got to know more about Elsie over the next weeks and months. She was a lovely girl, bright and cheerful and conscientious. After a good education at the Priory College in Hornsey, London, she had done a year at Pitman in Southampton Row studying shorthand and typing, for which subjects she had won prizes. She was lucky that both her parents had been in business, and did not block her desire to be independent and to earn her own living. They were quite progressive in that regard, for Elsie was of the class that could easily have done very little, but she had two much older stepsisters, Daisy and Edith, the children of her mother's previous marriage to a Spanish professor who had run an academy in London. I had not met either of Elsie's step sisters as they had both left home some years before, Edith to marry a Cornishman and move down to that county; Daisy to travel as a missionary to China.

After her graduation, Elsie told me she had been employed at a bank in the City of London. When the family moved to Salcombe, she had first obtained a position in Lloyd's Bank in Kingsbridge as a clerk, before becoming Mr McIlwraith's Private Secretary.

Elsie adored dancing and music and poetry. She was quite athletic, fond of walking, badminton, tennis and swimming. She loved the sea and books. She told me that she wrote poetry, and confided in me that her greatest wish was to be a published poet. She gave me a copy of Byron's poetry in which she had marked, "The Corsair", for my birthday, and I set myself to learning it to please her, though I struggled through it. The next time we met however, I was able to quote "O'er the glad waters of the dark blue sea, Our thoughts as boundless and our souls as free..." which I know pleased her. I showed her my copy of the Australian writer Adam Lindsay Gordon's poetry which I had bought in Australia. I have to admit that I had bought it on a whim and had barely opened it, but I reread it now and found his manly words more to my taste.

Over the course of the next months I spent more time with the family, enjoying the musical evenings in which they delighted. On these occasions Annie Lucie would play the piano and Elsie the violin, which she loved, though she was also a creditable pianist. Annie Lucie in particular had a fine contralto voice with which she often entertained us. I was only just beginning to appreciate classical music and I learned so much from them. On a trip to Kingsbridge I bought some sheet music of Chopin as a small gift, and they were delighted and sat down to play it straight away.

Elsie and I talked over how we saw our future. She was an intelligent young woman, and though she was fourteen years younger than me, I felt that she was already beginning to understand me.

I bought her several books of poems over the months which I know she treasured, and I came to understand just how important poetry was to her. One of the books was by a new poet called Rupert Brooke, who wrote of the First World War. He became a particular favourite of hers, and I admit I grew to admire his work. Generally though I was completely ignorant of poetry, but gradually, as in music, I began to learn from her. Elsie was clever because she started me on the sea ballads of John Masefield and the soldierly ballads of Kipling and I grew to enjoy them enormously.

In one of our many talks I admitted that I was aware of the shortcomings of my own education, and said that I too wanted to spend some time with books. She knew already that I had always enjoyed reading. "My main priority is to build my business," I said. "But I have seen other men work to the exclusion of all else and I know they end up with nothing other than the business." She knew without my having to say it, that I said this sort of thing because I already saw her by my side.

I was anything but a romantic man, but I did my best to please her. I picked flowers and brought them to her. I took her for walks on the beach when I could, and often we sat and watched the sunset together. She loved Salcombe just as I did. Elsie was giving her heart to Salcombe and to me, and in those days it seemed as if I could move mountains.

One summer's evening we took the ferry across to East Portlemouth and walked around to Gara Rock which was somewhere she had not visited, and she was intensely moved by the beauty of the place. Through the years it became one of her favourite walks. She loved to sit on the cliff top and just look out to sea. It inspired her and she wrote several poems about Gara, some of which were published in later years.

But much as she loved Gara she was perhaps happiest in the harbour, where the brooding majesty of Bolt Head had always fascinated her.

When we could we took the dinghy up to Sunny Cove which Elsie loved as much as I did. Sometimes we went further afield and rowed across to Splat Cove or walked up on Soar, or out on Bolt Head.

When I think back to those days it seems to me that the summers were always hot, and the sea sparkling, and I hear my darling's bubbling laughter ringing out. Though we were both very busy, and I in particular was working punishing hours, we always found time to enjoy all the activities we both loved. We fished off the quays or took the small family dinghy out, often mooring up and dropping over the side to swim. We swam off Fisherman's Cove, or Smalls, or took some food with us and walked around the cliff path to Sunny Cove.

When the mackerel were shoaling we joined two or three other local boats and rowed backwards and forwards outside the Bar, trailing lines behind us. Sometimes Aaron or Edmund came with us, and we gutted the fish on board, taking our catch home triumphantly to share between our

Splat Cove, Salcombe, looking up the harbour.

families, followed all the way back across the Bar by crowds of screaming seagulls. We were young and we were in love, and we did everything that holiday makers always do in Salcombe, and for both of us those days were heaven on earth.

Both sets of parents were important in our lives, and we did not neglect them. Annie Lucy enjoyed making picnics and sometimes we walked around to South or North Sands and joined them on the beach. We dropped in to see my parents at the Lodge, and always came away with an armful of flowers or vegetables as presents for Elsie's parents.

The first time we ate with my parents, my mother tried to accord Elsie the never before heard of honour of insisting she sat in her special chair. Our eyes going from one woman to the other, Aaron and I sat spellbound. Vaguely we were aware of some ancient feminine rite of passage, some ritual that excluded us by reason of our sex, being played out in front of us. Dimly we both realised that this was something that could go disastrously wrong, but my future wife rose with graceful magnanimity to the challenge by politely insisting in her turn that she would be happier if Ellen took pride of place at her own table. Cheerfully and without any fuss, she carried in dishes of food for my mother, and afterwards, despite Ellen's protests, helped her with the washing up, and hearing their chatter from the kitchen afterwards, even we males understood that some momentous affair of state had been settled. Ellen the matriarch had tested Elsie, but she had passed the test with flying colours, and Ellen now welcomed her unreservedly, with open arms and heart, into the family.

Elsie's parents in turn had made me so welcome that "Torre View" had become almost a second home for me. Edmund Symmons and I had talked over all sorts of subjects in our meetings over a period of several months, and to an extent I felt that her father and I had got the measure of each other. He was a tall, sparse man still with a full head of greying fair hair which had a tendency to flop over his forehead, and an elegant, almost foppish air, but he had a very good business brain. He did not give the appearance of being a particularly robust man something which I guessed had   influenced his early retirement, since Elsie had told me that he was not yet fifty years old. Then again the fact that he had no heir to take over the business might have had something to do with it.

Over the next weeks we talked man to man about business.   Mr Symmons asked me my plans for my firm and listened as I told him about the contracts I was engaged in and what I had in mind for the future.   He said very little, just listened with his handsome, leonine head on one side, but I saw that what I said was being taken in and analysed very carefully. I knew that he and his wife adored Elsie and though they were happy to give her the freedom to work outside the home, they both wanted to make sure that she would be well looked after by her future husband.

I asked Elsie if she would marry me on Sunny Cove one Sunday afternoon and to my utter delight she accepted me.   Her straightforwardness was one of the many things I found so appealing about her.

I was invited to dinner at "Torre View" that evening and Elsie and I agreed that it was the ideal opportunity to ask her father for his permission for us to become officially engaged. I admit I was nervous as I walked down from the Lodge later, stopping for a moment and leaning on the sea wall, looking out over the peace of a glorious evening. The sun was sinking down over the horizon and staining the sea all colours of pinks and blues and greens. I longed suddenly to have Elsie beside me, watching this with me. Not just for now but for the rest of my life.   Buoyed up by this thought, and the certainty that I was doing the right thing, I went off to my dinner engagement, the tiny red leather box containing the diamond engagement ring I had just bought, safely in the pocket of my jacket.

The meal was delicious as always, but I have no idea what it was. In spite of Elsie's gentle teasing of me over dinner, in an effort to get me to relax, all I could think of was what I was going to say to the man who sat across the table from me. I think we all knew what was coming.

After dinner Elsie's father and I stayed in the dining room while, as pre-arranged, Elsie led her mother out of the room.

I spoke a little about what I hoped to achieve in life, and that I considered that now all I needed was the right wife. I spoke of my admiration for Elsie, and my affection, and I said truly that I would never do anything to hurt her, but would always love and cherish her. I asked Mr Symmons if I could marry Elsie.

He must have known that I was sweating on his answer. He must also have known that even if he had said no, it would make no difference to me. I was going to marry Elsie. I had made up my mind to that the first time I had set eyes on her and I think he knew my character well enough to know that I would allow nothing to come between us. But now, with his greying blond head on one side, and his thumb hooked into his watch chain pocket in a characteristic pose he looked at me long and hard as if he was considering his answer. He had a very droll sense of humour, and he was also a controller, used to ordering mens' lives, but to do him justice he took pity on me, and nodded, smiling as we shook hands. It seemed to be only moments before Elsie and her mother burst into the room. I guessed they had been listening in the hallway.

We were a happy and united family. I gave Elsie her engagement ring which delighted her, and was greatly admired by her parents. Mr Symmons, who now invited me to call him Edmund, brought out a bottle of champagne, something I had never tasted before. "To the happy couple," he said, as we all raised our glasses. I looked across at my future wife's radiant face, and vowed there and then that I would always look after her and make her the happiest woman in the world. My parents had known what I intended that evening, and had been shown the ring, and I could not wait to get home to tell them. I knew already that the news would make them very happy.

We were now engaged, and Mr Symmons – Edmund – had a little gathering to announce the fact to Salcombe society. The family had been in the town for less than a year, but he had made many acquaintances at a better level than I. He was a gentleman retired on his own means, though he had been in trade, and he numbered Mr McIlwraith amongst his acquaintances. So the man who employed my father and myself, and who had now become my customer and I met properly on a social level for the first time. I have to admit to a feeling of great satisfaction as we shook hands.

There were reasons why our marriage should be delayed. Since Elsie was only just twenty to my thirty four years we had made up our minds to wait until she came of age. Secondly I had to find us somewhere to begin our married lives. I had the glimmerings of an idea but as yet I had taken no concrete steps towards its fruition. Now I determined that I would.

I talked my plan over with Elsie when we met up after work the next evening, and we both went to have a look at the crumbling remains of the mock Napoleonic tower in Newton Road. My plan was to renovate this tower and build a house which would be a suitable home for my young wife.

Elsie was as excited as I had hoped she would be at the prospect. The tower was little more than a ruin, but its' views over the estuary were completely uninterrupted. I knew that Andrew McIlwraith owned the tower as well as still maintaining a tranche of land included in the "Cliff House" deeds even though he had generously given the rest to the town. I had long thought the land the tower stood on would make a wonderful position for a house, and now, as Elsie and I fought our way in amongst the tangle of undergrowth below it, and stood in the shelter of its tumbled down walls, I knew I was right.

We climbed the tower's uneven and precarious stone steps and looked over the harbour. Even to such as we who lived daily with the beauty of the Haven, the view was astonishing. Spread out before us lay Millbay and the golden beaches on the Portlemouth side. On our right hand we looked towards the jagged shapes of Bolt Head and Start Point and the brilliant blue of the unbounded horizon beyond; on the left spread out before us was the town and Snapes Point and the estuaries and rolling green hills up towards The Bag and Kingsbridge. It was a magnificent sight and we both agreed that we wanted above everything to convert the ruins and build a house there. But as Elsie asked as we walked home, "Will Mr McIlwraith sell it?"

A few days later when the opportunity arose, I asked Andrew McIlwraith about it. He refused outright to sell me the tower but after thinking through my request for a while, came up with a suggestion. The bequest of "Cliff House" and some of its land to Salcombe had given him a problem, in that he knew that he would somehow also have to find a way of ensuring that the Board of Trustees whom he had appointed would have an income for repairs and restitutions of the property in future years. He decided therefore that he would give me permission to build a house on the site of the tower to my own design, for which he would pay up to £2,000, and I could then rent it on as long a lease as I wished at a reasonable rent. The rent would go towards maintaining "Cliff House". It was a neat compromise.

I asked him if I could talk it over with Elsie. I was disappointed that he would not sell it outright, but I still thought it was worth doing. My wife to be was of exactly the same mind. I spoke to Mr McIlwraith again and we fixed a rent of £50 per year.

At this meeting he also told me that he had been contracted to oversee the construction of a house to be named "Orestone End" for a Mrs Foster, on similar terms to those he had just agreed with me, and he wanted my firm to build it. But at that time I was at full stretch and did not have the necessary labour force free, so I reluctantly had to turn it down. However I later built "Little Orestone End" for him. His butler lived in that house.

Much more building work now came along and Mr McIlwraith, who enjoyed having construction work done, employed our firm on a great many projects. He offered me 2.5% on all work my firm did for him to remunerate me for drawings and consultations that often kept me busy half the night. Looking back I am surprised how quickly I learnt about construction, often simply by a process of trial and error.

In the meantime, like so many engaged couples Elsie and I settled down to work hard and save money for our future, though especially during the winter season, we attended many social engagements including several dances at "Cliff House", which now promised to become a great asset to the town. As for me, I had the drawings of a new house to do and the costings and building work to begin on what we had from the first called simply "The Tower".

My fiancée and I decided to marry on June 1st, 1921, which was Elsie's 21st birthday. We were both working pretty hard. As well as several house building contracts, I had the men and myself on overtime on "The Tower". This was the beginning of the boom years in which more plots in Salcombe had started to come on the market, and enquiries were coming in from all parts of the country. Many of the plots were being bought by wealthy people who had now begun taking holidays and wanted a place to escape to. Elsie - "my girl" as I lovingly nicknamed her - was working long hours for Mc McIlwraith who now asked her to act as his bookkeeper as well as his secretary.

With money earned in this way, we took a day off to go to Plymouth with the idea of buying all our furniture for the house, as we had nothing except for some items that Annie Lucy and Edmund had kindly given us. But post war prices had soared because of shortages of supplies on almost all goods. Though we had what we considered to be a fairly large sum of money with us, all we managed to buy on this first expedition was a set of chairs and very little else. Later however we managed to purchase all the essentials, paying £70 for an oak bedroom suite, which, a year later when things were more freely available again and prices had tumbled, we could have bought for half that amount. Elsie had fallen in love with some Clarice Cliff china, which was more expensive than we had budgeted for, but which we managed to afford. We also bought some very modern looking smoked yellow drinking glasses to tone with the bright yellows and oranges of the china.

Whatever money I had earned in the past had immediately been reinvested in the business, so things were tight. Although I had now used up almost all my savings, both Elsie and I agreed that we would pay cash for all our purchases, a policy that we continued throughout our lives. If we needed something we waited until we could afford it, so that although we enjoyed dances and occasional outings we had no financial worries. In the meantime the date of our wedding was growing closer, and as I had determined that we would begin our married life in "The Tower", my work schedule was particularly heavy.

The War Memorial that had been Mr McIlwraith's pet project was unveiled in April 1921. I think everyone agreed that the simple granite cross he had chosen fitted admirably with the backdrop of the harbour. Salcombe people rose to the occasion and turned out in force, and the memorial was inaugurated in style.

Unveiling of the Salcombe War Memorial. April 7th 1921. J Fairweather
To right of monument is Andrew McIlwraith.

Elsie and I married at the Holy Trinity Church on a glorious summer's day. Innumerable friends, family and quite a number of my business acquaintances attended the wedding and the church was packed. We came out of the service to a street full of townspeople and well-wishers. Rose petals were strewn around us as we walked to the waiting motor car which was to carry us away. I remember seeing my wife's dark hair bedecked with petals as we made our way through the crowds, though what I remember most was her face, lit up with happiness as I could feel my own was.

Wedding of James Cranch Murch and Elsie Muriel Symmons at Holy Trinity Church, Salcombe.
1st June 1921.

Below: Crowd outside Holy Trinity Church.

My brothers had hung a lucky horseshoe on the back of the car we had rented from the Central Garage and they ran alongside us laughing as we drove out through the street, where quite a crowd of people had gathered to watch us pass, and wish us luck in our new lives.

We had two weeks' honeymoon at a hotel in Lynton, before returning to Salcombe where I once more immersed myself in work.

That summer was glorious I remember. We had no rain until October, and my new wife and I enjoyed just being in our beautiful new home – even though there were several rooms which were largely unfurnished.

We both continued to work overtime. Elsie did all the "Cliff House" accounts as well as those for another house at Gidley for Mr McIlwraith. As a thank you for her hard work, he gave her a grand piano which pleased her no end as it was a luxury that we would not have been able to afford. I bought her both books and sheet music whenever I was in Kingsbridge and "The Tower" echoed to the sound of her playing. Often in the evening when we had finished work, I would sit quietly in my chair, smoking the pipe Elsie had bought me and looking out across the harbour, as my wife played the piano. Watching that dark head bent over the keys as the beautiful chords of a Chopin nocturne, or the bitter sweet majesty of Tchaikovsky filled the room, I don't think any man could have been happier or more content.

I had some worries about work which at that time seemed almost insoluble. The Salcombe water supply came from Hanger Mill and various local springs. It was rationed for drinking at that time, with none allowed for building work. To construct "Uppercot", which Miss Norton was due to occupy that September, we had to cart water in barrels from South Sands, loading it onto the barge, offloading it at Council Quay and driving it up through the town on horse drawn carts. It was hard, heavy work, and I did my share of it.

Building supplies were still hard to get hold of. In consequence of a long drawn out strike, I found that no roof tiles were obtainable. I asked around, trying to find any supplier who had some, and after a few anxious day I was offered sufficient round tiles to roof "Uppercot". I accepted these gratefully. I often think of this flap when I pass this house, as "Uppercot" is the only roof in the locality with these tiles.

I was so happy being with my young wife. We lived an idyllic life and did most things together. I could rely on Elsie. She was absolutely straight. She had a wonderful character and I never heard her speak ill of anyone.

My joy was compounded when we learned a year after our wedding, that she was expecting a child. The tragedy that perhaps only parents who have been in this position can understand was to lose this child, a daughter.

But a year later my wife was once again pregnant, and this time the baby went the full term. Our son, who we named Peter James, was born on 23rd January 1923,

We now had a great deal of work on both sides of the harbour, so I obtained a 16' boat for the firm and put in a second hand engine, which proved to be very temperamental.

A few months later however I acquired an old ship's lifeboat from the "Mauritania" which turned out to be one of the most useful and reliable tools we ever owned. It had come from the client for whom I had constructed a house at Gullet. Since his home was tidal he had bought it to use as a bathing platform, mooring it up in the channel so that his family could swim off it at any tide. This was such a success that he asked me to build changing rooms and a sunbathing area on the boat to extend its use.

When in time it fell into disuse, he gave it to me as a thank you for the work our firm had done for him, stipulating only that I strip off the superstructure I had built to convert it to a barge which I had told him would be of most use to us. Once this was done, the boat became a sturdy work horse, capable of carrying six tons. From the first it was in constant use.

Securing a contract for a house which was later named "Barn End" at East Portlemouth, I bought a new motor winch for haulage from the foreshore, as we used many tons of beach shingle and sand for the house's difficult foundations. My brother Frank had by now retired from the Navy, and as we had previously agreed between us, came to work with the firm in 1923. Frank was a very good joiner, but had no experience of house building, and so I kept him in the workshop, where he was invaluable. "Barn End" was the first job he worked on, and it was a baptism of fire. The client had decided he wanted to have ship's teak for the framing at the building's gable end, and Frank and I barged the timber in from Kingsbridge. But the tide was running strongly that day, and we swamped the teak as we came down the harbour. The result was that my brother and I had to unload the very heavy, sodden timber and spread it out to dry in the street, a process that ended up taking half the night. We finished just in time to grab a couple of hours sleep, and then came back to work. But we did succeed in drying the timber. Using good, dry timber was almost a fetish with me.

Our next Portlemouth job was the conversion of "Water Side" from two old cottages to a single residence, and there again both the motor winch and the barge were very useful tools.

I was still doing a lot of work at "Woodcot". One of the latest projects that Mr McIlwraith had planned was a 26' square boat house and slipway. We hand cut the stone for this from Limebury Point which he owned, and barged it across the estuary. I roofed it with boarding on Belfast trusses. Once again this was the only roof of its kind in the locality.

The old wooden access bridge across the road from the higher gardens at "Woodcot" to the lower grounds was in very poor condition and next Mr McIlwraith turned his attention to this, obtaining outline permission from the local Council to replace it with a stone one.

But when I began preliminary investigations, I realised that the cliff face would not stand the additional weight we proposed to load onto it.

Wedding group. From left front: Aaron and Ellen Murch, page, Annie Lucy and Edmund Symmons.
Back row: Frank and Edith Murch; Fred and Mabel Murch; James and Elsie Murch; matron of honour, bridesmaid, Daisy and Edith Symmons.

Re-working my calculations, I decided that in order to construct a stone bridge over the road, we would first have to build a wall about 20' high for some distance along the edge of the lower garden.

I did many drawings and submitted them to Mr McIlwraith. The plan resulted in a lot of interest and brought quite a few objections from the townspeople. I understood their concerns. I too disliked the idea of shutting off the magnificent view which had previously been accessible to all, but the land belonged to Mr McIlwraith and it was his to do what he wanted with. I think most people but he and I would perhaps have abandoned the idea in the face of such adverse feeling, but Andrew McIlwraith was determined, and I had already got my teeth into the job and was not going to be beaten by it. I tried every other idea that I could, but had to admit in the

My family James, Elsie and Peter Murch. June 1924

end that there was no other way it could be done. In the end my employer had his way as usual. He had been such a benefactor to the town that no-one could gainsay him this work on his own property.

A great deal of stone was needed for the wall. Again the stone came from Limebury, and we cut and shaped it by hand on site, once again using the barge and the motor boat to transport it. Each load was dragged up on site manually, using a system of pulleys which we had constructed to bring it up from the water's edge. It was exhausting work, and it went on for day after day after day. I would go home in the evening having been at the wall all day, and I would look down on it from "The Tower". I could see it from "Torre View" and from the lodge. It was the last thing I saw at night and the first in the morning and often it would intrude into my dreams. It seemed to grow infinitely slowly, yet gradually it neared completion. I don't think I have ever been so glad to see the back of a job. But it was still only half finished. There was still the difficult work of building the bridge that had started the whole business, ahead of us.

I made many drawings, and Mr McIlwraith got lots of interest in them. Now the wall was built and the furore it had caused had died down, it was almost a relief for the local people to concentrate on the designs that had been submitted for the bridge. That part of my work was over. I just waited to see which design would be chosen.

Finally one of my first drawings depicting a simple curved stone bridge was approved. My intention was to build stone walls on top, but at the last minute Mr McIlwraith changed the design to iron rails, which meant that I had to build the bridge 12" thicker than I had intended to balance them. This re-design came from Mr McIlwraith's granddaughter, then a girl of eleven or twelve. She went on to become the noted architect Elizabeth Jennings.

Once again all the stone we used for this job was brought in from Limebury Point, using our own boats. With the help of two labourers I did it all myself, this time having to barge the stone to the Kings Arms Quay and move it by horse and cart to the site, since the new wall blocked off our access from the sea. I made the centres for the arches in sections in the workshop as the walls were buttressed and these formers were propped up over the road as we continued building. We were forced to stop from time to time to allow passers-by safe passage below us.

With access secured, Andrew McIlwraith began his plan to re-design the land fronting the water. He wanted a fish pond to supply the house, and had several ideas for the way he wanted the gardens to look. My father was involved at all the stages and he and I and Mr McIlwraith worked together, spending a great deal of time establishing the best layout for the gardens.

The first step was to remove the large forcing houses which I had helped build years before as an apprentice, and move them to the upper gardens. All the glass for these greenhouses had been cut with a curved bottom edge to deflect rain water, and I noted with satisfaction that almost twenty years later the timber was still sound.

Steps in Lower Garden above sea at "Woodcot".

Completed bridge running from top gardens to lower at "Woodcot".

We constructed the fish pond and my father got to work replanting and cutting new flower beds. The garden itself was a sun trap and boasted splendid views, brought into prominence by a Camera Obscura, so it was a good idea to maximise it for the family's enjoyment rather than simply use it for the glasshouses.

About two years later we turned the western lower garden into a formal one, with a lily pond about 40' x 20'. My idea for this was to use simple, very large blocks of granite in its construction, in keeping with the elegance of the overall design, and this was approved straight away.

The granite had to be brought up from Penryn, and the gigantic blocks were manoeuvred into position with the help of what seemed at the time to be almost every able bodied man in town. When it was assembled I took water from the spring near the Lodge to supply it.

These lower gardens, thanks to my father's hard work in overseeing and planting them, now began to look spectacular. Aaron had made this project the culmination of a lifetime's knowledge and there were pathways rimmed with great swathes of colour and banks of shrubs and edging plants that really made the most of the landscape. He was pleased with the way it had turned out and Mr McIlwraith allowed Ellen to go and see the results of his labours, which pleased her mightily. She was proud of Aaron's achievement, just as I know she was proud of the houses I had built, and the careers of her other two boys. In these days for the first time in her life she had some leisure time and she would often go down into the town to chat to friends or relations. It did not hurt if they commented favourably upon the work that her family were doing. Not long afterwards Frank was nominated and accepted as a member of the Salcombe District Council, which only added to her pleasure.

Mr McIlwraith was so pleased with the finished job at "Woodcot" that he had it photographed, and the photograph appeared in a London magazine. He gave a copy of it to both my father and myself with the remark that this work was our monument. I have to admit that I was pleased with it, particularly because my father and I had worked so closely together for an end result which satisfied the client so much.

Seeing that the whole family had something to celebrate, Aaron suggested quietly to me one evening that now might finally be the time when we could get the leg on my mother's chair replaced. We had tried several times over the years but she had always objected on some grounds or another – usually ending the debate by stating tartly that "there were better things to spend money on". Whatever these better things were Ellen never did them, for she and my father retained their frugal ways all their lives. The one thing that had changed now and which I think pleased Ellen more than anything was that Aaron had been able to build her a flower garden of her own outside the lodge. She loved this little garden dearly, and could often be found just sitting outside admiring her flowers, while the window sills of the house were now full of red and pink geraniums in burnished copper pots. But the chair was a different thing altogether. Once more our suggestion was met with the same objection. Ellen was not going to part with her chair long enough to have its leg changed. She did however muster the good grace to accept some beautiful red velvet material and gold tassels from Elsie, so that she could make a new cushion to replace the old one, which by now was threadbare. That was enough for my mother.

We were next retained by a Mr Craig at "Castle Point". He was a charming man who had lived in South America most of his life. He had seen the work we had done for Mr McIlwraith, and he asked me to build similar walls and gate pillars for "Castle Point". He wanted stone from near the Old Castle, which was on his land, brought up and used.

It was winter and I did not like the idea of barging the material down the harbour and up through the town, so we rigged up a wooden runway up the cliff face and hauled the stone up using our motor winch. Our client was intrigued with this method of accessing what was again a difficult building area and was on site daily watching our progress. Some years later he asked me to build "Hipple Field" for him. He told me he had decided to use our firm as he admired my guts in taking on difficult jobs and seeing them through to completion.

I had earned myself a little breathing space. My reputation was growing and work was coming in thick and fast. Camp and I took on more masons to meet the demand. I considered myself very lucky. I had waited some time to get married, but I knew I had chosen the right partner. I had seen other marriages in which couples ended up pulling in opposite directions. My married life was happy and I did not have to watch my back. I was able to give all my attention to my work and build the firm, which was what I had always wanted.

Like all new parents we delighted in our new born child, and spent much time watching and playing with him. Peter was a healthy baby, with a head of silky, dark hair that showed his colouring would one day be like his mother's. He was like her too in his long limbs. Coming home to Elsie and little Peter made my world complete. His cot was in a front room. Often at night when the paperwork was finished, Elsie and I would tiptoe into his room and watch him sleeping, and then, as I held my girl, I felt humbled by all the gifts Providence had bestowed on me.

In the Spring of 1923, just after Peter's birth, I bought a rather old gunter rigged 16' sailing boat named "Handy Andy", which had a reputation as a fast racing craft. I paid £35 for her and determined there and then that I would race her successfully. I bought her with two suits of sails including racing sails which had a hollow yard and boom. She was an open boat with no buoyancy tanks so if she had filled up, she would have sunk, as she had already done once with a previous owner.

My aim was to enter "Handy Andy" in the restricted class. To fulfil the criteria for this class meant that the boat could not exceed 200 square feet of sail, and could not have a spinnaker, though a portable boomed jib was permitted. The total weight of the boat was not to exceed 3cwt, which included ballast, and to be eligible it had to be sailed by its owner. It fulfilled all criteria except for the sail size, but I got around this by cutting 10' off the mainsail. I raced her with a crew of two. It was always easy for me to find fit young crew, as I just told off two of my apprentices on the principle of "you and you will volunteer". They soon got to enjoy racing, especially when we won.

I was still working very hard, but with Elsie's encouragement I now began to devote some of my leisure time to racing. I loved to sail, and I have to admit that my strong competitive streak was definitely engaged by the competition at this time. I think that some of the sailors in Salcombe harbour at that date were amongst the best in the world.

Sometimes Elsie came out in the boat with me, though by this time she was expecting another baby, and so her participation was limited to appearing at "Cliff House" for the prize giving ceremony and smiling widely at what turned out to be my frequent wins. Ever since our marriage she had given me books and encouraged me to read whenever I had time, and I was now, thanks to her, building a decent library, full of the classics, poetry, history and the biographies of great men which I particularly enjoyed, as well as a growing number of shelves of construction books. I had been collecting books before our marriage, but sadly had lost several of my favourites when one of the ships I was on was wrecked, so my dear wife now brought replacements for me, for my birthday and Christmas. She marked my racing wins too with new books, and I had a lot of satisfaction in looking at the book shelves I had built which now began to be quite full.

In 1924, I won the Summer Series Cup outright, receiving the Challenge Rose Bowl which was the helmsman's prize for the aggregate for most points in all classes, as well as first prize in both Salcombe and Kingsbridge Regattas, which brought me prize money of £3 in each. I also won a silver cup. Kingsbridge Regatta was the more exciting, as we sailed in a gale and I took a chance and did not reef the sails. Only three started in that race, and one boat capsized and stayed down soon after the starting pistol had sounded, leaving only myself and one other to finish the race.

Salcombe Regatta was also sailed in a moderate gale that year with seven starting and only two finishing. That afternoon as well as my own boat, I raced Mr McIlwraith's "Foam", in the twenty foot class. I came last which dented my pride considerably, but I considered myself fortunate to get around the course in a rapidly building gale and racing a boat I had not sailed before.

In December 1924 our second child, a boy whom we christened Alec Symmons was born. Again we were lucky in that he too was a healthy child.

Soon after both Frank and Fred became fathers for the first time. Frank had a son called Arthur. Fred called his boy David. It was good that they were both so close in age to Peter and Alec, and their mothers introduced the babies early on, pleased that they would have cousins to play with as they grew.

In my limited spare time, I continued racing. For the next three seasons I finished second in each race class. But little by little we local sailors found that the races had started to fill with trophy hunters from outside the area. It seemed to me that the sporting element had gone out of racing. I made up my mind that I would sell "Handy Andy".

Both my sons loved being on the water, and I often took them and their cousins out. Elsie and I had taught them to swim as a condition of being able to go boating, and though young they were competent swimmers. Peter in particular loved boats and all his life was always happiest when he was on the water, but they were still too young to sail a boat like "Handy Andy" by themselves, and so I made up my mind that I would find something that we could enjoy as a family and sold the boat.

I had, as my girl laughingly said, "sown my wild sailing oats," Now perhaps, she agreed, it was time to change… I bought a Canadian style canoe with a motor which was a wonderful vessel for trips to the beach for the boys and their cousins, and for fishing. Elsie came out with us all the time, and we had lots of fun just messing about on the water. I have to admit to hugely enjoying seeing this new generation discovering all the joys of the harbour for themselves.

As soon as the boys had demonstrated to me that they could swim well enough, by the time honoured Salcombe test of being able to swim the harbour, I built a paddling canoe for each, with the promise that when they were older they could each have a sailing one. But Peter worked out how to get a sailing canoe for himself more quickly. Elsie and I were going down the harbour in the motor boat one sunny afternoon, when we saw Peter running proudly at great speed before the wind with a strange sail ballooning at full stretch on his canoe. On closer inspection the sail proved to be one of Elsie's petticoats, so to avoid him using any other of her undergarments, we gave him a proper sail.

About this time I designed a house at East Portlemouth for a Mr Bartlett, a London solicitor, spending a weekend with him in London to settle the contract. But a snag arose, regarding water supply for the house, and he later abandoned the proposed project.

I later built "Upalong" for Mr Clark on the same site.

Mr Bartlett had bought a very smart motor launch at this time, which he kept in the harbour. It was 30' long, with a very powerful engine. He had also had a 12' clinker built dinghy constructed. When he decided not to continue with his house, he wrote to me explaining his decision. In the letter he mentioned that he now wanted to sell both boats. I offered him £12 for the dinghy which he accepted, allowing me the 5% agent's selling commission. The launch remained on the market, but did not sell. Some months later he wrote to me again and asked me to accept the boat at no cost, giving it to me, as he put it, as slight recompense for the trouble he had put me to. I accepted the boat. As the storage of the launch in a boathouse had been costing him £30 a year, I guess he thought he was well quit of it.

I took out the launch's engine which drank petrol and put in a Morris Cowley conversion, which did well up to the 1939 war.

I turned the little family rowing dinghy into a sailing boat with a centre board and it went on giving us all pleasure for over thirty years. It was always Aaron's favourite boat I think, and he loved taking it out in the evening to fish.

As a family we had great fun with the boats. The launch was moored off "Cliff House" together with the two motor boats, the sailing boat and two canoes. These were such happy days.

I did not neglect my business however. I did all the office work and drawings in the evenings and at weekends, and never went to bed on Saturday until I had checked the time sheets and invoices and so on. Elsie helped me tremendously. Her bank work meant that she had a wonderful head for figures, and her shorthand skills that she could take dictation quickly. We bought a typewriter which was a real boon. I got into the habit of dictating work at lunch time which Elsie then transcribed so that she had the letters and invoices ready for my evening return. She did all that as well as taking care of the house and the boys herself, though we did have a cleaning woman who came in to help two mornings a week.

My brother Frederik was still at sea. He had trained as a hard hat diver and his expertise meant that he was continually being transhipped for assignments. He had always been on three year secondments and he remained so. But after all these years of living in Plymouth, he and his wife with their young son David, had decided that they needed a family home of their own in Salcombe. There was a piece of land vacant on the corner of Bonaventure and Herbert Road, very close to "The Tower", and I had earmarked this for him some time before. On his last trip home, he had purchased the site and asked that we build a home there for him.

To a large degree he left the design to me, and I drew up a five bedroomed house arranged over two floors with an attic and cellar. The size was approximately 2093 sq feet in a site which extended to about 58'x 100'. Fred then went back to sea once again on a long secondment, and I was left to liase with his wife Mabel who with David was very much looking forward to moving in. In the meantime, as I had agreed with my brother, I invited them to live with us in "The Tower", since we had room to spare. I converted part of the downstairs into an apartment for them and they stayed there while their house was being built. Since David had been friends with our two boys since birth, it made for fun and games for all of them.

In 1927 we were invited by a firm of Manchester architects to tender for the erection of a new Methodist Church for Salcombe on quantities supplied by them. This was a chance to get a really good job and with the aid of my wife, I got busy pricing the quantities, something I had never dealt with before. I subsequently got the job which proved to be about the happiest we had ever done.

I had as was my habit put aside any spare money I had almost from the start. With the new Methodist Church contract secured, I decided to put in a bid to buy the old Chapel in Island Street, which was in need of repairs and would now be redundant. I was lucky because at that time my bid was unopposed, and so for not a great deal of money I became the proud owner of a redundant chapel. It had no immediate use and stripping out the interior fittings I earmarked the good timber for re-use in the new Methodist building. The floors of the old chapel gave us a great deal of good quality, well-seasoned timber. I set the apprentices to removing nails, cleaning and sizing this timber. Once this was done, we sorted the timber into different grades and lengths, and stacked it in the chapel until it was needed on the new site.

We made all the interior fittings for the new Methodist Church, which was rather a challenge because ecclesiastical joinery work was in a class all by itself. We now employed three journeymen including my brother Frank who was responsible for all the machining and fine detail work, and five apprentices who were now given a wonderful chance to show what they were made of, which they really appreciated. I had made up my mind that all the internal woodwork was to be in warm, richly figured Columbian or Oregon Pine, the majority of which had come from the old chapel. This was hard wood which was tough to work, but the machines I had installed helped a great deal and meant that we could even run out all the mouldings ourselves. I kept the apprentices inside in the workshop under Frank's charge, and had the rest of the men begin work on the foundations.

But the site was not without problems which taxed even my ingenuity, for when we started to dig the foundations, we discovered several previously un-guessed at running springs which meant that the deeper the men dug the more the ground flooded, making the site apparently unworkable. On the plus side there was no danger of the Trustees abandoning the job, but the problems seemed insurmountable, and we were all worried.

The Trustees got in touch with the architect, who wrote to me suggesting a meeting for the following week, and saying that if I had any suggestions as to how we might get around this problem, they hoped I would have them ready for their arrival.

I was not going to lose this job if I could help it, especially as I felt that my reputation was at stake, and I began to think the problem out carefully. I mocked up several possible solutions, and tried them out in our bath. Finally I came up with the idea of building a raft on which to "float" the building, six feet wide at the bottom, diminishing to two feet at damp course level, the whole to be set about four feet down, with all the concrete reinforced with metal railway bars for additional strength. It would put up the cost of the build, but I felt that this was the only solution to the problem. I submitted my drawings to the architect, and gained his approval for the idea before putting it before the Trustees.

The Trustees met and then sent for me. I was rather bucked to hear that they had agreed that if I considered it would be the sound job of which I had assured them, they would go ahead with the revised plan. They also agreed the £390 additional cost.

Throughout all of these negotiations, my partner Jim Camp, who happened also to be a Trustee of the church, resolutely refused to join in discussions. He accused me of drawing twice as much as he was from the job – not quite accurate – and he therefore maintained that I should carry the whole responsibility for the work, which I was glad to do. He was pessimistic about the problems on site. I made sure that I waited until the job was back on an even keel and the problems resolved, and then I did draw twice the amount he received. Our partnership was beginning to flounder, and I made the decision then that I would buy him out as soon as I could afford it.

Having made up my mind to use railway metal to help shore up the foundations, I wrote to the Great Western Railway as soon as I got the go ahead for the extra work, asking if I could buy some of their discarded metal rails. But in spite of repeated requests, I had no reply. In the meantime my wife and I went to Plymouth on a very hot day and walked miles around scrap yards, finding no metal of any length since it had all been cut down for shipment. It was towards the end of the afternoon, when we were hot, tired and rather dispirited, regretting very much that we did not have a motor car to travel in, that we bumped into a commercial traveller I knew.

We got talking and I told him of our mission, and he assured us that he would be able to find the necessary materials.

We accompanied him to Milehouse where he introduced us to the Chief Tramway Engineer, a friend of his, who told us that we could have all the old rails we needed, even offering to have them cut to length if required. This was not needed, but, greatly heartened, I gave the order to the traveller's firm, "Service and Co." Within three days we had 14 tons of metal rails delivered from Lostwithiel, together with fish plates, bolts and spanners. The cost of all this delivered, was £43, so all ended well.

We began building. Owing to its elevated position the new church was a very public site from the first. From the foundations to the top stone above the main entrance was some height. Knowing in advance what we would be facing, I had ordered new wood poles and planks, also long 6' by 3' pudlogs (the tie bars for the scaffolding), to overcome the buttresses. I had always maintained the principle of not asking any of my workmen to do a job I would not do myself, but I have to admit I was none too happy assisting the principal man up the 34 step ladder, and steadying him at the top. But I gritted my teeth and got on with it.

I had been asked to supply all the joinery for the interior. When it was learned that I proposed to make all the fittings myself with my men actually based in Salcombe, I was given the order for all the seating and furniture for the church as well.

The Methodist Church had been collecting money for years for this project, but even so I was astonished that they were able to raise the additional £12,000 required for the interior fittings. The job was paid for as

Wesleyan Church, Salcombe. Fairweather

soon as it was finished, with no retention. Through the years I was more than pleased to discover that there was no sign of any settlement around the church, despite the unusual solution I had come up with for its construction.

The Schoolroom was officially opened at Christmas, and the Church at Whitsun. Both events drew large crowds. Many people congratulated me on the work. I also received a complimentary letter from the Methodist Trustees as well as the architects, both commending me for a job well done.

Interior of Wesleyan Church. 1. Fairweather

Interior of Wesleyan Church 2. Fairweather

I have to admit that I was pleased with the end result. However I discovered that there was a downside to all this adulation, as I soon found out that I was thereafter expected to attend what seemed to me to be countless ceremonies of thanksgiving at the church on all public holidays!.

CHAPTER TEN

Even before finishing the Methodist Church, we had obtained the contract to build a new Cottage Hospital in Kingsbridge. Our original tender was for about £13,000, but we were asked to re-tender against a Torquay firm, with revised quantities. I had only two days to do this, which I think was probably an arranged thing, but I was determined to secure the contract, and Elsie and I worked with hardly a spell for sleep. I altered the quantities, and Elsie revised the prices, and we got our amended tender off with little time to spare, and secured the job.

Kingsbridge and District Hospital.

It was a happy site, and towards the end we were given the contract for all the furniture to equip it. As usual we made this ourselves, using up all the offcuts of the Columbian pine from the Methodist Chapel, which pleased me as I hated waste and it was magnificent wood.

The Hospital was officially opened by Lord Mildmay, amid a fanfare of publicity, and I received a complimentary letter from him a day or so later, as well as ones from the hospital trustees and the architect, all congratulating me on a job well done.

Whilst building the hospital, my firm was also employed in constructing a tea room seating 150 for Gunns in Fore Street, Kingsbridge, which was later demolished by bombing.

I also did a £2,000 reconstruction of "Whinfields", for both jobs I was in sole charge, so together with other smaller jobs on our books as well, my hands were full.

In quick succession our firm built "The Tides Reach" Hotel at South Sands and the "North Sands Hotel". Soon afterwards we quoted for and secured the contract for a hotel at Gara Rock, and constructed the "Gara Rock Hotel".

The "Tides Reach Hotel" left, and the "South Sands Hotel" to right, South Sands, Salcombe.

I still did not own a car at this time, and so used the catch the 10 a.m. bus to Kingsbridge every day, returning home at midday. I was probably foolish not to buy a car, but I seemed to be running the company on a shoestring despite the big projects that I was engaged in.

I had a little money saved though, and I now made up my mind to buy some land that I had had my eye on for some time. Towards the end of 1927, I paid £475 for the large garden in Newton Road adjoining "The

Tower", mainly with a view to building a garage, but also to increasing the

"Gara Rock Hotel", Gara, Nr. Salcombe. 1926

size of our garden. The space gave my growing sons a much bigger place to play, which made them happy. My father Aaron planted vegetables there, and in time it became a very productive kitchen garden for my family and my parents, usually with enough surplus produce to give to Elsie's parents, as my father often popped in to visit Annie Lucy. He reserved for her the warm, genuine friendship that he had long had with his daughter-in-law, and the two of them were often to be found chatting in the garden of "Torre View". Our two mothers got along, but they were very different people, both strong and determined in their own way, and consequently did not see much of each other, but Aaron as usual was everyone's friend.

I put it to my parents that I might build them a small house next to the "The Tower" for their retirement, and they were genuinely delighted by the plan. It was in my mind that one day in the future it might provide a smaller house for Elsie and me. I admit now that I cherished the idea that one day my two sons would follow me into the business. Occasionally I allowed myself to daydream of this time, but almost immediately my ambition to continue to build up the business drove me on again.

Once these big projects were finished, we constructed another house at East Portlemouth, and followed that by building the Methodist Chapel there, as well as six houses in Herbert Road, Salcombe. We were also finishing the house in Bonaventure Road for my brother Frank at that time. The tragedy in my elder brother's life that he seldom spoke of, was that his son Arthur was sickly. Years later he developed tuberculosis. As it was his doctors had recommended the boy get as much fresh air as possible which is why Frank had agreed this site for his home. I have to admit that having the whole family close to "The Tower" pleased me greatly. I felt I had achieved what I had always wanted, to be able to take care of them all, and I took a pride in that.

Things seemed for once to be going our way. Then came the day that the newspapers immediately christened "Black Thursday" October 24th 1929, when the American Stock Market crashed.

I had walked down into town very early on some small errand, and stopped to buy a newspaper. I was so absorbed in a building problem that I was wrestling with that I did not even glance at the news boards in front of the shop. I registered that there were a few knots of men on the street, but beyond a quick "good morning", and raising my hat a couple of times to ladies I passed, I paid them little attention. I was probably not what you would describe as the most sociable of men anyway, and I was usually on my way to some site or other, and more often than not pushed for time, so I rarely stopped to talk.

I guess through the years my personality had become known in Salcombe. My position now as one of the town's leading employers I knew had to a degree alienated me from the people I had grown up with. I spent my time with the wealthy and influential men who were my clients, the majority of them incomers, and I was aware that there was some bad feeling amongst those in town who envied me my success. But I also knew, as they did, that I came from them and ultimately would always be a part of them. The bottom line was that I lived for my work, and that and my family was all that was important to me. I knew I had a reputation as a hard bastard, but I had also heard men say that I drove myself harder than I drove the men, and I felt I could live with that. I was not the sort of man who went to the pub or involved himself in idle pursuits. I was probably, if the brutal truth be known, not a popular man, and I certainly had no close friends, but I also knew that I had earned respect in the town and that I counted as more important.

It was a bright, sunny day even though there was a chill wind. I was enjoying this time in the fresh air, and I decided on a whim to go back home on the slightly roundabout route, and climb the steps behind Cliff House.

I looked down over the estuary as I walked. The sea was shining, tipping the waves with sparkling silver as it seemed to me only to do in my home town. A noisy flock of seagulls followed a fishing boat in. It was too far away to see whose boat it was. I watched as it ploughed against a running tide until it came level with Mill Bay beach.

I passed the memorial my eyes as always going to my cousin's name on

Mill Bay beach, Salcombe. c 1934 Valentine.

the granite cross, and turned into Cliff House and up the path beside it. The steps were shaded by tall trees. The leaves were just beginning to turn their autumn colours. The grounds of "The Tower" ran down to the steps and I glanced up at my kitchen garden and saw the camp my sons had recently made there. I noticed that their forays into the workshop had resulted in some sound building timber being used. I deliberated this briefly, torn between indulgence and the need to teach them that such good timber was valuable, but perhaps because of the sunshine, I came down on the side of indulgence, though I made a mental note to have a word with the men to make sure it did not happen again. Looking more closely I saw that the camp's construction was good, and I chuckled, convinced that Alec was behind it. Even at five years old his constructions were always sound whereas whatever Peter built seemed inevitably to fall down.

I came to a place behind the red tiled cupola where the path levelled out and sat on the wall, staring out to where the Bar and the dark bulk of Bolt Head was just visible over the roof tops, but without really seeing it. My problem was how best to utilise building materials on a site in East Charleton that seemed to be made almost entirely of shifting shale and sand. I knew I would have to build deep foundations but just how deep? How much would the job stand?

I glanced at my watch, a new and prized possession Elsie had given me for my last birthday, and seeing that I had a little time to spare, opened my newspaper.

The headlines jumped out at me: "Financial Panic as Wall Street crashes millions of dollars wiped out overnight".

I could only stare in disbelief. Alone amongst all the nations after the war America had seemed to be thriving. What the Press was now referring to as the "Roaring Twenties" had brought the United States seemingly unending prosperity. New schemes had been introduced to guarantee employment. Police had cleaned up the corruption that had stemmed from Prohibition with the arrest of gang bosses including Al Capone. Only a few months before had come Herbert Hoover's presidential address with his proud declaration: "We in America are nearer to the final triumph over poverty than ever before in the history of any land."

And shoring it all up the New York Stock Market that for the last eighteen months had enjoyed a bull market that had appeared unstoppable, with shares rising with lightning speed and investors stampeding the markets as they opened, borrowing and mortgaging everything they owned in order not to miss out on this new gold rush.

Edmund and I had been talking about it only a few nights before. I knew that my father-in-law had more than once been tempted to invest. I think he had dabbled in the London Stock Market in the past, but this running bull market worried him. The Dow Jones had dragged in ever more new and often naïve investors, many of them buying shares on margin for as little as ten per cent down. Frequently one set of securities, still unpaid, would be used to fund a second set, then a third, until the U.S Stock Market had begun to seem little more than a gigantic casino for speculators trading on borrowed money.

Share prices had continued to rise, despite President Hoover's attempts to cool things down. The last newspaper report I had read had said that shares now stood at an all time high and that in one day alone the value of stocks and shares traded had reached $13 million. And now this....

"It would only need one to take fright..." Edmund had said prophetically, and he had been right. I scanned the editorial, still scarcely able to believe what I was reading. A few investors had realised that prices had risen far beyond their real value, and had begun to sell. Others speculating on a small safety margin and already edgy, had quickly followed suit to escape financial ruin. It had been enough to bring about the collapse.

I got to my feet and carried on up the steps, the newspaper under my arm. I knew the fall out from this disaster could not fail to reach England, but to what degree would the country be affected? As I walked up the road I tried to think it through from every angle, wondering if our business was secure enough to weather such a storm, knowing I had to talk to Jim Camp...to Frank... But suddenly, more than anything else I wanted to get home, to see Elsie.

She was standing in the dining room, her face pale. On the table were the accounts books she had been working on. The radio was on a side table, and as I came in, she switched it off, and its green glowing dial faded infinitely slowly to black.

She saw by my face that I had learned the news. "I'm trying to think how it will affect the firm," she said, her voice level, her bookkeeping skills uppermost. She stumbled slightly as she moved towards me, something which seemed to be happening more and more lately.

"It's bound to hit house building – But I think we'll be in as good a position as any to survive" I answered. "At least we don't have loans, thank God. And thank God also that we didn't have any money to invest..." I added with what seemed even to me to be a rather hollow laugh.

She nodded pensively. "The radio said that police riot squads are in the streets in New York... everyone's panicking. People have seen their life savings wiped out in hours...It's horrible. There have been eleven suicides... investors have been jumping off skyscrapers – you know those very tall buildings..."

"I know," I said. She came into my arms, tall enough that her eyes could look straight into mine.

"I just keep thinking about those people," she said quietly. "The announcer said that investors were selling everything they owned to buy food. There were men standing in the street selling their cars for almost nothing..."

I was due back on site, and I had to leave. I kissed her. "I'll be back as soon as I can", I promised walking towards the hall.

She called me back. "Jim do you think Daddy has invested ...?"

"I'm sure he hasn't" I reassured her. But I wasn't sure. The more I considered it the more I thought it was the sort of thing that Edmund would do, for the excitement if nothing else.

For a while, although the newspaper headlines continued to be gloomy and alarming, it seemed as if things might not be so bad. I was a cautious man however, and I determined straight away to tighten up on our already tight stock control. Even though my partner was not interested I had always carried out regular stock checks and insisted that Elsie keep a detailed inventory of our business assets for him. I never threw anything away that I thought might one day come in useful, and I knew we were sitting on good stocks of timber, and had plenty of the smaller items such as nails and screws, which I had bought advantageously over the years, or painstakingly got the men to straighten out for re-use when we cut up old timber.

When the workshop closed that evening I walked home to spend the first of several nights poring over the account books and stock legers.

I did not see Edmund over the next few days. It was left to Annie Lucy to tell me that though my father in law had fought shy of investing, unbeknown to him his broker had done just that on his behalf. He had lost money he knew, but he did not yet know how much.

I walked down to "Torre View" on my way back from a nearby site. I saw that Annie Lucy wanted to get me alone to talk, and so, on the pretext of taking some cabbage seedlings to Aaron, we walked up to the lodge together.

"We still don't know exactly how much money we have lost", my mother in law said as we turned the corner. "But I've got a plan. I've decided to open up "Torre View" to visitors... "

It seemed to me a good idea, and I told her so.

"The house is too big for the two of us anyway" she said. "Every summer now there are more visitors wanting accommodation in the town..."

I nodded. "It will give you an interest as well," I said. "It should be a good venture... You know I'll help if you need it," I added.

She squeezed my arm. "I know it's no good asking you not to tell Elsie, but just make sure that she doesn't let her father know," she said. "Edmund trusted his broker, but now he feels a fool for doing so".

Things seemed for a while to go on as normal. We heard many rumours around Salcombe of people who might have lost money, but nothing was confirmed. Then, suddenly two weeks before Christmas, the slump began and there was no work to be found anywhere in the locality. .

I thought back to my days in Australia and a strike that had suddenly dried up all work   I had told myself then that if I had £500 in the bank I should be safeguarded against such an event, but then I had only myself to look after. Now I had my family and the men who had been loyal to me throughout. Many of the workmen had wives and young children...I didn't want to lay anyone off if I could possibly help it...

But on the other hand I knew that we would have to make economies where we could if we were to keep the firm going. I had a series of discussions with Jim Camp, and in the end we decided that the fairest thing would be to lay off all the single men. I put it to the rest that if they would agree to take a 10% cut in their wages, I would demolish the old Methodist Chapel in Island Street, and build five new cottages on the site on spec. I knew that that would be enough to keep us building for some time. I talked to the single men and gave them my word that I would find work for them as soon as I could.

In the meantime I set the men to pulling down the old chapel, demolishing it by hand to preserve the stone, passing ropes through the top windows and pulling on them until the heavy stonework came crashing down into the safety nets we had hung above the street. It was difficult work as the buildings all around were occupied and I knew that one wrong move might damage the surrounding homes.

As it was the demolition of the chapel attracted a great deal of attention. The men worked always with a group of interested onlookers as well as the passers-by in the busy street. Though we tried hard to keep them back, children were drawn to the site like moths to a flame, delighting in the noise and dust. There were several businesses in the immediate vicinity including "Hannaford's" butchers shop on the corner which had to carry on their trade regardless. There were also gas street lamps which presented their own hazard. I have to admit I was relieved when the chapel was down, though in its time it had been a marvellous and very well attended place of worship. I know that many of the elderly including my mother, who had known it for so long, were heartbroken to see it go as it held so many memories for them. It was in its way the end of an era. Ellen reminded me several times that all three of us brothers had been baptised there.

I had been working on the drawings and plans for the cottages that would replace the chapel, and as soon as the site was clear, we began to re-build, pouring in a great deal of concrete to deal with the water that had once literally made the area an island. In accordance with my plan not to spend money on additional materials if at all possible, I sourced everything from our own workshops. All the joinery was done by the apprentices which gave them work. Later I found some employment for the single men as well around Salcombe, including building the Orangery at the "Salcombe Hotel", which was a job I had quoted on some time before and which I forced to fruition by reducing the contract price considerably.

It was a long haul, but finally work came along again, and eight months later the men were back on their normal wages. I never heard a complaint during this reduced wage period, and my plan certainly saved the firm from having to close and forcing the men onto the bare 17/- a week unemployment pay, which would have meant great hardship for all. At last we could breathe again, but it had been a tough few months.

Elsie and I had always wanted our boys to have the best education we could afford, and had made up our minds long before that they would go to a public school when they were older. They had attended a local kindergarten school, and then had gone to the Boys School in Salcombe for a while. I had made enquires about several schools, but one of my clients based in Cornwall had recommended Truro School in that city, highly. I had visited and talked to the principal and I liked what I learned. I decided the school would provide an excellent education for Peter and Alec.

At about this time an endowment insurance policy I had taken out in Australia became payable. It was only for £200 with profits of £80, but I had for some time wanted to build a garage for "The Tower", so I decided to use the money for this.

I was getting more and more tired, and was beginning to feel run down. All the years of overwork were starting to take their toll on me. In the late summer of 1931, my health broke down and Dr Twining told me firmly that I needed to rest. I knew I had been overworking. I had never taken a holiday and I had put in at least a twelve hour day ever since I started the business. I had always worked the full 53 ½ hours with the men, chiefly supervising, but sometimes when we were particularly pushed, working alongside them. After they had gone home I began the drawings and dictated letters and quotes to Elsie, as well as dealing with all the money matters. I tried to keep it from my wife, but I had recently begun to have nightmares in which I saw the faces of the injured men on the ships after Gallipoli.

I was also concerned for Elsie. Uncomplainingly, she had done everything she could to help, and I knew that I could not have achieved nearly so much without her. As always "my girl" had been there when I needed her, even though she also had the responsibilities of the house and the welfare of us all to consider. The hard work she put in at least enabled me to be out on the water when I could at weekends, which was my only relaxation and something I enjoyed hugely.

I made up my mind that we would take a holiday. We discussed at length what we would like to do, but the only holiday that appealed to me was a sea trip.

I organised a rota for the men, making sure that all projects were well in hand. The next thing that was coming up was my father's retirement, which, since he was by now in his 70's was long overdue. I had promised to build my parents a house and I had already started the drawings for this. Everything was ready to start on our return. In the meantime my parents kindly agreed to look after the boys at the lodge, an exercise which I discovered later seemingly consisted of them being greatly indulged, spending a large part of each day with Aaron, helping him in the garden at "Woodcot", then in the evening fishing or exploring rock pools on the foreshore. If I knew my father, there would also be stories of his time at sea, and I smiled to myself thinking it did not seem so very long ago that he had told those stories to my brothers and me. He and my mother still enjoyed good health, though both, particularly Aaron suffered from rheumatism.

All was set. We left for Southampton on 2nd August and embarked on the "SS Montclare" for a thirteen day cruise to Madeira, Tenerife, Las Palmas and Gibraltar, returning via Liverpool during the third week of August 1931. The trip did us the world of good and we enjoyed it immensely.

After we docked at Liverpool we returned to Salcombe. Soon afterwards we walked up the road to collect the boys and told my parents and my eager sons all about our trip, giving them the small gifts we had brought back for them, and hearing their news.

The next night Annie Lucy and Edmund invited us all for dinner. As always when we were together, our talk was wide ranging. We talked of guests that my in-laws had had staying with them. Through their business contacts and friends in the East End both had met a great number of new acquaintances. These were often quite influential especially in the Arts, for their home had gained something of a reputation for attracting rather an intellectual set including musicians, writers and artists – the sort of people they had often entertained at their London home.

It was at this dinner that Edmund mentioned Franz Hummer an old friend whom he had known for some years but had lost contact with. He was living in Berlin, and I remember Edmund saying that he hoped he might be able to visit "Torre View", so that they could catch up with each other. It was an interesting conversation for the boys, as Edmund mentioned that Franz had written about hyper-inflation in Germany, which led on to talk of the growing financial crisis in Britain, and the demands on the gold reserves which had consequently dwindled alarmingly. We had read in the newspapers on our return that drastic cuts in salaries had been proposed for public workers in Britain. The government however had now begun its summer recess so it looked unlikely that we would hear much more for a while.

One of the topics I remember we discussed at length during the meal was the trouble in Spain. We had been off the coast of Spain for a few days during our trip and this had perhaps brought it to our minds. We knew of Annie Lucie's connections to the country through her first husband and his extended Spanish family, and we discussed the abdication of King Alfonso and the current state of Spain as a Republic and debated what the unrest would mean to the Spanish people.

It was good to be back in Salcombe again. I had enjoyed being with the boys that evening. They had an excellent relationship with both sets of grandparents and I thought they had conducted themselves well during what was quite a grown up dinner party. Both had engaged with Edmund and showed that they had some knowledge of financial and world affairs and Peter in particular had put up a few interesting questions. I had seen Edmund smile that half mocking, kindly smile while they were talking that meant he was enjoying the conversation... my wife was happy and looked particularly beautiful after her holiday. I was a happy man.

We said our goodnights and thank yous, and walked back to "The Tower". The air was still and calm and the summer warmth lingered. The moonlight shone on a full, sleepy tide. I was not feeling tired and as Elsie and the boys went to the house, I walked down to the kitchen garden where I had planned my parents' home and did what I usually did when I was engaged on a project, which was to try and visualise the building I was going to construct. Aaron had left an upturned bucket beside his vegetable patch and I sat on this enjoying the night air, and smoking my pipe. It was one of those evenings when everything seemed right and in its proper place in the world.

Two days later on August 24th 1931 amid rumours that the run on the pound was driving Britain towards the abyss of national bankruptcy, the Labour government fell, to general concern.

As a result of emergency talks with Buckingham Palace, an all-party "Government of Co-operation" led by the outgoing Prime Minister, Ramsey MacDonald, was formed to cope with the emergency and to take whatever steps were deemed necessary to restore confidence in sterling.

MacDonald resigned when the majority of the cabinet, backed by the TUC shrank from endorsing what he declared were the necessary draconian spending cuts. He advised the king to invite other the party leaders to join in forming a new government which would embark on full retrenchment policies, but in the ensuing chaos, Britain was forced off the gold standard.

Over the next weeks with a 30% devaluation in sterling, there was general discontent, riots and strikes by public sector workers, and many clashes between police and demonstrators.

The crisis lurched on over the next few months. Elections at the end of October saw the National Government staying in power after the largest election rout in history ousted Labour. Ramsey MacDonald carried on as titular prime minister, but every member of the former Labour cabinet except one lost his seat. Sir Oswold Mosley's New Party was destroyed and Mr Lloyd George lost his influence.

They were troubling times, and what made matters worse was that no-body seemed to be able to get a grip on what was happening. News from Germany in another letter from Franz Hummer, told of continued hyper-inflation. Edmund said that Franz had complained that the elderly Hindenberg, the old man of German politics had beaten the presidential challenger, even though a Herr Hitler had vastly increased his share of the vote. It seemed from Hummer's letter that many people were putting their faith in this Herr Hitler to get Germany back on a stable footing. It was yet another indication of how shaky the world's economies were since the Stock Market crash.

I started on my parent's new home, as Aaron's retirement was now imminent. I had always used my own income when I constructed something for my family, but for this house I took a mortgage of £800 from the "Forresters' Club". I had drawn up plans for this house with all the rooms looking out over the harbour just as those in our own home did, knowing that Aaron in particular would enjoy that view. Both Elsie and I were pleased to be able to do this for my parents. As for the old people, they just could not wait to move in. I often found my mother standing looking at the place where her new front door, the first of her very own, would be, while the sound of the men hammering and banging drifted out from inside.

The house was finished in good time and Aaron and Ellen moved in, naming their new home "Sunnydale". They lived there rent and rates free for the rest of their lives. Elsie was as keen as I was on this idea and insisted on our helping the old couple with fuel and so on. They had some savings, but used them very sparingly, living mainly on their pension. But my father still worked hard, and usually managed a plentiful crop of vegetables which he shared between us and Elsie's parents, who now had visitors to feed as well, at "Torre View".

After the lean period of the last years we suddenly became very busy, as gradually the country began to claw its way up out of the Depression, and work came flooding in.

Ferry passing enlarged Marine Hotel and Cliff House. Fairweather

We began to take on more and more men over the next years. By now we were employing up to sixty carpenters, joiners and masons in addition to a great number of sub-contractors, which made the firm one of the largest in the South West.

We built four cottages at Batson, two large houses in North Sands Valley, rebuilt "Woodcot", remade the road to Snapes Point and did lots of work at "Gullet", including amongst many other projects, completing a wing to the house, rebuilding part of the original building after a fire, constructing three cottages and one bungalow, extending the stables and cow byre, and creating water reservoirs.

Peter was due to sit his scholarship examination for his new school, and I hired a car so that the whole family could accompany him to Truro for the day. Alec was officially too young to sit the exam, but the headmaster allowed him to take it with the older boys, as I had told him that I hoped that in time he too would attend the school.

When we had dropped off the boys Elsie and I took the car into Truro.

We spent some time in the cathedral admiring the building and its magnificent stained glass windows, and later stopped at a restaurant for a cup of tea, but our thoughts were continually with our boys, especially Peter.

Less than a week later we received a letter with the glad news that Peter had passed his examination, and asking him to attend for an interview with the School Governors. Alec we were told, although too young as yet to be considered for a place had also returned a good result. We learned later that over eighty boys had sat for just twelve places, so the competition had been fierce. Peter was the first boy outside of Cornwall to gain a place at the school, so Elsie and I were particularly proud.

It remained now for him to pass his interview and a couple of weeks later we once again set off for Truro.

This time I opted to take the whole family by rail and we set off from Kingsbridge at 7.30 a.m. The interview, which was to be at 11 a.m, was to be conducted by Sir Arthur Quiller Couch, then Chairman of Truro School Governors.

The boys were seated in a waiting room with their parents. The interviews were conducted behind closed doors, and the headmaster stayed outside with us, chatting and ushering in the boys one by one as their names were called. Since Alec was not invited to this meeting, I suggested that he and Elsie went for a walk in the school grounds. Elsie was a bundle of nerves and I thought it better that she did not distract Peter. They did not venture far away though, because from time to time I saw the feathers on Elsie's smart new hat bobbing outside the window as they walked up and down!

It came to Peter's turn. He was obviously quite nervous, but tried to conceal it. I nodded at him in what I hoped was an encouraging manner as he went in, but I felt quite stupidly apprehensive myself.

I sat looking out of a nearby window at the sweep of green lawn in the school grounds, and made myself think of something else, though all the time I was straining to hear any sounds from the other side of the door.

I heard laughter, then finally the door was opened and Peter came out. His eyes were shining and he was smiling.

I was invited in to meet the Committee.

"You have a bright lad," Sir Arthur Quiller Couch told me approvingly.

I remarked that I had heard laughter while my son was being interviewed.

"I asked Peter if he was sorry Australia had won the Test Match," he said, referring to the series which was currently being played in England. "But he said no. He told us that you had lived in Australia for some time and though you described them as "rather undisciplined" as a bunch, he knew that you had respect for their fighting ability."

I didn't say anything to Peter but I admit I was feeling fairly confident about the outcome of his interview, and now I determined that we would make a day of the trip to celebrate.

We had lunch in Truro, and then went by bus to Falmouth where we saw the "Cutty Sark", which was then lying some way offshore. Peter was fascinated to hear that I had known her before her re-construction and asked many questions about the state of the ship then and the seaman who had sailed in her. He was mad about boats and ships and was barely able to tear his eyes away from her.

But I had another treat up my sleeve, and I surprised my family by hiring a boatman to take us all out to look over her. For Peter in particular to actually go on board a big sailing ship such as his grandfather had sailed on, and particularly one with such a reputation, was wonderful. It brought us very close. Glancing from my sons' faces alight with excitement, to my wife, I felt so proud of my family. Elsie was just over thirty then, and she was a strikingly attractive woman. She was always so elegant and today, dressed in a matching coat and dress in dark lilac, her figure still willowy and slim despite two children, she looked eye catchingly lovely.

We had tea and buns in a café and then made our way back to the station to catch the train home.

We arrived back at Kingsbridge railway station at 9.15 in the evening to find that the fair had come to town in our absence, and so we did the rounds of this to finish off the day. Both Elsie and Peter managed to hit one of the tin targets on a stall and each won a goldfish. We ate candy floss and shared a stick of rock between us. Eventually we caught the late bus back to Salcombe, all of us very tired, but happy. It had been quite a day!

We heard quite quickly that Peter had been awarded a scholarship for early tuition and had been granted a bursary worth about £15 a year, which Elsie and I both agreed would help greatly with his school fees.

Work in general was thin on the ground just then, and it was an anxious time for many firms. However our firm was still very busy, and I did not need to apply for exemptions for any of our men as I know several other local builders did at that time. We built the "Tides Reach Hotel" as well as two blocks of Council houses. In total I think our firm built almost all the homes around Salcombe and the Estuary.

In due course Alec followed Peter to Truro School. As the paperwork continued to increase, we got in a day girl to help in the house, so that Elsie was freer to help me with correspondence and office tasks. I was busy all the time. In the evenings after the workshop closed I began the drawings that would secure future commissions, dictating all the quotation letters to Elsie who typed them up for me to sign. I thought that we were well fixed.

My only worry was a niggling concern about my wife's health. From being a graceful woman, she had unaccountably become clumsy of late. We made a joke of it, but she had begun to leave a trail of broken dishes and other damaged items behind her. She would reach for something, and it just seemed to slip through her fingers. She said that sometimes it felt as if suddenly there was no strength in her hands. There were days too, when her legs jerked uncontrollably, or she was tortured by cramp. But she was so brave. She insisted that it was nothing to worry about, and that the symptoms were probably caused by being so busy. She refused outright to go to the doctor and so there was nothing that I could do.

I was going backwards and forwards to "Gullet" where I still had a lot of men working, using our little motor boat. The trip only took fifteen minutes, and it was a pleasure to travel this way. I continued to rent a car to make trips to Truro for half terms and other visits, now Alec had followed Peter there, and also for travelling backwards and forwards to Plymouth North Road Station to collect the boys and return them to school. It would make sense to buy a car both Elsie and I agreed, and I began to look into it. I had a word at Cranch's Garage where I viewed a couple of vehicles.

Things were changing fast in Germany, and the country appeared to be often in the news. Herr Hitler was now Chancellor of the German Reich, but there was trouble between his National Socialists and the Communists. We read in newspapers that Hitler's Storm Troopers had been burning books considered un-German, and replacing them with copies of his own book, "Mein Kampf" in bookshops. Trade Unions had been purged, and after a mystery fire at the German Reichstag, the Nazis had made the Jewish race their scapegoats, hounding Jews from office and robbing them of the rights.

Edmund had always been a prolific letter writer and kept in touch with many of his old friends from the East End. It was thanks to this correspondence that we learned a great deal about what was actually happening in Germany. One of his correspondents was a Jewish businessman called Moishe Abrahams. Moishe was a wealthy jeweller with stores in several major cities. Seeing which way things were going, he had fled with his family to Switzerland. It was Moishe who told us of some of the dreadful things that the Nazis were doing to the Jews. He wrote to Edmund that marriages between Jews and Germans had been declared illegal, also that Hitler's men had been forcibly sterilising "imperfect" Germans. Jews had been herded into concentration camps. All the time in counterpoint, Franz Hummer's occasional letters told of a country which was gradually getting over its troubles and growing stronger - by June of that year Germany had become a one party state in fact if not in name as the last Social Democrat was thrown out of the Reichstag and the National Party was absorbed by the Nazis. Hitler, the Austrian corporal was no longer a figure of fun but a force to be reckoned with.

Meanwhile newspapers declared that Hitler had announced that

Germany would take no further part in the Geneva Disarmament Conference, giving his reasons as "humiliating and dishonouring demands of the other Powers". He used the same excuse to announce Germany's withdrawal from the League of Nations.

Fierce fighting had now broken out between opposing sides in Spain. But news from the New World was better, as Franklin Delano Roosevelt assumed office in June 1933, his ticket being a New Deal Work Programme.

In 1934 the elderly Hindenberg died, and Hitler, who was now boasting that the German Reich would last a thousand years, became supreme leader. In England too the Fascists were rising. From a relatively unknown, Sir Oswold Mosley had held rallies of the British Union of Fascists, attended by what was estimated to be a crowd of 10,000. Pathe News said that it included about 3,000 of Mosley's committed supporters who gave the fascist salute and thunderous applause to their leader's calls for a dictatorship.

Driving through central Plymouth one hot August day in 1934 I came upon a rally of Moseley's Blackshirts. A Plymouth business acquaintance had told me their leader had spoken at several venues around the city. He said that neighbours in the street near their headquarters were angry because the Blackshirts had cleared the garden of flowers, and laid it all down to concrete so that they could practise their drill. But I heard that during one meeting at Millbay, a group of Communists had gate-crashed the meeting and scuffles and fights had broken out, pre-empting the later battle between 100,000 Blackshirts and East Enders in London, in 1936. It was not until after the war that we discovered that one of these Plymouth Blackshirts, rather a non-entity of a man by the name of William Joyce, was the traitor who had been broadcasting the propaganda attributed to Lord Haw Haw.

But unpleasant things such as that were all forgotten in the excitement of the opening of the magnificent Tinside Bathing Lido in Plymouth. The boys had been pestering me for ages to take them to see it, so one half term holiday soon after it opened I took them in for a swim. It was a beautiful day, and they thoroughly enjoyed themselves. I did not swim, but I must admit that the sight of those splendid white concrete curves shining so brightly in the sunshine, and thronged thickly with bathers seemed to me to be a tremendous boost for the city. A few weeks later on a return journey after delivering the boys to school, I took Elsie for a tea dance on the pier, which we both enjoyed hugely.

By October of that year there was fierce fighting in Catalonia which included bombing by German aeroplanes. The situation was only brought under control by the arrival of a warship carrying Spanish Foreign Legion soldiers. Martial law was declared throughout the country. Monarchist officers on the retired list on King Alfonso's abdication were invited over the wireless to resume service with the colours. Alongside the headlines telling of the kidnap of Lindbergh's baby, the newspapers reported that Germany had begun a massive re-armament programme.

In October came news that the Italian leader Mussolini's troops had marched into Abyssinia.

Our firm received quite a lot of work from the Ministry of Defence at this time. This included maintenance of buildings taken over by the Navy. We were also employed in making a great many blackout frames and boarding for local businesses which coincided with the issue of gas masks to various classes of civilians in a major civil defence operation throughout the country.

However much we tried to close our eyes to it, events in Germany showed that the clouds of war were once more gathering. Notices of meetings and the occasional exercises relating to civilian Air Raid Precautions appeared outside places where people gathered. In October 1935 I had notification of a civil defence black out exercise in Plymouth. Since our firm had been so heavily involved in the production of black out equipment I was interested to see the result. and hired a car from Cranch's garage for the night of the exercise.

I set off just after midnight, taking with me a rug, a thermos flask of coffee, and a sandwich. It was a very dark night with occasional flurries of rain. The countryside was quiet and deserted as I drove through the small villages. Just outside Modbury I came across a lone cow standing in the road, having obviously escaped from a nearby field. I slowed to a halt and it looked at me balefully for a moment, but I saw a lantern light approaching and guessed that its owner had been called. Unlike sheep which ran everywhere when startled by a vehicle, the cow seemed to be quite content to wait to be recaptured.

I came into the city in pitch blackness. Without street lights it was difficult getting about, and I drove very slowly towards the centre, pulling off into a side road as soon as I could, for it was impossible to see another vehicle approaching.

I parked and switched off the engine. My eyes had become accustomed to the darkness by now and I could make out the occasional patch of white paint work on the houses. Without light to distract me my hearing seemed more acute. I was aware of the quiet hum of machinery from somewhere nearby and thought there must be a bakery or some factory of that kind in production, but there was nothing to show where the premises were.

I heard footsteps approaching the car and sensed rather than saw a man walk past. I guessed he was one of the wardens responsible for making sure that the public heeded the black out, for there was no-one else around.

I waited for what seemed like hours. There was not enough light to read my watch. I was growing chilly and pulled the rug over my knees. I reached for the thermos and with difficulty in the dark poured myself a cup of coffee, cupping my hands around it for warmth. There was no sound. The darkness blanketed the city, muffling all sounds of life. I ate my sandwich. All of a sudden I heard the rumble of aeroplanes above. I wound down the window and listened. As they came overhead the drone of their engines filled the sky. It was an eerie, uncomfortable sound in the black night. The planes circled over again and again for perhaps an hour. Then the noise of the engines faded. There was silence for a while until the wail of a siren coming from the direction of the dockyard sounded an "all clear".

I started the car up. I was cold and tired and I looked forward to getting home to bed. A few lights had come on again, and the street lights were once more illuminating the road. One or two houses had their lights on... All in all the exercise was unsettling, and I was glad to get back to Salcombe and see the lights shining on the water in the harbour and the riding lights on the boats. I had told Elsie not to wait up and I let myself into the house quietly. I tiptoed into the bedroom and saw that she was sound asleep. But now I was home I could not settle. As dawn broke I went outside with my pipe and leant on the wall below the house looking down at the sea. I just needed to feel the normality of everyday life, to forget for a moment the possibility that the friendly planes that had circled Plymouth that night, might one day be replaced by enemy ones.

According to one official I spoke to later, it seemed as if the results of the exercise had passed muster. I think it reinforced the idea that it was possible to black out an entire city for protection. The bombing in Spain had shown that any future war would involve aircraft and bombs and almost certainly gas such as had been used in Spain. It was an uncomfortable time, not helped by the further issue of gas masks which every household now owned.

This lingering sense of unease continued into 1936, which was marked by an astounding series of events.

The country was riding high after the pageantry that had accompanied the Silver Jubilee celebrations of King George V and Queen Mary. Like so many tens of thousands of others around the country we had listened to King George's Christmas broadcast to the nation and around the world, but by January 20th, he was dead. George had been a stuffy king, I think not much loved, but certainly respected at least for his position if nothing else. He had, as people said, "always done the right thing" and for that had been honoured.

Elsie and I saw his funeral on Pathe News at the cinema. 124 naval ratings pulled the gun carriage conveying the body of the sailor king on his journey to Windsor where he was to be laid to rest amongst the tombs of his ancestors. The new king, Edward VIII, slender, fair haired and still almost boyish-looking walked immediately behind the carriage with his brothers, the Dukes of York, Gloucester and Kent. Queen Mary, heavily veiled, followed in a carriage. As kings, princes and leading politicians walked in the cortege the camera lingered on the grieving face of the new king. No-one then could know what trouble this man was to bring upon his nation.

Flags were at half mast, and yet again I heard Chopin's Funeral March, this time played on the organ in the Holy Trinity church in Salcombe. There was sadness it is true, but not the sense of desolation that we had felt on the death of Queen Victoria. I tried to explain to my sons how it had been in those days, but I felt already that it was part of another world. My consolation was that both boys voluntarily joined the many citizens in Salcombe in wearing black armbands out of respect.

We heard Edward VIII's first broadcast in March. We thought his voice lacked the solid timbre of his father's, but his address was masterly, going straight to the heart of every Englishman. We could only pray that with the news that the Nazis were marching into the Rhineland in defiance of the terms of the Treaty of Versailles, he would be equal to the task that lay ahead of him.

Elsie's symptoms seemed to improve and we enjoyed a good Christmas. She went to the doctor and he told her that she was just a little run down, and assured her that there was nothing to worry about.

In March 1936 I secured a job worth almost £5,500 at "Ringrove". I would have to travel there each day, and I decided on the strength of this that I would finally buy a car. I chose a 12.6 Austin which cost me £50. New legislation had now brought in compulsory testing for all new drivers within the new Road Traffic Act in 1934, though existing drivers were exempt. Since Elsie had also been a driver, we both applied for and received licenses.

After a few months this car caught fire as I was driving up Fore Street in Kingsbridge. To replace it I bought a Standard 16, which cost £90, though I got a £30 allowance against what was left of my old car

In April 1936 there was a shipwreck near Salcombe which attracted considerable attention both locally and from farther afield. The wreck was that of a majestic Finnish barque, the "Herzogin Cecile" which had been the winner of the Windjammer Grain Race from Australia.

She had beached originally on rocks between Screw Hill and Hope Cove, a week after putting into Falmouth and 80 days after she had left Port Lincoln, Australia, as the race winner. Her skipper was a Captain Erikson, and he was on the ship with his new bride, Miss Pamela Bourne, an authoress, and the daughter of the late Sir Ronald Bourne. A female friend of Mrs Erikson's had joined them in Falmouth and was also amongst the party.

We had heard the lifeboat alarm swiftly followed by the sound of heavy footsteps running down the hill outside the house. Looking out I saw a couple of the crew struggling into their jackets as they ran. Almost immediately I heard more men following, and I guessed by the number of people I heard passing "The Tower" in the next few moments that there would be plenty of willing hands to help launch the boat.

Elsie was awake by this time and I made a cup of tea for us and we sat talking on the bedroom window seat, as the lifeboat crew rowed out to sea. Thick fog rolled around the estuary, tainted pink by the fading of distress flares and rockets drifting round from the direction of Hope Cove. It was just after 3 a.m. There was nothing we could do, and eventually we went back to bed. I fell into an uneasy sleep. Knowing what the shipwrecked crew would be going through from my own experience, I could only hope that they would be safe.

With the shipwreck on our minds we were both awake at daybreak. It was still foggy I noticed straight away. It was a Saturday and most of the men would be in the workshop all morning which meant that I could be a little more flexible than normal. I suggested to Elsie that we might drive over to see the shipwreck after I had gone down to the workshop and dropped in at the site we were currently working on near Bar Lodge.

I heard more news of the stricken ship when I arrived at the workshop. "She's a four masted barque" one of the men related to the lifeboat coxswain said. I asked her name but he didn't know. "The fog was too thick to see..." he said. "She hit the Ham Stone and she's down at the bows... The lifeboat is there and is standing by. Tugs are on their way..."

"I 'eard that the Hope Cove life-saving apparatus is ready but 'er hasn't been fired yet." Ern added.

It was not long before we knew the name of the ship. "She's called the "Herzogin Cecile". She's big – the largest on Lloyd's List" Frank told me having met up with one of the reserve volunteer crew back from the site when he went down into the town.

She was indeed a big ship we soon found out, of steel construction with a total length of 334 feet and a beam of 46 feet. Her main mast was almost 200 feet high and she had a total canvas spread of 56,000 square feet. She was the winner of eight grain races. On her last trip she had crossed the line in 53 days. Days later I heard that the "Herzogin Cecile" had survived a hurricane as well as a severe snow storm off the Lizard the previous year. She had had to heave to and try and ride out the storm which had lasted 30 hours. It had left her with 18 sails torn to shreds or blown away and two injured crew members.

I went home just after ten to collect some papers. The fog was getting thicker. I was in the sitting room talking to Elsie and our new bookkeeper, when I saw the lifeboat coming in over the Bar. We all went to the window to watch as the little boat battled its way gallantly into the harbour. She was very low in the water and I made out the heads of a great many people, so that it was a wonder that the open boat was not swamped. It was not until an hour or so later that I heard it confirmed that the Salcombe lifeboat had taken off 23 members of the barque's crew and the one woman passenger. The boat had been out on rescue for six hours.

The lifeboat crew must have been exhausted but immediately they had their passengers on dry land they set out again. This time their focus was the captain, his wife and seven of his senior crew who had remained on board, but they returned with only a small proportion of the remaining shipwrecked mariners. "Capt Erikson would not leave his vessel and Mrs Erikson would not leave his side", the young woman passenger who was a friend of the bride told her rescuers. She praised her friend, saying that she had been calmness personified during the disaster, going below to pack a suitcase even as water poured into the breached ship. She was grateful to the lifeboat crew she told them, and she hoped that all would be rescued, even the two ship's cats.

With the crew safe, news spread quickly. We heard from the coxswain's wife that the rescue was an extremely difficult one. "She's on the rocks off Soar Mill Cove," she said. "The seas are very high out there." She added that according to her husband, the fog was still very dense with visibility of only a few yards.

The lifeboat was expected back again in about an hour and a half. Elsie and I sent a note to the "Salcombe Hotel" to congratulate the rescued on their survival. We asked if there was anything we could do, but it seemed things were in hand. Thanks to the example of the captain and his wife, such calm had reigned on board that most of the rescued had even been able to pack a change of clothes.

I got back to the house in good time and Elsie and I set off around the coast to see the wreck.

The road was heavily congested. Crowds had gathered on the hills above the "Herzogin Cecile". Cars had parked haphazardly everywhere, and crowds packed the cliff tops. The fog was thick but a slight breeze was blowing from the sea. At first we could see nothing, but then we glimpsed the shadowy outline of the four masts and we saw the ship with our lifeboat circling her, the crew straining over their oars in the choppy sea. The blanket of fog rolled back briefly, and a muted groan of dismay rose from the crowd at the dreadful sight of that beautiful ship stuck fast on the rocks below us. With her bows pointing out to sea, her sails tightly furled on her yards, and her white painted hull she looked like a ghost ship. In a later break in the fog I made out her name plate with "Herzogin Cecilie" in curling gold letters. I wished the boys were here to see this. It was a piece of history. But it was undeniably sad and one felt somehow an intruder as if the ship were a dying being that we were callously watching for our entertainment. Elsie had tears in her eyes as she looked. There was a rumour in the crowd that the breeches buoy had been engaged though no-one knew how many if any had been rescued that way. Someone said he had heard that she was carrying a full load of grain. A policeman said that he had heard that two of the ship's holds were waterlogged and another partially so.

We drove back so that I could return to the workshop to pay the men. The crowds had grown tremendously by this time and there was a queue of cars which must have extended to more than a mile. The police were there and were coping admirably. I heard after it was all over, that it was estimated that as many as 50,000 people in total had come from all parts of our region and farther afield to see the ship.

I was met by the smell of newly planed wood when I got back to the workshop. The apprentices had done well with the rough timber I had set them to finish, and the floor was knee deep in wood shavings. The men working on the doors for the current build were wading through them as they moved around, and I told off the youngest apprentice sternly to clear the floor, conscious that the shavings were a hazard. The men asked me what we had seen that morning and I told them, and the loss of that beautiful, graceful ship the largest of its kind in the world we now knew, cast a dampener on all our spirits. Seeing that barque on the rocks had been a terrible sight. I hoped against hope that she could be rescued, but I did not think it would be possible.

Frank said that there had been talk in the town of divers being sent down, but that it seemed unlikely that they would be used owing to the position of the ship. Two French tugs, one from Brest and the other from Le Havre were rumoured to be on their way, but people were already saying that their journey was unnecessary.

Over the next days as the stricken ship still lay on the rocks, there were reports that a salvage tug had arrived, and then that the crew was taking off the ship's gear, although her position meant that it was extremely difficult to get boats alongside.

It was estimated that about 300 tons of grain still remained dry in her holds, and we heard that efforts were being made to offload that. The personal effects of the officers and men had been retrieved. The local agent of the Shipwrecked Mariners' Association having been in touch with the Finnish Consulate was now taking responsibility for the crew. The captain and his wife together with a skeleton crew were still aboard. It was rumoured that two young apprentices had returned of their own volition to help which all thought showed a good spirit. Word was that Mrs Erikson was even cooking meals in the galley for them all, but only at low tide, since at high tide the galley was flooded. Though the captain's dog was apparently still on board, it was said that the two cats had been placed on board the lifeboat. Amusingly the ship's canary had been taken off by breeches buoy.

We heard that the captain strongly believed that his ship could be rescued, and that he had made several trips on shore to make telephone calls to talk over this possibility. He had apparently been in touch with the ship's owner in Finland, but word had it that the owner had told him bluntly that he could not afford to repair and re-float the ship.

There were rumours that private money might be forthcoming to rescue the vessel, but negotiations apparently came to nothing, despite continuing desperate efforts by the captain. Captain Erikson's firm belief was that with the grain unloaded, excess furniture and fittings removed, and the ship patched up, it would be possible to float the "Herzogin Cecile" off the rocks with the tide. Opinion was divided in Salcombe. It was said around town that the ship might last all summer on the rocks in normal weather, but the first storm would most likely finish her off.

In the meantime it was estimated that more than 400 tons of grain had already been unloaded by a lighter sent from Southampton. It was taken to Plymouth where it was sold. Mr Vivian, the local Lloyds Agent said that if the fine weather held, more grain might be salvable than had previously been thought possible.

More grain was taken off, and there was suddenly talk of London buyers who had shown interest in saving the ship as a training vessel. Full of hope, Captain Erikson travelled to London for meetings with them.

The wind got up and the wreck was buffeted by strong waves. Word in Salcombe was that salvage negotiations had broken down. Suddenly all the optimism ebbed away. It now seemed unlikely that anything would happen in time to save the ship. It looked as if the "Herzogin Cecile" would meet the same fate as the "Hallow'een" the sister ship of the "Cutty Sark" which had been wrecked in the same place fifty years before.

Then came the news that divers sent down to the hull had said that the "Herzogin Cecile" was not as seriously damaged as had been thought. The talk around town was that the Admiralty had offered to pay the cost of salvage and run the ship for ten years so long as Capt Erikson would remain as captain. Buoyed up by this optimistic news, the ship was dragged towards Salcombe and beached at Starehole Bottom where it was thought it would be more sheltered from the prevailing winds. Capt. and Mrs Erikson and members of the crew attended a fund raising dance at Cliff House where film of the wreck was shown. It was said that the couple were very gratified by the hospitality Salcombe had shown them, and newspapers took pictures of Mrs Erikson on the balcony of the hotel, and did an interview with the composed heroine of the sea.

Grain taken from the "Herzogin Cecile"'s hold by the "Rosslyn" which had been employed as a salvage ship was transhipped to a Dutch motor vessel, the "Express" which was moored in Salcombe. It was said that when the "Express" had finished loading it would pick up the remaining cargo

.

and take it on to Rotterdam. The "Thea" at that time lying in Salcombe would continue with the work.

Another Dutch vessel, the "Delta" was now being employed. To guard against asphyxiation due to the waterlogged, rotting grain in the holds workmen were wearing breathing apparatus, but they had had to be stood off by two days of bad weather which prevented the boats from coming alongside. The amount of grain remaining in the hold that was considered salvable had been revised upwards to 1,000 to 1,500 tons. The ship was now secure in Starehole Bay. Several Cambridge undergraduates arrived in the town, keen to help, and they spent their holidays helping local men unload grain from the ship.

The wreck had touched the public imagination and boats went out packed with visitors to view her. She was a tragic sight by now. Crowds still came from far afield to park up and look down at her last struggles with the sea. Local farmers began charging admission to the fields and set up collection boxes to raise funds that were to go towards the ship's rescue. Lloyds Bank in Salcombe was holding a growing sum of money which it was rumoured might soon be receiving a £1,500 boost, though others said that it seemed now that any possible private investors had pulled out. Determined to keep things moving, Capt. Erikson promised that he would take between six and ten British apprentices every year on the ship free of all payment until the whole of the money raised by the appeal had been repaid. But to all those who heard this last desperate statement came the same thought: it was all over. The captain was going to lose his ship.

As if in response to this negative emotion the weather turned. The ship was heavily buffeted by a strong southerly wind and accompanying heavy swell over a period of several days. The damage this caused was obvious. Looking down at the "Herzogin Cecile" it could be seen that her deck had risen up alarmingly amidships, and fore and aft she had sunk seven or eight feet into the sand. Reports said that it seemed likely that her keel was badly cracked and that the ship's back was broken. It was also evident that the steel plating of her hull was breaking up under the terrific strain. Studying her from the cliffs one day during a particularly heavy pounding by crashing waves, I saw several rivets flying from her hull.

We heard that the Dutch vessels, "Duurwold" and "Prima" which had been unloading grain had left for their home ports. Bad news came that the ship's pumps were now proving quite ineffective against the incoming sea which had filled the holds, further swamping the remaining grain. The Cambridge undergraduates who had done sterling work, left. It appeared now that after all the hopes and untiring work, this once magnificent ship was to be surrendered to the sea.

Still Captain Erikson refused to admit defeat. Then we heard the shocking news that he had collapsed. He had been helping to unload grain in the holds but had refused to wear a mask, and had been overcome by gas. We learned that he had soon recovered on being brought into the fresh air, but many felt that his symptoms were brought on as much by despair as by the grain fumes.

Then a gale burst over the ship. Her hull, which had overcome so many storms on its voyages to the Antipodes, and which had been so damaged when she went on the rocks, could take no more. It was all over now. The barque would never sail again. We heard that motor vessels from Finland were on their way to begin dismantling the remaining valuable accessories such as the heating and lighting plant, the capstans and winches, all of which we guessed would be re-used by the ship's owner, a Mr Gustav Erikson, in other vessels which he operated.

I collected the boys from the station and in the car on the way home, their chatter was of only two subjects: the tumultuous reception given to the arrival of the "Queen Mary" on her maiden voyage from Southampton to New York in a record-breaking Atlantic crossing which had succeeded in winning back the coveted Blue Riband for Britain, and the "Herzogin Cecile", which I had been keeping them abreast of in my Sunday letters, and which they were both desperate to see.

Though Peter was all for going straight out to the wreck when we arrived back in Salcombe, I had to rein him in as Elsie had as usual when they returned from school, made their favourite supper for them. The next morning though, both were up early and I decided to take them straight out to see the ship before I went on site. Elsie came with us and we all stood together on the cliffs amongst a vast, silent crowd watching as the ship's masts and her figurehead which was to go back to Finland, were removed. Finally, probably inevitably, despite all efforts to save the ship, the sea had won.

The boys went back to school, and the "Herzogin Cecile" was left now to the mercy of the wreckers and souvenir hunters. Dozens of small boats went out to her, their passengers helping themselves whatever they could lay their hands on. Spars, blocks, pieces of taffrail, lanterns, riding lights, rope, anything that could be removed, was taken. One of her big lanterns was taken by someone in Robinson's Row and it was eventually hung up over their front door where it still is today. By this time Robinson's Row was a slum. From time to time the disgrace of this area was reported in the newspapers. It had been agreed that something should be done to clean up the street, but no ideas were forthcoming.

At the end of July civil war broke out in Spain and the army rose against the Republican government. Hundreds of volunteers left Madrid to fight the rebels under the command of the Fascist General Franco, and German planes bombed the Basque city of Guernica. The loss of innocent lives was horrifying. Annie Lucy took it particularly hard because she had relatives who were involved. She told me in the days following that two of her former husband's grandsons currently living in London, were both talking of going to Spain to fight. Their mothers were desperate, but the boys would not listen to reason. I know Annie Lucy tried her best to help but the boys raced to join the International Brigade that was gathering volunteer fighters. What made it so much worse was that, as had happened in so many other Spanish families, one boy had chosen to support General Franco, while the other was for the Republicans. The gruesome pictures coming out of Spain at this time showed young men and women of the International Brigade being butchered like animals. I know that Jaime Garcia Fernandez was killed at this time, but the other boy, Jose-Maria Fernandez simply disappeared.

In October there was news of jobless men walking from Jarrow to protest about the closure of the shipyards and steel works. We in Salcombe knew how they felt. But they were from the industrial north which had taken over the mantle of shipbuilding from towns such as Salcombe, so the sympathy was mixed. But even so the thought of so many men out of work was an uncomfortable one.

Almost like a harbinger of things to come, the Crystal Palace went up in flames that November. It had been built for the Great Exhibition of 1851 and it was a monument to the Victorian age and to Victoria the Empire builder. I had visited it briefly when I had gone to London with the Volunteers so many years before. It seemed impossible to believe that the glittering, light filled palace I had seen had been reduced to the charred heaps of molten glass and twisted metal pictured in the newspapers. The only good news was that no-one had been killed, and reports said that even the thousands of birds inside the building had managed to escape as the glass in the windows shattered. Talking about it with Elsie, I discovered that Edmund had taken her and her step sisters there several times when she was very young, but she remembered little about it except for the orchestras that had played to accompany the visitors.

But in December 1936 news of the gathering European crisis was temporarily forgotten in the drama that was being played out in the British royal family, as rumours of a romance between King Edward VIII and Mrs Wallis Simpson a still married, divorced American, hit the newsstands.

I had taken the boys to the new cinema in Newton Abbot to see Chaplin's "Modern Times" as their half term treat, and we had all found it amusing. I discovered that a Marx Brothers film, "A Night at the Opera" was being shown and I took Elsie to see it, thinking that it would make a jolly counterpoint to all the gloom. However the Pathe News showed pictures of a grim faced Prime Minister on his way to Buckingham Palace to discuss the situation with the King. There was news that a weekend Cabinet meeting was now being hastily convened

There was a buzz of talk in the cinema as people turned to look at one another. This was unprecedented: something was definitely going on.

We did not have long to wait to learn what it was. We had warning to turn on the wireless, and at 10 p.m on December 11th, we heard the broadcast that announced our King's decision to abdicate. Broken with sorrow, his voice was barely recognisable, as he explained that he believed that it would be impossible for him to rule without "the support of the woman I love" and that therefore he had made the decision to give up the throne of England for a woman who it had been decided, could never be his wife.

Elsie's eyes were full of tears. It was such tremendous news that neither of us knew quite what to do or to feel. I think in the end Elsie's reaction was typical of most women's. They wept a little and then I think they sympathised. I think perhaps most men felt as I did, that however loved this man had been as Prince of Wales, he had not in the end done his duty.

We learned later that Mrs Wallis Simpson had left the country for France, and less than four hours later the King had followed her, sailing out on the Admiralty Yacht "Enchantress". As most people wryly agreed, it was a very aptly named boat to carry the two who it was said would hereafter be known as the Duke and Duchess of Windsor.

The King's departure in December 1936 after only eleven months on the throne left his brother Albert to succeed him.

CHAPTER 11

Albert, whom it was announced would be taking the title of George VI, was not a natural for a king, as he had a stammer that made public speaking an ordeal for him and for those listening. However as the country learned more about him in the weeks that followed, the general verdict became that he was probably a better man than his brother. His queen, the former Lady Elizabeth Bowes-Lyon was a woman who was generally liked, and their two little girls, Elizabeth and her sister Margaret Rose brought a cheerful family image to the royals. There was also a sense that George VI had stepped into the breach after his brother had behaved so badly, which meant that public feeling was largely for him.

There seemed to be a lot of so-called cultural visits by Germans about this time. I wondered subsequently how many of these were aimed at discovering as much as they could about our armaments and the country's readiness for war.

One of my joiners had been to a football match at Plainmoor Football ground in Torquay to watch a game between Torquay United and a German team. He told us that before the kick-off the German team had all lined up and given the Nazi salute, and that in the evenings the players had paraded through Fleet Street in the centre of the town, chanting "Heil Hitler" and again giving the Nazi salute.

In April 1937 it was announced in the newspaper that the German Ambassador, Herr von Ribbentrop was arriving in Torquay by train to inspect the crew of a German naval training ship that was paying a courtesy visit to the town.

An apprentice living near Ashburton had seen him arrive at the "Manor House Hotel" in Moretonhampstead. He said that the Ambassador had been driven in a huge black bullet proof Mercedes Benz saloon car which was so large that it would not fit into the hotel's garage and had to be parked at a larger garage nearby. He told us that the car had been driven by a tall, uniformed German chauffeur wearing a black jacket with silver swastika buttons, and that the sight of this powerful car and its smart driver impressed everyone who saw it.

The Coronation on 12th May 1937 was recorded on film, and Elsie and I went to the cinema in Salcombe to see it. We had to wait several days after the service itself to view it, though I read in the "Western Morning News" that the town of Teignmouth had scored a coup, with an aircraft landing at the aerodrome at Haldon with a film of the event for screening at the Riviera Cinema in the town on the actual day of the event.

Once more Salcombe's streets were hung with red, white and blue bunting in honour of a coronation and we had celebrations and a band with dancing afterwards. The boys loved all the fun, especially as they had a day's holiday in honour of the occasion. Both of them dressed in fancy dress to join in the party. Tables were set out in the street, and we brought out our own chairs from "The Tower" to help seat everyone. There was a gala atmosphere with entertainments, culminating in fireworks that went on right into the night.

Ships dressed overall in Salcombe Harbour

Over the years things had become really cramped at our workshops on the Kings Arms Quay. We were very busy and I knew we ought to employ more joiners. We needed bigger premises, but I was determined that any new workshop should have the same advantages as our existing one with access to the sea so that timber could be unloaded directly to our store. I had been keeping an eye out for such premises for some time now but nothing suitable had come up.

Then I heard of two cottages and a near derelict fisherman's store in Thorning Street off Island Street that were to be sold.

I spoke to the agent and went straight down to have a look, deciding there and then that the buildings would fit the bill well. The store, which was a ramshackle wooden construction built mostly of odds and ends of shiplap boarding, abutted the small quay which had reasonable water access. The cottages adjoining it were also in a very poor state of repair. It was all only fit to be pulled down, and was therefore ideal for my purpose since I had determined to utilise the space to create a two storey building with big workshops.

I took Elsie to see the buildings, and she agreed that they would be perfect. I spoke to the bank and secured an agreement in principal that they would lend me the money, and then went back to the agent to settle a price subject to the council's agreement to my redevelopment plans. Then I walked round to see Jim Cranch, catching him at his home on Victoria Quay and told him what I proposed, saying that I would put the buildings in my name, but agreeing that I would pay the firm's cost price for both the mens' time and the building materials to develop the site.

That evening after work I went back to Thorning Street and sat on the quay with my notepad. I lit my pipe and drew on it looking up towards Batson and into the quiet hills above. These were the days long before the Council had begun extending the road to Batson, creating the new car and boat park that local people still know as "the Dump", since the town's rubbish was used to infill it. The water was full and deep in the channel then. Big boats still moved up and down to Shadycombe at high tide. I bent my head over my notepad and began working on plans to submit to the council. There was a quiet excitement growing in me. I knew that in these old buildings I had found the premises that would mean I could expand the business.

Later this year the British Home Fleet visited Torbay, followed by the American warships "Arkansas", "Wyoming" and "USS New York", and I took the boys to see these huge ships. I think we all felt pleased that the British and Americans were putting on such a show. It was only sabre rattling, but it did bring home the fact that one day soon we would probably be at war. Like so many other fathers with sons I dreaded what might happen, but Hitler with his seemingly relentless drive to secure more territory for the German people, his rallies and floodlit demonstrations appeared unstoppable. His recent appearances with the Fascist Italian dictator, Benito Mussolini in a joint show of strength were even more worrying. The display of anger at the black runner Jesse Owen's win at the German hosted Olympics the previous year was now seen in its true context in the light of things we had begun hearing about his treatment of Jews, gypsies and the mentally ill. The British public had begun to be uneasy with our government's staunch policy of appeasement. Though it was tempting to do anything one could to avoid another war, there were those, particularly the ex-servicemen, who had begun to feel that maybe it was time to be firmer with Hitler. Even so I think that most Britons still did not really believe at this time that war could happen.

There was an international surplus of shipping in this year and several merchant ships appeared in the harbour. We heard that many ships were laid up in the River Dart which at least meant that their harbour dues would bring in some revenue for Dartmouth, though the situation would do little to reduce the town's dire unemployment problem, which in those days was worse even than Salcombe's. Dartmouth had public health problems which affected a small but not insignificant part of the population. The Public Health Inspectors had investigated the town. The local newspapers carried a report in which they said that in one residential area ten families shared two water taps and two outside toilets. There were areas of Salcombe that were bad in those days but I think Dartmouth was worse.

The Council agreed my plans for redevelopment of the site in Thorning Street, and I set to immediately to begin work, largely demolishing the buildings and reconstructing as soon as I could.

Demolition work and subsequent re-building through the last years had meant a growing pile of salvaged items, and I bought a site in Loring Road, and we built a pair of semi-detached houses on spec. just to use up the many second hand windows and doors which were surplus from "Woodcot", "Ringrove" and "The Anchorage". Then we built "Ferry Hill" and another house in Herbert Road.

In January 1938 there was a disastrous fire at Buckland Abbey, which despite the best efforts of three fire engines, destroyed most of the ancient building. Thanks to the valiant efforts of the fire crews many treasures including Drake's Drum as well as old deed boxes recording the existence of the Cistercian Abbey since Elizabethan times, were saved. Sadly, hundreds of treasured old books were incinerated.

The worsening situation in Europe was on everyone's mind. So many people spoke for peace, but in each mind was the thought of war. Events in Spain where the civil war was still raging, had convinced both governments and people that any future war would be fought in the air as well as on the ground. The gas attack in Spain had also left a legacy. The government announced a further issue of gas masks. It was a small step but one which again fuelled fear. People said that the British government was unprepared for war, but the newspapers ran articles saying that England had in fact been stockpiling armaments for some time, and had ordered a thousand Spitfires to be built. You could not believe half of what you heard.

In March 1938 Germany annexed Vienna. Fred was home on a brief visit and we turned on the radio to listen to the BBC broadcast. The announcer's voice was sombre: "The sound of jackboots rings through the streets of Vienna... The army of occupation is said to number 200,000... Vienna is gaily flagged, waiting for the arrival of Herr Hitler himself ... crowds greet the Nazis with revelry of swastikas and cheering... young girls throw flowers, older women weep, delirious men give the "Heil" salute..."

We looked at each other. "... The poor deluded fools..." Fred said it for both of us.

"Still Drake's drum was saved," I said, to lighten the mood.

We both laughed, thinking of the trick Aaron and Frank had played on me so many years before.

"I wonder if we will hear it soon?" Fred mused. And the pair of us fell silent.

I left Fred to talk to Elsie and went back to my drawings, but the broadcast stayed in my mind. I thought what charisma that insignificant looking man Adolf Hitler must have and realised that everyone had underestimated him. According to the news broadcast he was now absolute rule of an empire of 74 million people... I lost myself in my drawings, able as always to shut out everything except the idea I was working on. If things were going right, I could see, almost feel the building I was drawing, sense when something was not right. It had been that way with the new workshop which was now completed and into which we were transferring tools and equipment. From the first it had gone exactly as I planned it and I was very pleased with the end result. It was a very workable building.

Fred put his head around the door. We talked a little about various small matters including the new greenhouse my brother wanted constructed in the garden of the house I had built for him in Herbert Road. Like Aaron, Fred had always been keen on gardening. Mabel had named the house, taking the lead in household matters as she always did. It was called "St. David's", an unusual name that owed its provenance to the name of the lifeboat that had rescued Mabel's father from drowning many years before. Both my boys got on well with their cousin, and were often to be seen around town together on some nefarious scheme which usually included trying to pilfer wood from the workshop for some design or other. It had always been tacitly agreed that Frank and I would keep an eye out for Mabel and David, though Mabel was one of those tough, capable Plymouth wives who always took care of things herself

We said goodnight. At forty, Fred was the only one of us still in the services. His leave was about to come to an end and he was due to be posted off on another three year trip. I knew that the chances were that war would be declared within that time, but I did not know if he would still be on active service.

I realised how little we two saw of each other. We wrote regularly, but his work took him to many different ships. He had qualified as a hard hat diver, continuing the obsession he had had as a child to be under water, and he was part of a small team of men who were invaluable to the Navy. If a ship had scraped coming into port, or had trouble with engine or screws, it was divers like Fred who went down to have a look at it. I thought back to the time he had dived for a lady's purse as a little tacker, and smiled to myself.

I got up from the table and went to him, clapping him on the shoulder in what was for me an unusual display of affection. "Goodnight, Fred", I said.

"'Night, Jim," he returned. He went out into the hallway and took his cap from the hallstand. He let himself out and I heard him whistling in the street outside. I listened to the sound of his boots on the stones as he made his way back to his own house.

Salcombe Harbour from Limebury Point.

The early summer was blazing hot. I got in some fishing with Frank. The fishing was particularly good that year and the mackerel shoaled near one of our favourite fishing grounds, off Jones' Wall. One evening, we hit it just right, and we couldn't stop hauling in fish. The dinghy was full of flapping mackerel. If anyone could have seen us, two grown men knee deep in fish and clowning around as if we were boys, they would have thought we had gone mad. At one point Frank stuffed a big, still flapping mackerel down my shirt, and I retaliated by trying to push one down his trousers, all the time the pair of us laughing fit to bust, dancing around on our slippery catch trying to keep our balance in the dinghy and falling all over the place.

Frank and I began to go out in the boat together if the boys were not at home. Elsie no longer came out on the water and I missed her company. She had become unsteady on her feet, and several times during the last trips in the motor boat, had fallen. There were times when her limbs twitched and jumped and were twisted with terrible cramps, and she had now begun avoiding social occasions since these happenings came out of the blue, and she was a proud woman who did not wish to be the subject of pity. Again she made light of it, and we managed to close our eyes to the problem.

The German threat to Czechoslovakia was building. Prayers for peace were held in both the Methodist and Holy Trinity Church. Elsie wanted very much to attend, but in the last months she had become dramatically worse. It was about this time that Dr Twining, her physician, suggested that we take her to a specialist. He would not be drawn further, but I left the surgery convinced that he knew what was wrong with her.

He made an appointment with a specialist in Plymouth, and we travelled down to see him. So many trips to the city had been full of happiness for us as a family, and I know we both feared that this one was not going to turn out the same way. We were subdued as we travelled down. Half way there Elsie's legs went into acute spasm. I stopped the car and pulled over. I tried my best to help her by massaging her long slender limbs but in the end I could do nothing but wait, sitting on the running board of the car and smoking my pipe while in the passenger seat my wife tried to endure her agony silently, tears of shame running down her face. I think this was perhaps one of our lowest moments.

The consultant was straightforward. He told us that Elsie had Multiple Sclerosis and that she had probably had it for something approaching a decade.

We were both shocked, and yet somehow almost relieved to have an actual diagnosis. He gave us a moment to assimilate the news before he explained it to us. MS was a disease of the nervous systems, for which there was no cure, he told us. It cruelly struck young people, particularly women, before the age of forty.

There was so much I needed to know, so many questions whirling around in my brain, but they all boiled down to the same one: was my adored wife going to die?

It was as if he had read my mind: "Multiple Sclerosis will not kill your wife," he said firmly.

We talked for a while. Both Elsie and I were still stunned. It was just too much to take in.

The consultant was very kind. As we got up to leave, he reassured us that both he and our doctor would always be available to do what they could to help.

I had thought to take "my girl" out for tea afterwards, or give her some little treat to cheer her up. But that was when I was fairly confident that we would come away with some tablets to treat whatever was wrong with her, or that perhaps at the worst, she would be told to take bed rest. But this was something altogether different. Neither of us had the heart to do anything else but go home.

That evening we sat quietly together looking out over a moonlit sea and listening to a record playing on the gramophone I had bought only weeks before. So recently I had thought I had everything. Now it was all being taken away in the cruellest fashion. I would lose my beloved wife as surely as if she had left me for another. As the beautiful note of the Tchaikovsky Piano Concerto No. 1, which was one of our favourites, swept over us, I think it was for both of us a final acceptance of the new life that was now to become ours. I could only be grateful that both boys were away at school and they had been spared this.

As if she too was thinking the same, Elsie said, "The boys... How are we going to tell them...?

In the weeks that followed I realised that my brave girl had surrendered. It was only now that I understood how hard she had fought all this time just to appear normal, and I was humbled by her courage. She was changing all the time now. Her speech became indistinct, as if her vocal chords too were dancing to the cruel rictus that often jerked her limbs. Day by day now my adored girl was being taken from me and it was something I could not bring myself to watch. I began working longer and longer hours, finding things to do in the workshop or the store that delayed my homecoming. I had always done my drawings on the dining room table in the evenings while Elsie kept me company, playing the piano, or sitting in an easy chair by the fireplace, sewing or reading a book. Now on the excuse that I might be tiring her I began shutting the door and working alone late into the night, then tiptoeing upstairs to the bedroom we shared, hoping that she was asleep so that I would not have to see the desertion and loneliness in her dark eyes. There was absolutely nothing I could do to help her and it was just too painful to see her suffering. I could not take the pain and because I was a man and could not deal with my emotions, I locked them inside me.

I slipped away by myself to talk to her consultant privately. His words dispelled any lingering hope I might have had. My wife was still a relatively young woman, he said, and she would probably live for many years yet. The quality of life that her illness would leave her with was another thing. I must be prepared for her becoming an invalid, ultimately unable to do anything for herself. There was nothing more he could offer. No words of comfort. There were none to be had. One thing I knew that I would never do, and that was obey her anguished cry on the day we had come back from the consultant: "Leave me, Jim. Just walk away. I don't want you to see this".

The boys came back from school on holiday. We had shielded them from the worst of Elsie's illness, but they already knew that she was very sick. They were concerned and protective as I had known they would be, but Peter particularly adored his mother, and it was hard for him. I tried to encourage them to go out as much as possible, and they spent a lot of that holiday messing about in boats, fishing, swimming and being with their wide circle of friends locally. Both of them had adopted the fashionable Oxford bags in those days, and considered themselves the bees knees as they flapped down Fore Street. They were both tall, good looking young men, but they were still so young, so untried by life.

A small number of Elsie's closest friends were now told of her condition and they rallied to help her. They organised get-togethers, lunches, and charity dos at "The Tower", which quickly became a hive of activity.

Though it was not a subject that Elsie took to easily, she had begun by now to realise that she needed a woman to help her dress and generally to aid her with everyday activities. Both my mother and mother in law had been looking after her, but I readily concurred with Elsie that besides the fact that both were getting older, it was not right for them to be tied to such a role, even though both protested that they were happy to do it. I think both Elsie and I felt that she could maintain her dignity easier with a paid helper.

Finding a nurse was yet another big step, but Annie Lucy had already considered this and she recommended the daughter of some friends from London who had done some nursing training and was now looking for work.

Betty Thompson arrived a few days later. She was a big, solid girl with a good sense of humour and a strong practical streak – exactly what we needed at this time of transition. Although they were very different characters, she got on with Kathleen Crispin who was our cook, cleaner and general help, and the house often rang with their irreverent laughter which did us all good.

Elsie had been retiring for a sleep in the afternoon, climbing up to our bedroom on the top floor. It was Betty who realised that this climb was becoming harder and harder for her patient, and she suggested to me that I made a small bed sitting room on the ground floor where my wife could withdraw and rest during the day if she needed to.

I broached the subject with Elsie and found to my surprise that she welcomed the idea. There was a fair sized room on the seaward side of the dining room which we had sometimes used as a little sitting room as it had magnificent views through a large window across the harbour and out to sea.

With Elsie supervising and two apprentices doing the work we shifted out furniture and brought in a velvet covered chaise which Annie Lucy had given us. The chaise was a bed in all but name as it was long and well upholstered. If Elsie was in pain it would be possible for her to rest there without having to worry about getting up to our bedroom. We pretended that it was only a temporary measure but I think we both acknowledged that we had crossed another Rubicon. To make the change less painful, I determined to make what was already becoming known as her room, into a place where she was comfortable and could receive friends. As a surprise I made her a little desk where she could write and placed that near the window so that she overlooked the sea as she was writing.

Her creative abilities were undimmed and she wrote many poems and had quite a few published in those days. She regularly received "The Poetry Review" and several other similar publications and kept abreast of new poets. She kept up a lively correspondence with several writers, some of whom her father had published, and this too kept her spirits up. Her parents when in London had been on the fringes of the Bloomsbury Group of writers and artists, and she kept in contact with people like Virginia Woolf and Dame Edith Sitwell who sometimes visited her. I admit I found some of them rather strange people, though I later came to know them quite well. Dame Edith Sitwell who visited several times – once bringing along her brother Osbert draped in a long, dark woollen cloak despite the day being warm – was perhaps the most unusual of them all with her sharp, beak-like face, bird bright eyes, turban, dark, exotic clothes and enormous rings. I found her far from easy to speak to, but I knew that her presence stimulated Elsie.

May Schofield, who was perhaps Elsie's best friend, visited whenever she could. She was married to a Naval man, Gray, who was some years older than her. He was a veteran of the Far East runs like Fred. Lady Clementine Waring C.B.E, who now lived at "The Moult" had also become a close friend and she too visited whenever she could, and her visits and her breezy, confident manner, cheered Elsie. Lady "Clem" as we all came to know her was an interesting and very clever woman and I know the two of them had a special relationship. Curiously, we discovered that Lady "Clem" was the sister in law of Dame Edith Sitwell. Seeing how these visits cheered Elsie, I arranged for as many people as possible to keep her company when I was out. We had an open house and the front door was kept ajar so that a friend could just pop in without the formality of having to summon Kathleen to open the door and announce her. I had got into the habit of having my lunch back at the house and eating with Elsie either in her own room if she was bad, or occasionally if she was in one of her increasingly rare remissions, in the dining room. When she ate at the dining table, she insisted that Kathleen laid the table exquisitely, with flowers and starched white napkins, something which the rather slapdash girl did to the best of her ability though she grumbled at the fuss.

That summer of 1938 was glorious. The house was perfumed by Aaron's flowers and the sea sparkled. Holiday makers arrived and took their places on the beaches to make the most of the sun. Edgar Cove's boat rentals on Council Quay was very busy. Rented sailing boats criss-crossed the Estuary and the Regatta that year had some very exiting racing. It was as if the whole country had resolutely turned its back on thoughts of war, and was making the most of the sunshine.

Sunny Cove, Salcombe, with Edgar Cove's bathing huts on beach. 1938

The hot weather continued. Kathleen had the kitchen door open from morning till dusk and still complained of the heat from the Rayburn. At night we slept with the bedroom window wide open to catch any zephyr of wind that blew up the Estuary and faint and far away came the cooling, seductive sound of the waves breaking on the Bar. The household routine went on as normal. Hope sprang eternal. Surely, people said, having seen worldwide slaughter once it was not possible than anyone would wish to revisit that horror. But there was also a groundswell of feeling that we were doing everything we possibly could to prevent war, but it was not enough. We were like blind men marching slowly, in step, towards an abyss.

Meanwhile I did everything I could to try and find a cure for my wife. I could not accept that we had to just write off her life like this. I was a man on a mission. I sought names from Dr Twining and her consultant and I wrote to everyone. When that failed to yield results I drove Elsie to Bristol and later to London to visit various alternative therapy clinics. She was examined and prescribed powders and herbs as well as other treatments, but ultimately although these remedies sometimes brought a little relief, they did nothing. A homeopathic doctor in London whom we visited did his best to alleviate her cramps and other distressing complaints with homeopathic medicine. For a while these had limited success, and so for about three years, he sent various boxes of pills weekly. In those days before the National Health Service we had to pay for all consultations and medicines, but I was prepared to pay anything in the hope that we might hit on something which would help her.

It was about this time that I bought a shed in Coronation Road which I justified by telling myself that I needed somewhere to store old pieces of equipment that I had hoarded against the day that I might need to use them for spare parts. I put an old armchair in there. Knowing that Elsie was well looked after and had company, I began to spend time there, ostensibly making an inventory of stock, but in reality often sitting alone after work in the near darkness of the gathering night, smoking my pipe and thinking ... anything rather than go home.

Her illness estranged me from my wife. Annie Lucy, who doted on her daughter visited at least once a day. Ellen visited often. Edmund came too, though less often. He, like me, found Elsie's illness hard to bear. He was a changed, older man since the Stock Market Crash. He had lost money, and some of his jauntiness had gone. For the first time it was possible to see him as an old man. It was Annie Lucy, with her practical, down-to-earth good sense who realised what was going on and took steps to deal with it. My mother in law was wise enough to understand that I was in effect grieving for my wife as if she were dead. She knew too that I despised myself for what I thought of as my cowardice in not being with Elsie, but it was a fact that the sickroom scared me. It was Annie Lucy, realising that I needed some practical problem to get my teeth into, who supplied the answer: I was to be kept busy constructing a luxurious suite of rooms for my wife.

The only bathroom was upstairs, and so the first task I was set was to convert the tiny room next door to Elsie's room, which had served as little more than an oversized hall cupboard, into another bathroom. It was a challenge but I managed it, adding a big window to give the room more light. I was pleased with myself when I had finished, and keen to turn my hand to re-designing the room that the two girls called, "Madam's Parlour".

I built a wall of bookshelves and brought in Elsie's books and arranged them as she wanted. Elsie and Annie Lucy chose a shade of moss green which reminded me of the colour of the dress my wife had been wearing when we met, and we had the room redecorated. Elsie added soft silk and velvet cushions in deep reds and mauves, and a spread of rich green and reds for her chaise. Kathleen and Betty raided the house and brought in lamps and a small occasional table which was big enough for the two of us to eat off if we wanted. Edmund donated a very comfortable old leather armchair. Entering into the spirit of things Elsie's friends added other small items such as paintings and a gilt framed mirror which I hung opposite the window to reflect the sea far below. The final result was a fantasy scene from the Arabian Nights. In this boudoir my darling wife looked like a beautiful, broken doll.

Annie Lucy continued her practical support. I blessed her for that just as much as for the daily, often humorous little notes she wrote that brought Elsie comfort. I saw in Annie Lucy that same indomitable love for her child that I knew in Ellen, and I was humbled by the power of it.

My mother too, was a tower of strength at this time, making sure that Elsie had everything she needed and doing little bits of shopping for her, sometimes just sitting with her and talking, telling her tales of when we boys were small, which Elsie loved to hear. Aaron, dear Aaron came humbly to her door, overawed by the colours and richness of the decorations, terrified of her illness, and it was Elsie who called him to her, knowing that Aaron himself was suffering because he could not bear to see her in pain. He expressed his love in the only way he knew how, through his garden. He took it upon himself to make sure her room was always full of flowers. He brought Elsie offerings of lilies, dahlias, roses, wild flowers and the deep red and purple fuchsias that she doted on particularly. He channelled his love for his daughter in law into digging and planting for her, as if by those acts alone she could be made whole.

But the monster we were fighting was not about to give in. In another cruel twist MS, that silent, yet ever present intruder into our lives, attacked Elsie's eyes. There were days when, without warning, she would wake up without vision. She who had gloried in the sights of nature, and who loved reading, could no longer enjoy even these small gifts. This was the hardest trial of all for her to bear. The blindness came and went, but each time it happened it frightened her more. There were times now when she railed against her fate, and clung to me, weeping like a helpless child.

We were together as much as possible now. My mother in law had showed me another way to behave and I tried now to make amends for what

I still saw as my cowardice. I bought Elsie books and gramophone records and the "Devon Violets" perfume she always wore and her friends did the same. Sometimes we listened to the radio, or I read the newspaper to her. She would ask me about the job I was working on and how it was progressing. She wanted to know about any construction problems that arose and how I had dealt with them, details of materials shipped or moved through the town, and I told her everything, realising that it was important to her to try and keep abreast of things, especially now she could no longer manage the bookkeeping, which she had always done. Holding onto a semblance of what had once been our normal lives was our way of keeping things under control. It was as if we sat with Pandora's box in our living rom. We walked around it, we touched it, we even stored things on top of it, but we never opened it. The nearest we got was sometimes in the evenings when we listened to music in the twilight or when the moonlight shone on the sea. Then, sitting silently, holding each other's hand, there were times when both our hearts were full to overflowing with sorrow. I would have given anything I had to make my girl well again. It sickened me that I had worked so hard and saved and that I now had enough money to buy almost anything I wanted, but the one thing that would have made my life right again, I could not deliver. To my shame I took this sadness with me in my daily life. I could not speak of it, I shut it inside me where it festered into bitterness. I did not mean to, but I understood by the faces of those I worked with that sometimes I hurt them with my harshness. I was not the sort of man to dissemble. I was a "hard bastard" with few if any, redeeming virtues. My agony caused me to take out my pain on those around me. I could not do otherwise.

As if to emphasize the fragility of the world situation the hot weather climaxed abruptly in August in one of the worst thunderstorms I had ever seen. Thunder rumbled around the Estuary and shook buildings. Both sheet and forked lightening tore open the skies, hitting several buildings in surrounding hamlets and setting at least three houses alight. Through my binoculars I saw the corpses of several blackened and smoking cows in the fields near Snapes. After the storm came terrific rainstorms. Salcombe was awash and there was concern about the flooding that would occur at high tide especially down at Custom House Quay and Chapel End steps which flooded badly in those days. We heard that Torquay was virtually marooned by flood waters. I was told later that whole families had to be rescued by boat in Newton Abbot, and in several other towns traders had to wade through almost waist deep water to rescue their wares.

In March 1938 Hitler had annexed Austria unopposed. But the pledge that Britain and France had made then to defend Czechoslovakia against German aggression marked a new and more dangerous phase as Hitler now demanded the Sudentenland, the German speaking area of Czechoslovakia.

I think everyone realised that things had reached a turning point. There was some disagreement and even anger about the subject. Most people cared little about Czechoslovakia. Few people could even find it on a map. The attitude in the town was: What does it have to do with us? Appease the monster and he will go away. I heard many people still arguing that war was never going to happen. Then we heard that the four powers, Britain, Germany, Italy and France were to meet in Munich.

By September of that year the German threat to Czechoslovakia was building but at the last minute an agreement was reached at Munich between Mr Chamberlain, Herr Hitler, M. Deladier for France, and Benito Mussolini. The news broadcasts trumpeted it as a major coup. I went to the cinema the next night and saw the Pathe News broadcast of Prime Minister Neville Chamberlain's return from Munich. He was standing in the doorway of the aeroplane that had brought him from Germany, waving a piece of paper, a broad smile on his angular face. A cheering crowd welcomed him as he announced that the piece of paper represented an historic Anglo- German Accord that meant "peace in our time".

For a while people breathed more easily. Prague had agreed to cede Czechoslovakia's German-speaking Sudentenland to Germany. The country had simply had no choice in the matter. The politicians had sold Czechoslovakia down the river, but war had been averted – for the moment. Later film was of Mr Chamberlain repeating the gesture on the balcony of Buckingham Palace with the King and Queen in front of wildly cheering crowds. But the groups of local Salcombe people who left the cinema that night showed none of this exuberance. As I walked back through the streets to "The Tower", I passed a couple of fishermen and heard one say to the other: "Poor bugger…I think 'er really believes 'er's brought world peace."

Already by the next morning, the newspaper headlines were of his detractors, amongst them the Opposition voices, including dissident Tories, Winston Churchill, Anthony Eden and Harold Macmillan.

We all knew by now that war was inevitable, and so it was simply a matter of hanging on until it came. Nobody knew what was going to happen. I think, like so many other businesses, we decided subconsciously to try and pack as much work in as possible while the going was good, and we were very, very busy in the eight or nine years leading up to the war.

Guessing that prices would inevitably rise and materials become increasingly hard to find once war was declared, I was on the look-out for good, cheap building material. Hearing that a laundry in the Naval Dockyard in Plymouth was to be demolished, I drove down to look at it. It was September 1938, and as I drove through the city I passed part of the 6 miles long line of trenches which had been dug as an emergency air raid shelter for the civilian population. It was an uncomfortable sight, as was the First Aid post which had been established near Charles Church from which uniformed staff came and went.

I passed several lorries laden with sandbags as I neared the Docks, and saw that many municipal buildings had piles of sandbags rising around them. Fred had said that he was expecting to be called back to his Devonport base, and I was interested to see quite a number of men with kitbags on their shoulders walking towards the dock gates, and guessed they were some of the Reservists who were being called up.

I stated my business at the entrance and was directed to the old laundry building. There I was met by a dour Scotsman, who unlocked a padlocked door and showed me inside. I could see at a glance that the timber was excellent and I thought it good value at the price asked. It was always a bonus to find laundry timber as it was steamed, bleached and well-seasoned, so it worked well.

I concluded the deal, arranging for transportation the following week by naval lorry, then drove down Union Street to visit a small shop where I had often bought unusual fittings and specialist screws. I made my purchases, then, pleased with my efforts, headed for home.

On the island bounded by Cornwall, Bedford and Bank Streets was the newly enlarged Messrs. E Dingle & Co., store. The owners had recently taken over the "Underwoods" provision store only two years after having absorbed the clothiers, "W. J. Vickery & Co", and they were now one of the biggest retailers in the county. I had heard people who had shopped there say that it rivalled the great London department stores, and was a boost for the West Country.

Driving down George Street, I saw a shop with a sign saying "Air Raid Protection Depot" over the door. There were two dummies in the window dressed in green coveralls and wearing gas masks. Around them was a display of Tilley Lamps, torches and cooking stoves. As I drove on I made a mental note to check our equipment at "The Tower" and in the workshop. It occurred to me that I should make sure that Mabel was suitably prepared since it now looked as if Fred would probably spend the war in Plymouth. I thought about David, the same age as Alec and decided that it was the sort of thing that a boy of that age could be made responsible for. He was a sensible youngster, already mad to join the Navy like his father, and I guessed like my own sons, would enjoy this chance to be the man of the house.

The preparations for war continued but the workshop was still busy. There had been several articles in the newspapers lately about the need to prepare defences both in the locality and in private homes. In order to familiarise myself with the basic requirements for building air raid shelters I had applied for and received several government pamphlets with instructions as to how these should be constructed.

In addition to fear of air raids, there was great concern about possible

German gas attack. But making a gas proof room was simplicity itself, according to an article which appeared in a "Woman in the Westcountry" article in the Western Morning News, which Elsie showed me. It was only necessary to hang heavy blankets dampened with water outside the door to a room to make the conversion. This technique would prevent gas leakage, the article maintained, especially if any cracks were filled. Cracks were to be filled with wet brown paper moulded into a type of "putty" if the real thing was not available. Fireplaces were to be stuffed with paper, rags and a bag of wet sawdust, then cardboard or plywood was to be used to close the opening.

The article at least provided a solution to a mystery that had been puzzling me, because in the last few days we had been inundated with housewives asking to buy bags of sawdust from the workshop. I would cheerfully have obliged for nothing as we were generally glad to get rid of any sawdust that was left over after the fishermen had taken what they needed for packing their crab, but I discovered that the indomitable May Schofield had already arranged for several tea chests full to be collected for use in her Civil Defence classes. Since I had recently seen her bicycling around the area with a home-made hot box strapped to the rear of her bicycle to demonstrate how a meal could be prepared even while one was cycling to work, I could have believed anything of her! But it was indicative of the mood of the nation at this time that defence was a priority.

For a second year we had glorious weather. In that hot summer of 1939, it seemed that the world was on a knife edge, but the sunshine brought people out of their homes and onto the water and the beaches in apparently carefree mood.

The owners of some of the bigger houses in Salcombe began approaching me covertly to ask our firm to build air raid shelters in their grounds. Though the government had announced that it would supply basic shelters, I think a lot of people – especially those who could afford to pay for it - wanted the security of concrete shelters. The first we built was at "Whinfield", which was I think the best, but many others followed.

Miraculously Elsie went into remission at this time. She laughed and was happy and despite my misgivings, insisted on going to visit our parents' homes and even walking as far as to North Sands. We made plans for her to go out in the motor boat, and for me to drive her to Gara Rock. We both acted as if life had returned to normal. I think perhaps a little part of us did believe that.

The remission lasted perhaps six weeks, but then Elsie's condition began worsening again. Her symptoms were strange and often appeared totally disconnected. She had trouble speaking, then first one leg, then the other and then both arms lost all sensation. After our brief happiness it was hard for us to bear.

With the threat of war looming I made sure that contracts were finished and paid for. The firm was currently building two houses on spec. but though we had already laid the foundation I decided to stop work on them.

It was a time of rumours and counter rumours. Then something happened at Slapton which at the time was of little significance but which with the benefit of hindsight was memorable.

I had a small commission to build a rosewood bedroom suite for a customer, and I had to go to Totnes to collect the timber from Reeves' Wharf. The area was buzzing with gossip about a beach exercise that had supposedly taken place at Slapton a couple of days before, and on the way back curiousity made me take a detour to Slapton Village, cutting in past Stanborough Hundred and taking the winding coastal road that led past the Ley to the sea.

I had missed lunch and was hungry so I decided to have a pasty at the "Royal Sands Hotel". Some fishermen I knew were drinking there and I asked them about the story.

"Royal Sands Hotel", Slapton. c 1938

They were only too keen to talk and I learned that a major military exercise had indeed taken place on the beach involving soldiers with heavy naval support. I remembered hearing 'planes overhead myself, but I was told that at Slapton there had been an almost continual fly over and the whole village and surrounding area had been kept awake most of the night.

The rumours of the exercise had spread like wild fire, and with the arrival off shore of big ships one of which was recognized as being one of the three Bibby Troopers that had been a familiar sight at anchorage off Dartmouth, locals flocked to the high ground to watch. More ships arrived disgorging hundreds of soldiers who stormed the beach. The aircraft carrier "HMS Courageous" which it was believed had sailed from Portsmouth was recognized and Fleet Air Arm Swordfish aircraft which it was guessed were acting as bombers flew overhead, much to the astonishment of the locals who by this time included sightseers from many of the surrounding villages.

The staff at the "Royal Sands" furnished more details when I went to pay for my pasty. The soldiers had been from the 9th Infantry, the Lincolns, the King's Own Scottish Borderers and the Second Battalion of the Middlesex, one of the barmen who was ex-Army himself told me. They had landed from the warships "HMS Southampton", "HMS Sheffield", the battleship "HMS Revenge" and a flotilla of destroyers. An elderly man drinking at the end of the bar said that he had counted twelve aircraft in all. It had been a big operation.

But soon after the men had been landed on the beach, the weather which had been fine and calm during the late afternoon and early evening, suddenly turned. A gale developed and torrential rain lashed down. The watching crowd, the majority of them owing their livelihood to the sea, realized that the big ships were in danger of grounding and saw them withdraw to deeper water, leaving what was later learned were 1100 soaking wet soldiers huddled on the sand without shelter or provisions as night descended.

As the watchers returned to their homes the officers besieged the "Royal Sands Hotel" and queued to use its one telephone. Belatedly transport began arriving and eventually by the early hours of the morning the last soldier was collected from the beach and taken to Dartmouth Naval College – the only place that could be found to take in so many men - where it was said that staff worked through the night to feed them and dry their clothes.

At the time everyone had a story to tell about the event, but before long it was forgotten. It was only five years later that this abortive landing on Slapton Beach under the leadership of the then Brigadier Bernard Montgomery came to assume such import.

As much as it could, life went on as normal.

I walked with Edmund early one evening out to South Sands. We had grown into the habit of meeting now and then and walking together. Sometimes we walked without talking, at other times we engaged in lively debate about the smallest of matters. I had always enjoyed these discussions with my father in law.

At that time almost the only topic of conversation was the political situation. Whatever else people started talking about, sooner or later it evolved into talk of Herr Hitler and the Germans.

We had been speaking of the League of Nations which we both

supported whole heartedly, feeling that it alone would be a major way of resolving differences between nations.

"The trouble is that the League is impotent," Edward said glumly.

I nodded in agreement. "It would help if the Americans had joined," I said. "They are isolated outside the League".

"... And keeping Germany out... that was the start of it," Edmund mused, poking with the walking stick he had lately taken to using at a cuttlefish skeleton on South Sands beach. "That and their reparations for the war... maybe we should have scaled down what they had to repay, not rubbed their noses in it, though the Lord knows it was tempting". It was a view that had lately been aired in the press, but most people thought it smacked once more of conciliation.

The tide was low and there was a long beach of wave-rippled, shining sand. The cuttlefish must have been stranded because there were a large number of them.

"We used to collect them to send to London..." I said, staring down at one.

"What for?" Edmund asked. "What on earth could you use cuttlefish for?". He put his leonine head on one side. Though his hair was now almost pure white, it was still thick, still falling boyishly over his forehead. I saw Elsie in him, in his elegance and grace of movement, the way my wife had been and for a moment I felt again the anguish of my loss.

"You obviously have never owned a budgie", I said lightly.

"Budgie...?" he queried.

"People buy cuttlefish for budgerigars to sharpen their beaks on..." I replied. "My brothers and I used to earn money by collecting the skeletons, then passing them on to a man who took them up to London. We got well paid. We got two pence a bag for them."

Edmund smiled. "The politics of poverty," he said gently. "Everything has a value..."

"Especially if it's something a rich person won't do for himself," I chuckled.

We walked further, stopping to watch a sailing boat tacking near the Bar. It was a good day for a sail. The sailor was skilled. I didn't recognise the boat, but that happened quite often now. There were so many strangers in Salcombe.

We had reached the end of the beach and we turned and began to walk back when Edmund gasped.

Page 236: South Sands showing the Lifeboat House, and the "Bolt Head Hotel" c 1938

Looking round I saw that his face was grey and drawn suddenly, and he was clutching his chest.

"Edmund... what is it?" I caught his arm and guided him to an outcrop of rock so that he could sit down.

"My pills...in my pocket..." he gasped.

I felt in the pocket of his jacket and brought out a small silver container. I opened it and held it out to him, and he took a tablet and swallowed it.

I waited, weighing my options in case I had to get help. At least the tide was going out and he would be safe where he was for the brief time it would take me to get someone to him.

"I'm alright now," he said a few minutes later.

His colour was better. The grey had gone and his normal skin tone was returning, though he was still pale.

I said nothing, as we sat together looking out to sea.

"I've got a slight problem with my heart," he admitted after a while. "Don't tell Annie Lucy."

I stared at him. "How long has this been going on?"

"Some time..." he said. "But it's not bad. I've seen Doc Twining and he's given me these pills. I just don't want Annie Lucy to fuss...I'd be grateful if you wouldn't say anything."

Reluctantly I gave him my word.

"And don't let's talk about it," he said, getting to his feet. "...it's a beautiful day... too good to waste".

He was his old self again. We walked back up the beach and onto the road.

"It won't affect our walks, Jim", he said. "I enjoy our walks".

We went on, deliberately speaking of other things.

Private house work practically ceased at this time, as no-one wished to spend money in such an uncertain climate. Gradually I started laying off men, again targeting the single men first.

There was a feeling that one should do one's bit to help the country. I enlisted as a Special Constable, and was promoted to Sergeant a month or two afterwards. This was voluntary work, except for an allowance for patrol expenses, but it occupied a great deal of time, as I had to attend meetings in Plymouth, Exeter and Torquay on a regular basis. As a policeman there was also quite a lot of night work involved.

The German army marched into Czechoslovakia in October 1938 with a speed and organisation that betrayed lengthy planning. Hitler was acting on the terms of the Munich Treaty signed in the early hours of the preceding day. This gave Germany the Sudentenland, the largely German speaking border area of Czechoslovakis's provinces of Bohemia and Moravia.

The boys came home for the Christmas break. Peter was almost fifteen,

Alec approaching his fourteenth birthday. They were both tall like Elsie and myself. Peter had inherited Elsie's long, elegant limbs, Alec was stockier. Both were sporty boys. Peter loved music, Alec was developing into a talented artist. I waited to see what time would bring but I was already fairly sure that Alec at least would follow me into the business.

We had a good Christmas that year. The boys made a special effort to make it fun for their mother, and decorated a Christmas tree made from twigs and hung with silver paper. We had presents in her room as she lay immaculately dressed as always, but at the moment almost totally immobile, a heavy Spanish silk shawl that had belonged to Annie Lucy over her knees. I remember her smiling, her brown eyes filling with tears of joy as she watched her boys opening their presents. She adored both boys, but if truth be known Peter, the idealist who looked so like her was her favourite, just as Alec the more practical, was mine.

1939 dawned and I think many people were like us and wondered what the year would bring. May always a stalwart friend, now heavily involved in Civil Defence and voluntary agencies around the areas, came up with the idea of Elsie taking a First Aid Course. She talked it over with me first, explaining that she had persuaded the examiner to make a special case so that Elsie could qualify in her own home. She would teach the course herself, she told me.

Elsie was very keen and was a diligent student. May was so kind and structured the course so that the practical work of bandaging and instruction in artificial resuscitation could be conducted on days when Elsie was capable of doing it. The end result was that Elsie passed with flying colours. She was so proud of her achievement that she insisted I have her certificate framed and hung up on the wall of her room.

In January 1939 General Franco's troops swept into Barcelona. Thousands of civilians fled, fearing the fall of the city, but the troops on both sides fought on to the death. The collapse of the Republican forces at the end of March effectively handed power to General Franco's Nationalist Army. The 60,000 strong foreigners who had formed the International Brigade had ultimately been no match for the well-trained soldiers of the Nationalist Army whose numbers had been swelled by German and Italian troops, bombs, aeroplanes and gas attack. It was a measure of the courage and determination of the mainly young men and women of the International Brigade that Franco had taken three years to defeat them. But the casualties had been heavy. Assuming power Franco established a fascist government. One of his first acts was to order the mass execution of thousands of Republican sympathisers. No-one heard anything further of Annie-Lucy's nephew, Jose-Maria. The family could only assume that if he had survived the earlier slaughter, he had been executed in this cull.

Sergeant Jim Murch in the back garden of "The Tower". 1939

The British government war machine was gearing up. The country had been divided into areas to better handle the coming emergency. As Sir John Anderson, the Minister for Civil Defence, later to be known for the shelters that took his name, put it: "We are working on the assumption that there is a risk of war...but that does not mean that we expect war."

Spring as always in the West Country was a miracle of budding flowers and new life. Betty gathered primroses and dressed them in paper doilies as Elsie had taught her, and the bright little flowers, symbolic of new life, were dotted through the house together with the bunches of violets which Elsie adored.

I made plans to take Elsie up on the moors, but she suddenly took a turn for the worse which lasted several weeks. She recovered a little, but it was obvious that she had lost strength. Our lives were full of these small remissions which no longer seemed to result in gains, just more weakness and symptoms.

Elsie's great friend from school and commercial college, Esme Fulcher , who had been the matron of honour at our wedding, wrote to her. London was abuzz with rumours about what would happen and she was worried for her two daughters. She wondered whether we would take them in to keep them out of the city with its risk of possible bombing. We accepted of course, though privately I thought we had enough on our hands without acquiring two teenage girls. Though since they were sporty, not unattractive, girls about the same ages as our sons, I think the boys had the best deal when they came home for the Easter holiday.

I had been thinking for some time of building an air raid shelter for my family. I had already made plans for both sets of parents, but I was concerned that if Elsie was almost immobile at the time, we would not be able to move her to safety quickly enough. I pondered the problem and decided that I would convert a back store room which we had partially cut from solid rock into an air raid shelter.

I decided not to tell Elsie what I had planned so as not to worry her, but I had reckoned without my wife. Her dreadful disease had left her mind intact and one morning she broached the subject with me and came up with the same idea I had had.

The room was not large – perhaps eight feet by ten. It was underground and butted up to the road outside. With its back and side walls of solid rock, the room was always cold which was perfect as we had used it for storage but it also oozed water after rain, which was not ideal if several people were to stay in it for any period of time.

Still it was otherwise just right for my purpose. I brought in two apprentices to do the messy work of covering the rock in black bitumen to waterproof it, and then had the whole room freshly painted white. I sketched out a small raised platform extending almost five feet into the room at a height of about four feet which effectively doubled the size of the shelter giving us two seating or sleeping areas and then designed a small wooden couch with a sloping back which could be covered with bedding to make Elsie comfortable. The new air raid shelter was near the kitchen so that food and drinks could be organized if the stay was a long one. In all I was satisfied with the arrangements.

But at the moment I had more pressing matters to concern me, as heavy falls of snow in Devon had meant problems for us on the remaining work sites. Water froze in its containers and even though we built makeshift covers over brickwork, we often found that the mortar froze and areas we had thought finished had to be re-done.

The cold was so intense that moorland ponies had migrated to Cornwall, Fred, who was now in Plymouth most of the time, told us on one of his trips home to Salcombe. Seeking refuge from their frozen terrain the ponies had approached from the Roborough direction, turned left at the traffic lights, trotted along Saltash Road East and then into Bowden Park Road. Fred recounting this for Elsie told us that the ponies had finally found a piece of ground with grass on it and had made this their headquarters. When she asked concernedly if they had food, Fred laughed.

"The local children have made it their responsibility," he said. "They are taking bread and buckets of water, and feeding them turnips… I rather think the ponies are there for good!".

The snow continued. In places on the Moors it was reported that there were drifts seven feet deep and day after day the bitter east wind continued to blow.

I had a few men off sick but we managed to cover for them. Butcher Hannaford told us that Slapton Ley was completely frozen over and that people were skating on the ice. There was even a rumour that a local man had tried riding his bicycle across the Ley, but no-one seemed to know whether or not he had made it, particularly as gossip had it that he had been fuelled more by cider than common sense.

Against a background of aggressive diplomacy which had seen Germany gain effective control of Austria and Czechoslovakia, Britain and France followed a course of passive appeasement of Hitler. After the Munich Agreement in September both counties had hoped that Hitler would honour his promise to pursue his goals through diplomatic means. But when in March 1939 Hitler threatened to bomb Prague into the ground unless the Czechs allowed German occupation of the entire country, few observers were left in any doubt what Hitler's intentions were towards the rest of Europe.

In March Hitler's troops goose-stepped into Czechoslovakia. At the cinema Pathe News showed scenes of the populace hissing and booing the soldiers as they entered the country. Pictures of Czechs forced to salute Hitler with tears streaming down their faces were hard to take. The despair they felt as their country was overrun was evident. There were scenes of Jews at railway stations, trying, too late to escape the country. Britain was shocked, but neither our country nor the other signatories to the Agreement could do anything. Chamberlain protested weakly to Berlin but he refused to consider stronger action on the grounds that our country had no treaty with Czechoslovakia.

"The Tower" Salcombe, in the snows of 1939.

I think this was the beginning of a dramatic change in public opinion, certainly amongst the men I spoke to. I think Britain felt that Hitler needed to be taught a lesson. It was then we acknowledged that we had to go to war to stop the same thing happening to our country.

With Austria and Czechoslovakia in his hands, Hitler turned his attention to Poland, declaring that it was intolerable that the German Province of East Prussia on the Baltic was separated from the rest of the Reich by a corridor that gave Poland its access to the sea at Danzig.

The threat of force had made Lithuania hand back to Germany the Memel district which the Germans had been compelled to cede after the Great War. Fearing that Germany would use force to seize Danzig, the Polish government warned Hitler that any attempt on the city would mean war. Spurred by rumours of a possible German invasion of Romania, Britain and France decided at last on a unified show of strength to try and persuade Hitler to reconsider, by forming an alliance with Romania and Poland on March 31st, promising immediate military aid if Germany made any move.

I bumped into my father in law in the road between our houses and we stayed chatting and smoking, leaning on the wall and looking over the harbour, discussing the situation as so many others were doing.

" Danzig will be the flash point," he said.

I nodded. "I was reading the other day that Hitler openly stated in "Mein Kampf" that he wants the Polish Corridor".

We briefly exchanged news from our households and parted company. Me to return to work, Edmund to walk down into the town for a newspaper and a fresh crab for dinner.

CHAPTER TWELVE

On 1st September German troops swept into Poland from East Prussia in a devastating blitzkrieg.

Alerted to the broadcast the household gathered by the radio to listen to the bulletin.

"This morning the British Ambassador to Berlin handed the German government a final note stating that, unless we heard from them by 11 o'clock that they were prepared at once to withdraw their troops from Poland, a state of war would exist between us. I have to tell you now that no such undertaking has been received and that consequently this country is at war with Germany...."

Neville Chamberlain's voice was heavy, flat, the delivery very different to that of the man who had so recently confidently declared that he had won "peace with honour".

Outside the window a ketch tacked in over the bar and headed for the town. Elsie wrote a poem later that day that hypothesised that the unknown sailor stayed out forever and never learned that his country was at war.

We sat for a while together, a little group, just one of so many I guessed who were sitting as we were now around the radio, each of us trying to come to terms with the fact that our country was once again at war. Then Betty and Kathleen went back to work, leaving Elsie and me together.

"What will happen Jim?" she asked softly. I came to sit on the arm of her chair and put my arm around her. "We'll go on as best we can," I said gently. "It's all we can do". But to myself I was thinking: please God let it end before the boys have to get involved.

I was glad when I could get back to the workshop. Knots of people stood around in the street, their faces strained and worried. Even the children were subdued. Several people called out to me as I passed, and I acknowledged them but just kept on walking. There seemed little I could say. A couple of hours later when I went back through the town again on my way to another site, I paused by the war memorial. As always my eyes went to my cousin's name engraved on the stone. "At least you missed this one....." I said quietly, adding through clenched teeth: "Blast the damned warmongers, every one of them".

Later we heard King George's address to the nation, calling for us all to be calm and firm and united in this time of trial. He said his government had tried over and over again to find a peaceful way out of the differences between ourselves and those who were now our enemies, but that it had been in vain.

After the long build up most people seemed to take the situation equably. We expected something dramatic, after all we were at war. But throughout those glorious autumn months that followed, in what the newspapers soon nicknamed the "Phoney War", nothing very much happened.

My elder brother Frank stayed on at the firm for a few months after the war started. He was increasingly busy with Council work, and at this time was made Head of the Council. Fred was officially called back into the regular Navy as Chief Shipwright. He served at Devonport Dockyard through the Plymouth Blitz and for the duration of the war.

On the domestic front, our girl Kathleen Crispin, who had been with us for years, was called up for the V.R.N.S, and an older woman was sent to us, who lasted a very short time. Altogether we had eight different helps in the house during the war, two very good, but the rest indifferent at best. As the war progressed, Elsie gradually got worse, and spent all the time in bed, practically helpless except when we lifted her into a wheeled chair, placed by the window so that she could look out over the harbour.

She insisted however, that I must carry on with all my activities and kept her first aid kid under her bed, making me promise that if any casualties occurred nearby I would bring them into the house for help. For the time being Betty stayed with us.

Salcombe was a bustle of activity. Households were prepared with black out curtains and cut outs of cardboard to place over car headlights to dim then. Frank had organised the edges of pavements and the corners of buildings to be painted white to enable people to move around at night without lighting. We had stocked up with tinned food. We daily expected something dramatic to happen, but gradually as day after day of glorious sunshine continued and nothing very much happened, we relaxed.

We heard fairly regularly from Fred who said that Plymouth had made similar preparations. The fact that his was one of the most dangerous postings was brought home to us barely two weeks after hostilities began when the Devonport manned HMS "Courageous" was torpedoed at the mouth of the Channel with the loss of more than 500 lives.

A supply of Anderson shelters was delivered and seeing that quite a few townspeople, especially the elderly, were having trouble with their construction in their gardens, I detailed several men to help. I was also asked by several of my clients to advise on the construction of safe rooms inside their homes such as I had made at "The Tower". It was all work at a time when building work suddenly became non-existent.

We had been told that the town would have to take in evacuees. The South Hams already had its share of those wishing to sit out the war in beautiful surroundings. Several big houses had been let for the duration, and many homes had taken in lodgers. The reaction to these people from locals was mixed, but the general feeling was that they were not doing their bit and therefore there was some animosity towards them. In contrast the idea of giving shelter to children from cities where they would be in danger, was generally well received. Having not given the matter much thought, I had assumed that the number of children evacuated to Salcombe would perhaps number one or at the most two hundred. I was shocked when Frank in his position of Head of Council told me that in fact the town had been allocated 900 children.

The first concern was where to put them all, something which Frank, who now found himself doubling as temporary Billeting Officer, had to deal with first hand. The number was out of all proportion to the size of the town which at that time had around 2,500 inhabitants, and I know that my brother protested the amount vigorously in letters to the Home Office. Whether his complaints were noted or not, Salcombe actually received about 750 evacuees, which was still enough.

The majority of the children came from the Walthamstow and Dagenham areas of London. They were city children who mostly had never been in the country before. Preparations were made by the Urban District Council to billet them in houses around the area, and local householders rallied splendidly. Some householders were allocated up to three children. The only houses exempt were those where the householders were elderly or infirm which meant that at least we were exempt though I knew that Frank had designs on our one spare room in "The Tower".

The morning of the children's arrival dawned and I drove to the assembly point by the Holy Trinity church as one of those delegated to be on hand to help with transportation. All hands were required to give the young evacuees something to eat and drink after their journey and to take them to their allocated billet. Waiting with the car for the three youngsters I had been instructed to take on to a farmstead near Shadycombe, I watched the coach draw in. There were one or two adults with each bus, but I was shocked to see how young many of the children were. Tired and confused, the smallest ones clinging tightly to an older brother or sister they climbed silently out of the coaches and stood numbly in the street waiting to be told what to do. They were a sad sight with their gas masks in cardboard boxes slung around their necks and name labels tied securely to their coats. Some carried small suitcases, others had little more than a cardboard box or a brown paper parcel tied up with string. You would have had to have a heart of stone not to be moved by them.

My three charges were identified. There was an older boy, whom my paperwork said was eleven though he seemed very small for his age, and two little girls of five and three. All of them were very poorly dressed in thin, torn coats and down at heel shoes. Only the youngest girl was wearing socks.

I put them in the car with the boy beside me in the front. The smallest girl was sobbing and clearly exhausted. The older girl did her best to quieten her, but perhaps because he reminded me of my own sons it was the boy, trying manfully to take care of his sisters who tugged at my heart.

I pointed out things that I thought might interest them on the short journey, but apart from the continuing muffled sobs from the youngest, the other two were silent and uncommunicative. Even the sight of the sea and sailing boats drew little response. The only thing they said on the entire journey was when the middle child piped up with "Where are the shops, mister?"

We had to stop once in the entrance to a field for the youngest to be sick in the hedge. I guessed they had never been in a car before. Neither had they ever seen a cow, a fact that became abundantly clear by the piercing shrieks that greeted the arrival of a small group of curious Red Devons that ambled across to the gate to see what was going on. How these children were ever going to settle on the farm I was taking them to, heaven only knew.

The local schools could not cope with such a large influx of children. Frank had been involved in discussions with principals for some time, but it was now decided that the children's education should continue in church halls and even front rooms if necessary. It was evident from the start that some children required medical attention, and a hostel was set up to treat and care for those who needed it. To cope with the additional rations that would be required, Frank set up a Food Office, staffed by volunteer help.

At the same time the "Tides Reach Hotel" was taken over by the Shaftesbury Homes, and became the billet for about 200 men and boys from the London based Training Ship "Arethusa". For a while it seemed as if there were youngsters everywhere you went in Salcombe.

Most of the children seemed to adjust well enough, but in the weeks that followed there were a few instances where evacuees and householders did not hit it off and the billeting officers had to remove the children and place them in another household. Though there were cases where hosts were not as kind or understanding as they might have been, and certainly many of the children were homesick and perhaps difficult to manage, the vast majority of cases of failure were because the children had had a totally different way of life from their hosts and their own children. It was a shock to Devonians to realise that other Britons existed in such extreme poverty. I heard of several cases where householders had to resort to burning clothes that were full of lice and immersing filthy children in baths and scrubbing them vigorously with carbolic soap. Supplies of lice powder and nit combs sold out in all the local shops almost instantly. Bed wetting was also a problem, as was food, as the children seemed to have existed wholly on fish and chips and other such convenience food. I think vegetables were a step too far in many cases!

But in spite of the difficulties there were children who took to their new lives like ducks to water. Within the space of a few short weeks the Devon air and good food had started to work their miracles and most of the young evacuees soon looked much fitter and healthier than they had done when they arrived. Some of the older children especially those billeted on farms later stayed on to become apprenticed to their hosts and adopted their way of life. But the vastly differing life styles of hosts and parents were still from time to time responsible for upsets. The local newspaper raised a few chuckles when it reported the story of one boy who had written home to his apparently rather strait laced parents to say that he was enjoying himself very much as his host father was teaching him poaching!

There was a good response locally to the call for volunteers for Civil Defence, Rescue services, Fire Fighting and various other agencies, and the Womens Voluntary Services organised working parties to deal with any number of as yet unknown contingencies. I joined the Local Defence Volunteers when they were formed. At first we had neither weapons nor uniforms, so we were forced to improvise. Since this was Devon, amongst the weapons of choice were boathooks, oars, sickles and hammers and in at least one case a breadknife tied onto the end of a broom handle. In time however the LDV which was soon renamed the Home Guard, became responsible for a range of activities. Our remit included tasks such as setting road blocks, manning check points, investigating sightings of enemy aliens and parachutists, as well as conducting patrols and in general undertaking any tasks we were asked to do.

Several military units were now stationed at Salcombe and in the surrounding areas. Soldiers began mining local beaches, erecting barbed wire barriers, setting up check points in strategic areas, and building gun emplacements. It was at this time that the construction of an airfield and top secret radar station began on the cliff top at Soar, behind Bolt Head.

As Chairman of the Salcombe Urban District Council Frank was busy but not stretched. I know he wanted to do more, but in the meantime he spent a great deal of time meeting with the Defence Officer from the Commander in Chief's office, Plymouth to discuss what steps should be taken in case of invasion to deny the use of Salcombe's quays, beaches and other strategic parts of the harbour to the enemy.

Resident Naval Officers had been appointed to most of the major ports at the outbreak of hostilities, but some ports were overlooked or we guessed, like Salcombe, were not thought of sufficient importance to warrant such a position. But with the ever present risk of invasion on any part of the South Coast, and the frequent arrival of foreign manned craft it was obvious that Salcombe too needed someone to oversee what was happening in the harbour.

All men with any experience that might be of use in the war effort were asked to volunteer, and my eldest brother stepped up. This was what he had been waiting for. With his naval experience and as a local, with his intimate knowledge of the harbour, he was an ideal choice for the position which it now became necessary for someone to fill, and he was assigned the job of Resident Naval Officer, Salcombe, with the rank of Lieutenant Commander R.N.V.R. This was I suspect a unique appointment and one without precedent as it meant that Frank became naval as well as civil head of his home town, a circumstance which filled Ellen and Aaron with quiet, unalloyed pride.

The area under Frank's command extended from Torcross in the east to 4 degrees west, near the mouth of the River Erme, and came under the overall command of N.O.I.C Dartmouth.

Frank's first task was to set up a naval base in Salcombe.

"La Baranca" part of the Woodcot Estate, which faced the harbour entrance was deemed to be the most suitable building. Under the Emergency Powers (Defence) Act it was requisitioned and became the official headquarters of the Naval Base, Salcombe. A telephone exchange was installed with direct lines to other naval ports. All that was left was to staff it.

A few days before his appointment Frank had met up with a local Chief Petty Officer named Arthur Wood currently based in Devonport. He was a cousin of the Hannafords, and Frank had known him for many years. He was a good, sound man, just the sort my brother needed, and Frank asked him if he would like to come back to Salcombe to be part of the Naval Base. Receiving a resounding affirmative, my brother phoned Devonport to request that C.P.O Wood be seconded to Salcombe. There was some opposition, but Frank insisted that he must be allowed to choose who he wanted. Less than a week later C.P.O Wood was transferred back to his home town where he soon proved to be a valuable member of staff. Royal Naval ratings and Wrens were also drafted in to form part of the team, which instantly gained the affectionate nickname around town of "Mr Murch's Navy".

Two local launches which had formerly been in naval service were

The Resident Naval Officer, Salcombe.
Lt. Cmdr. Francis Murch R.N.V.R (Centre) with his team. 1939

requisitioned and armed with Hotchkiss guns. Nine local men were enlisted and sent to Plymouth to be kitted out. In addition to these harbour patrols, an inshore patrol consisting of four motor yachts operated between Dartmouth and Salcombe. After a night at sea, they would make for Salcombe or Dartmouth alternately.

Radio news broadcasts during May were increasingly dismal, as Germany launched its invasion along the Western Front into Belgium, Holland and Luxembourg, its troops advancing relentlessly towards France. British and French forces were surprised by an Ardennes attack which drove between Allied fighting forces. But I think most people were cheered by the announcement that Winston Churchill was to take over as Prime Minister from the now totally discredited Neville Chamberlain, who had presided over mounting military catastrophe. With "Winnie" back in charge as he had been during the First War, things could only get better, everybody said.

But in the meantime the situation was grim. Mid-way through May, the Dutch army capitulated after the bombing of Rotterdam. It seemed that nothing could halt the German advance into France, as their army pushed on to reach the French coast south of Calais, with the apparent intention of cutting off Allied Forces.

By the 26th May 1940 we heard that the British Expeditionary force had been driven back to Dunkirk and our soldiers were trapped on the beaches.

But in an extraordinary effort a flotilla of small boats set off to rescue them. The days during the rescues at Dunkirk were heady ones. So far away from the scene of the action, all we could do in Salcombe was listen to the radio and wait for news, our hearts in our mouths, pride brimming up in us as we learned of the sacrifice and the bravery of the rescuers.

Still buoyed up by the rescue of our men from Dunkirk, we heard two days later that Belgium had fallen. Barely two weeks afterwards we watched Pathe News with set faces as pictures of the triumphant German Army parading up the Champs Elysees, were broadcast.

Plymouth was by now crowded with foreign vessels, mostly of French or Belgian origin. In June 1940 a Commander Swinley, R.N, from Dartmouth organised the removal of some twenty French and Belgian craft from Plymouth to Salcombe.

Confined aboard their ships, the crews were supplied with food, water and other necessities by the Public Assistance Officer from Kingsbridge. As a Home Guard armed with a .22 I was part of a patrol of naval men on two launches which carried out nightly runs around these ships.

After a couple of weeks of this, two armed trawlers arrived in the harbour. In a 5 a.m. operation that Elsie and I watched from our bedroom window, all the foreign crews were gathered up and taken aboard the trawlers. From what we could see there seemed to be some resistance from a French boat which necessitated some to-ing and fro-ing from the Customs men. The boats were finally moved up to moorings in the Bag and I made a cup of hot chocolate for us both and went back to sleep. Meeting Frank in the town the next morning, I learned that a large quantity of arms and ammunition had been found amongst other contraband on the boats, and that the crew of one boat had handed over spirits and a quantity of smuggled tobacco to the Customs officers. Frank said it was believed that the items had been put aboard before the vessels left their home ports, so at least there was relief that it was not a local job.

With the collapse of France in June 1940, the enemy was poised across the Channel. The Prime Minister asserted that the war was winnable but he warned us that there would first be hard times. He broadcast to the nation, saying "Let us brace ourselves to our duty and so bear ourselves that if the British Commonwealth and Empire lasts a thousand years, men will still say "This was their finest hour". Dispirited, fearful, yet determined we rallied behind Winnie. He had a gift for raising spirits.

But even so the truth was that as a nation we were preparing ourselves to think the unthinkable: that we would soon have to fight the Germans on our own territory. Our future was in the hands of our Armed Forces, but particularly our brave pilots who daily fought the deadly war waged in our skies. We saw the planes taking off from R.A.F Bolt Head and heading out across the Channel. From time to time we saw dog fights overhead in defence of our harbour and homes. With the Nazi hordes just across the Channel, it was even more vital now to defend our town and its harbour.

At the beginning of October 1940 a crew were sent to Dartmouth to bring an M.T.B to Salcombe. The going was difficult and the crossing of the Bar was rough, but the ship was brought in safely and contributed to the harbour's defences from then on.

We had grown used to the planes coming off the cliffs by Bolt Head, and to the occasional sorties over the Channel. But we had seen few German planes and had so far not been subjected to bombing. This was now to change. The first bomb dropped on Kingsbridge on 20th October 1940. Within months Salcombe, Torcross, Kellaton, Middlecombe, Beesands and Aveton Gifford were amongst several areas of the South Hams to be hit.

Frank was now instructed as a matter of urgency to organise the laying of a boom defence across the harbour, but soon realised that little in the way of the necessary materials was to be forthcoming. He came to the workshop to enlist our help and we broadcast our needs to the town, ransacking fishermen's stores, quays and jetties, even the town's rubbish dump in search of large pieces of wood and metal that might be useful. Plymouth Dockyard came up with some coils of 6" wire and a few 5 cwt sinkers, but that was all and it still left us woefully short of materials.

We recruited the help of several local boat building firms and we all worked together. I took some of my men to cut down trees at Sharpitor for use as the booms, and we managed to acquire some empty tar drums from the Council Depot. Frank had determined that in addition to the booms, two boats would be moored up to form the necessary removable openings. The gate was to be closed at night when a boom would be placed between the two vessels. It is questionable whether this boom would have been effective at keeping out enemy craft, but it looked like a barrier and so from that point of view it did its job. The only thing that we knew of that was in any way similar to what we were constructing was the chain boom that had been laid across the harbour at Dartmouth so many centuries before. As we now began to realise the magnitude of the job we had taken on, we had to admire the ingenuity of those long dead defenders – and wish devoutly that we had a similar length of heavy chain to hand!

Having scratched together the materials needed, out next problem was where to put the boom. Local knowledge of the harbour dictated one thing, the War Ministry officials, having presumably studied the maps but as far as we knew never having seen the harbour, said another. Our hands were tied. Though Frank put up a stout defence we were overruled, and eventually had to place the boom where we were told, though all we locals insisted that the position chosen was too far towards the open ocean where the boats that carried the booms would be at risk from rough seas.

Unfortunately it went exactly as we had predicted. In a gale on 1st

November 1940, the 136 ton French cargo vessel, the "Placidas Farroult" which had formed part of the gate, broke adrift and was holed on Blackstone Rocks. On the next high tide, she slid off into deep water inside the rocks where she still lies. There was an immediate enquiry. Frank told me that the authorities admitted that he had advised them that the position of the boom was not the correct one. But the enquiry findings were that no-one was to blame. I know that the whitewash annoyed Frank as much as it did the rest of us who had been involved but there was nothing we could do about it. After a while we were given instructions to build a new boom further up the harbour in the place we had originally chosen. The necessary materials were now made available to us, I suspect as a peace offering. We had to admit that the rubber floats with nets suspended between them that we were allocated made a much more satisfactory barrier that our original Heath Robinson one.

Once the boom was operational, a mine observation building was constructed on the cliff behind Fort Charles. Again we realised that like the defenders of Dartmouth, the builders of Salcombe fort had chosen the best possible position for a view up the harbour and out to sea, as the mine observation building was ideally placed.

A few days later an electronically controlled mine field was laid from just inside the Bar down to Millbay. The Mine Control Station had a naval lieutenant in charge and was manned by naval ratings, a sergeant and 12 marines, all of whom took their orders from Frank. The area around the Old Castle which had been besieged in 1665 for four months and, except for Pendennis Castle in Cornwall, was the last Royalist stronghold in the country to surrender to Cromwell's forces, was once again to be a centre of resistance.

There were more fortifications going up around the harbour now. Two 6" Naval guns, manned by Royal Artillery soldiers billeted at the "Bolt Head Hotel" were mounted on bases at Splat Cove. The Home Guard assisted them as one of their duties, and I went out there several times to keep watch. The naval base kept the guns' history sheets which contained a record of rounds fired. Frank told me that the guns had come from H.M.S "Agincourt" which had taken part in the Battle of Jutland during World War I. Frank himself had been at this battle aboard H.M.S "Colossus".

The other defences at the naval base were rocket guns and two 12 pound guns, so, much to Aaron's amusement, it looked as if my boyhood training as GL No. 2 Gun Eastern King's Redoubt Plymouth might at last be useful! The additional gun positions and other duties necessitated an increase in personnel at the Naval Base. Some of the first batch of local ratings had been drafted away and others now arrived. The first detail of Wrens seconded were made responsible for telephone and coding work, as well as general secretarial duties, but they also doubled as cooks and stewards, when necessary.

Fort Charles. The Salcombe men in the Old Castle were the last but one stronghold in the country to hold out against the Round-heads.

Though Frank was no longer involved in the day to day work in the workshop, he made many visits to us, especially when he was after something. He came in soon after the completion of the boom, and commandeered some of our metal scaffolding. At that time I was doing very little construction work and, not being able to plead that I might need it, I had reluctantly to write it off as our contribution to the war effort, though eventually we did receive compensation for it. There were mixed blessings in being the brother of someone in Frank's position. His whole life was the care of his beloved town, and for a generally sweet tempered and genial man, he could be a devil if he was after something that was needed for its defence. The problem was that having worked for so long in the workshop, my brother knew what we had tucked away just as well as I did, and I could not keep anything hidden from him. On the scaffolding issue though, I stood firm. I could not conceive of any situation in which scaffolding poles might be of use, so Frank had to sketch out the design he needed to construct on the back of a cigarette packet to convince me. His instruction was to place over 500 "knife rest" defences on the mud around the harbour to prevent enemy aircraft landing. These knife rests were to consist of scaffolding poles bunched eight to a unit, placed so that three to four feet of the poles would project above the highest tide where they would prove a visible deterrent to any enemy invasion plans. It was an ugly, but formidable defence. It was also a very muddy job, so I was glad that he had not commandeered any of our men. I admit I gave my brother a wide berth for a few days until I saw that he had a team of Sappers in place to do the work.

Towards the end of 1940 a Company of the Royal Army Service Corps, No. 1 Motor Boat Company took over the "Salcombe Hotel". A number of Salcombe motor launches, including both my own, were requisitioned. The boats were needed to train soldiers in marine craft, or, as some of the locals standing around on the quay watching the mens' initial lack lustre performance put it dryly, " turn soldiers into sailors"

At this time Salcombe was subjected to isolated "tip and run" raids by hostile aircraft. A large yacht called the "Velda" which had been moored in the harbour at the outbreak of war was considered to be the object of one such attack. She was owned by an American called Irvin, who had pioneered the use of parachutes. America was still neutral at this point and since the boat was painted a bright white overall, Frank ordered her to be re-painted black, making sure that she had the United States flag prominently painted on her sides. Later she was taken over by the Royal Navy and used as an escort vessel.

There were several anti-aircraft posts around the district manned by the army, and there was a R.O.C Observation Post on the Berry. "Rockside", next to the Naval Base was occupied by the army. Once the airfield at Bolt Head was operational the army vacated it for the Royal Air Force, who used it for billeting their Air Sea Rescue crews. These were administrated by the R.A.F but came under the operational control of the navy. All these forces were posted around Salcombe to help with the town's defence, and many conscript naval trainees were billeted in commandeered houses. Since these were largely private homes, many did not have areas where the men could gather off duty and so I suggested to Elsie that we should allow them the use of our sitting room in the evenings. Elsie jumped at the idea, and after that many of these young men came over every evening. With our grand piano and fire it was a homely place for them to relax in. A couple of them could play the piano and they held regular recitals which Annie Lucy, who proved to be a very popular turn, attended when she could spare the time. It was great fun and a tonic for Elsie, who though she could sadly no longer play her violin, for a little while at least could forget her troubles in organising our very small household staff to care for our visitors.

Peter had passed his Matric and now left school. He found a job as a

Junior Clerk for Northcotts in Torpoint, then later with the same firm at Bangor in North Walves. He was paid £3 a week so was nearly self-supporting, though I drove him to Plymouth and back at weekends which he spent at home. Alec, having gained his Matric at fourteen, had gone on to do his Higher in Engineering drawings, as well as his Intermediate at London University.

Both boys talked of joining up as soon as they could. Both were keen to go into the R.A.F. Peter spoke of little else but flying. He was desperate to fly Spitfires. At about this time he told me that he had gone into a recruiting centre in Bangor and had taken and passed the necessary fitness examination. His papers had been transferred from Shrewsbury to Plymouth, but he was underage still and could only wait.

That year of 1941 proved to be the most terrible of all the war years. West Cornwall and the Scillies had taken their share of bombs, but March and April brought such horror and destruction to Plymouth that the face of the city was changed forever.

Many thought that the January raids on the city had been its Blitz, and dared to hope that perhaps the worst was over but now death and destruction without mercy rained down from the skies. On 20th March the King and Queen visited Plymouth and were reportedly much affected by the damage they saw. Only two hours after they had left, the gates of Hell itself were opened and thousands of fire bombs and high explosives rained down on the city. Showers of incendiary bombs destroyed street after street, blowing up centuries old buildings, shops, offices, and churches, destroying water, gas and electricity supplies seemingly at random, and terrified civilians fled the city and took refuge on the moors, as firestorms consumed their homes and livelihoods. In total 336 people were killed and countless more injured, and almost 20,000 properties were destroyed or damaged.

That same night of 21st April 1941 saw the first bomb dropped on Salcombe.

On 25th April and again on 1st May 1942 the airfield at Bolt Head was bombed.

At times we had information from the War Station at Prawle Point that suspect boats had been sighted, but they usually turned out to be French fishing boats carrying escapees from France or the Channel Islands. These boats were intercepted and escorted into harbour and their crews were taken to the Naval Base. After that they were checked by M15, Customs, Immigration officials and finally by the Medical Officers. French nationals were sent on to the French Resistance H.Q in London. You had to admire these men. Often their boats were very small and they had survived terrible crossings.

I was one of the few people who knew just how exhausted Frank was in those days. Since the early weeks of the war, he had given his all for his home town. He came into "The Tower" to see me one morning and I was shocked by how drawn and tired he looked. He said that he had realised that he needed to shed some of his responsibilities, and told me that he had decided to resign from his position on the Council. The only problem was that that would leave them a man short. By the time he left I found that I had agreed to stand for the Town Council!

But Frank's actual resignation was not so easily achieved. In a Council meeting in August 1941 which I attended, he put his case for his resignation from his position as head of the Council and also as a Council member. Taken completely by surprise several Council members tried to make him change his mind. He was well regarded and a popular Council head and no-one wanted to see him go. Unwillingly Frank bowed to overwhelming pressure, and agreed that he would serve until a suitable replacement could be found. That business being disposed of, I was nominated to stand and was accepted. Since Fred was also on the Council, with allowance being made during the war for his frequent unavoidable absences, it resulted in the curious situation of all three of us brothers serving at the same time, which has never happened before or since

Now that we had seen bombing in Salcombe I realised that we local building firms would have to take responsibility for the repair work to bomb damaged buildings. I talked to other builders around the area looking for support for the idea that we should all pull together. The general feeling was very much for this, and we agreed that we should work out a system between us to share the work. At a Council meeting in June 1941, it had been formally agreed that all building firms would pool resources of men and materials. I was now appointed head of what we called the "Builders Emergency Team", in charge of all bomb damage repairs in Salcombe and surrounding areas. Since I was also serving as a Sergeant in the Home Guard, a Special Sergeant in the Police force, in addition to still running the business and caring for my sick wife, I had my hands full. I had the chance to co-opt Jim Camp as Foreman on bomb damage repairs, and did so, as the pay for this position considerably augmented our firm's current low earnings. I knew that Jim Camp was a man who was universally respected for his craftsmanship, and moreover was someone whom other builders found it easy to work with, so I felt he was a good choice.

At the first meeting of the Builders Emergency Team we builders put our heads together and came up with a list of materials which we felt would tide us over most repairs. Accordingly the Council now approved the purchase of several rolls of Bitumen felt, and moved a motion that corrugated iron sheeting to the value of £50 should be secured. We felt confident that between us we had sufficient tarpaulins, scaffolding (even with Frank's pilfering for harbour defence!) planks, nails and tools to do most repairs. One of the first jobs this amalgamation of builders was called upon to tackle was to move the A.R.P siren from the Rate Collector's office to the Harbour Master's office. The builder who eventually carried out the work was subjected to a barrage of good humoured chaffing from the others, who all turned out to watch and see what sort of a job he made of it.

My father had been ailing for some months, but he had never complained. Ellen was having difficulty taking care of him. We all saw him regularly, but the main weight of his nursing fell on Ellen, who was not herself strong now. We had not realised that they had grown old, quietly and uncomplainingly as they did everything else, not wishing to be a trouble to anyone, but we realised now that they needed care. I had my hands full with Elsie and Fred was away so much. Mabel was looking after her own elderly mother, and so Frank volunteered to have both our parents at his home. It was here that Aaron died on 7th October 1941 with all his family at his bedside. He was the sweetest, kindest man I have ever known, and we all mourned his passing, particularly Elsie who I think had loved him from the first day they had met.

With the attack on the United States Pacific fleet at its home base in Hawaii and on military bases in the Philippines and the Pacific, America entered the war. Even the demoralising news of the fall of Hong Kong to the Japanese Army on Christmas Day, dampened only slightly our building excitement. Surely with America on our side things would change for the better we told ourselves. Even despite increasing hardship, rationing and shortages, the whole tenure of the war seemed subtly to change. Winston Churchill as always reflected the mood when he broadcast "As long as we have faith in our cause and an unconquerable willpower, salvation will not be denied us". We saw on Pathe News that he gave the "V" sign for victory, and I chuckled to myself thinking of Aaron and the day that he told my elder brother and me about the English archers at the Battle of Agincourt.

Most Friday evenings I drove down to Plymouth to collect Peter from the station, combining the trip with small commissions from the various services to save petrol. My habit was to drive through the city and work my way back to the station. One evening I arrived a little later than usual having been held up on site. Nearing the outskirts of the city I heard the air raid siren go off and pulled over with several other cars, to sit under the shelter of some trees. Straining my eyes I picked out the glint of a lone plane, high up above the barrage balloons that were tethered over the city. The ack-ack guns opened up, their explosions muted by the distance, but their positions indicated by the small grey puffs of smoke that hung suspended in the clear blue sky. Then, as our own planes scrambled for attack, the bombs began to fall.

Moments later the dull thud of the explosions reached us, and I saw flames erupt amongst the buildings as British planes chased the intruder out over the sea.

I came into the city centre as the All Clear sounded. Plymouth was a scene of total devastation. I had seen the wreckage growing week by week and Fred had kept us abreast of the major building damage, but even so I was shocked by what I saw.

In parts the city was a ruin, a desolate wasteland of dust covered stone and brick, towering, unstable part walls and jagged roof timbers. Teams of workmen and soldiers had kept the streets largely clear and a few cars and bicycles were managing to get through. Not long before a few remaining trams had been brought out of retirement since the buses were mostly unusable after a direct hit on the depot. One of these trams had been hit I saw now and its long pole flew sparking across the rubble until it was contained. To have known the city as it was, busy and vibrant, its streets lined with majestic buildings and then to see these ruins was harrowing. Stopping and starting, often having to detour around gangs of men busy clearing rubble, I made my way painfully slowly through the damage.

I passed the area where the bombs had hit. A layer of acrid dust hung over everything, and a stench of broken sewers was in the air. A.R.P men were searching the ruins, and teams of soldiers and Red Cross helpers with stretchers were picking their way over the smoking remains. I stopped to allow a couple of sturdy ATS girls to cross in front of me carrying an enormous tea urn, and one of them gave me a cheery grin.

I collected Peter whose train as I suspected had been held up, and we set off back to Salcombe.

Betty had gone back to London to join the ATS. We were suffering from yet another useless home help at that time. Food was by now severely restricted and we sorely missed Aaron's contributions to our table. Elsie spent almost all her time in bed now. The days when she had been well enough to receive friends seemed so far away. My mother and Annie Lucy did what they could, but the truth was that neither of them was fit now. The visitors who came were marvellous and helped with Elsie's care when needed. The indefatigable May Schofield was now teaching First Aid and Home Nursing courses in Kingsbridge. She still called regularly at "The Tower", and I saw her several times bicycling around the area with a suitcase of necessary equipment strapped to the back of her bike, and a determined expression on her face.

Peter was called up on his eighteenth birthday. The next day he travelled to Oxford and was cleared for flying duties. He began training at Scarborough and did some flying at Booker Airport. Then he was sent to Canada for flight training.

Meanwhile, Alec, still only seventeen, came to work with me. I set him to work with the men as an apprentice. He had passed his exams for Air Crew, and was with the local A.F.C with the rank of Sergeant.

Most of the craft that had come to Salcombe after the Fall of France had now been taken for other duties or returned to the French for fishing under U.K control out of Brixham. It was decided that one French trawler, the "Pierre Descelliers" which was one of the boats that had been lying in the Bag without crew for many months, should be commissioned. A crew arrived from Lowestoft one night in preparation for commissioning her the following morning as a patrol vessel. As there was no room at the Naval Base, they were put aboard their ship. The next morning, 13th August 1942, not long after her ensign was hoisted, a German aircraft flew over and dropped a bomb squarely on her, killing four of her crew and Mrs Chadder-Blank who was on the water boat refuelling the craft at the time. Frank was in the harbour in our motor boat and so he was on the gruesome scene of the sinking boat fairly quickly, and was able to transport the walking survivors to the Salcombe Hotel.

The base began preparing the "Pierre Descelliers"'s sister ship, the "Intrepide" for service. A week later, before a crew arrived for her, another enemy aircraft dropped a bomb on her. This time however, the damage was above the water line, so the boat was patched up and taken round to Dartmouth for its crew to embark which we all felt they rightly did with a certain amount of trepidation.

Salcombe sustained its most serious damage from bombing on 8th September 1942.

It was early evening and I had just finished the only cup of tea which, thanks to rationing, we allowed ourselves a day, when it happened. Our hopeless kitchen help had recently put a pair of my light coloured trousers and a white shirt of mine into the big boiling pan with a yellow duster. The result was that my trousers and shirt were dyed bright yellow. At any other time they would have been thrown away, or we might have attempted to bleach them, but with clothes on ration and no-body with any time to rectify the damage, I had put them on, thinking that I would see no-one as I hoped to spend a rare evening at home catching up with the paperwork.

I heard the siren, the plane overhead, then the whoosh of the bomb and the crash of masonry as it hit and all I could think from the direction of the noise and the cloud of smoke that followed, was that it must have hit somewhere near the Island. My overwhelming fear was that the workshop had been hit, and I opened the front door and ran.

I realised two things simultaneously as I tore through the streets. The first was that the area that had been hit was around the church. The second was that I was barefoot, and dressed from head to toe in canary yellow...

I reached the baker's shop on the corner and met the regular policeman. Since I was the first on the scene he asked me to take the Incident Officer's job as neighbours, fire fighters, rescuers and helpers began to arrive. The bombing was a bad one. I began my report of the incident while the bodies were being brought out. It read "bombs fell in the Church Street area, demolishing three houses on the southern side of the street, by and below the arch, and severely damaging houses opposite, and in Buckley. The Church and houses in the Island were also damaged"

The human cost of this raid was considerable. No 6, Church Street was the home of Gunner Charles Minney and his wife Mrs E A Minney. The parents were not injured and I saw them emerging shaken from the rubble, Mrs Minney still clutching the tea pot she had been using to pour tea. It was seconds later that they missed their child, and Mrs Minney's screams rang piercingly down the street. Eleven month old Kenneth Minney was rescued, having been blown across the room by the blast, miraculously still alive, though covered from head to foot in blood and dust from the fallen masonry around him. He was rushed to Kingsbridge Hospital but died there the next day.

Next door at No. 5 Church Street a 40 year old woman, Dorothy Rose Ball, wife, so the shaken neighbours told me, of Roderick Ball, was killed. In a tragic case two families living at No. 4 Church Street were killed. A direct hit wiped out David Putt, only three days old, his mother Grace, and grandparents Edith and William Henry Putt. I knew the family, and found reporting the scene hard. Two young brothers, Bernard and Derek Darnborough of 77A Fore Street, the sons of a Driver in the Royal Army Service Corps were also killed in this same raid.

Shortly after I had finished taking my notes my fellow sergeant, Mr Page, arrived with the other Special Constables, all dressed in full uniform complete with gas masks and with their jackets properly buttoned. They glanced in astonishment at my yellow clothing and bare feet, by now covered in dust, but they were luckily soon too busy helping out to pass comment.

Women were brought into the war effort in 1942, freeing up more men to fight. Local farmers who had once declared that they would never allow women to work their land, began to find that the girls were invaluable in coping with the vastly increased crop yields that were expected from them. Though some of the girls who had been city dwellers, found the work hard, the Land Girls in their distinctive breeches and jumpers soon became a normal sight around Kingsbridge and the Estuary.

Exeter was hit once more in May. Like Plymouth the city had suffered badly.

A telegram arrived at "The Tower" in May 1942. I opened it with the sort of trepidation we all used to show in those days, but it was good news. Peter had got his commission and his wings. His whole family were proud to see this achievement recorded in the local newspaper. He had been training as a fighter pilot, and on receipt of his wings now became a Pilot Officer. It made both Elsie and me proud, though we were worried for him.

He was still underage, but fortunately the Royal Air Force kept their youngest pilots on in Canada, mostly in Vancouver, for nearly two years instruction of F.A.A cadets before putting them on the front line. Peter wrote enthusiastic letters about Vancouver in which he described sailing around the islands off shore in his free time. He obviously loved Canada and we were pleased that he had this small respite from the war.

During almost the whole of 1942 there were air raids and increased activity in the Channel from E Boats and submarines. Salcombe was hit again on 19th September 1942. Several more French boats arrived in the harbour. On 1st December 1942, H.M.S "Jasper" an armed trawler, was sunk by enemy action. 14 survivors and one body were brought in by an R.A.F Air Sea Rescue boat. On 3rd December H.M.S "Pen-y-Lan" a Hunt Class destroyer, was sunk in much the same position whilst on escort duty. 19 bodies were brought in by Air Sea Rescue boats. Most of the survivors had minor injuries or were suffering from shock and were sent to hospital. Some of the dead were returned to their home towns, but Frank oversaw the burial of the rest in Salcombe with full military honours. Almost all the town attended the ceremony to pay their respects.

The greatest single loss of life around the Estuary occurred in Kingsbridge with the bombing of 2nd January 1943 when nine lives were lost at 61 and 63 Fore Street. 61 Fore Street was the local branch of Eastman's the Butchers. As the raid began staff took shelter in the shop's walk in freezer, but the premises next door, No. 63, received a direct hit which fractured the gas main. The Eastman employees were all gassed before they had a chance to escape.

Salcombe was hit again on 9th February. On the nights of 12th and 13th March 1943, more bombs fell on the centre of Salcombe. The incident could have been much worse if it had not been for the spirited defence by a pilot of 266 Rhodesian Squadron who intercepted and shot down a Focke-Wolf over Chivelstone. He then immediately turned and chased another FW190. We learned later that the pilot had shot this enemy plane down just as it reached the French coast. 266 Squadron was then tasked with the prevention of what we knew as "hit and run" raids which were currently causing havoc in southern England. These raids dropped bombs seemingly randomly on outlying areas with the presumed aim of bringing fear and showing Britain that no-where was beyond the reach of the Luftwaffe. In this raid Eleanor Catford, aged 63, and a civilian Fire Guard, was killed at 65a, Fore Street. Also killed in this raid were Polly Lapthorn, formerly named Gibson, the wife of another Royal Army Service Corps soldier, and her daughter Elizabeth Gibson, aged 15, as well as Catherine Susan Patey, a civilian member of the St. John's Ambulance, who lived at 9, Fore Street, together with Mary Richards aged 19, of "See-Moor", Grenville Road, the daughter of Able Seaman Ernest Richards R.N, who died at 65A Fore

Street.

On 30th March 1943 bombs hit Salcombe, Malborough and Bolt Head. A three year old child, named Anna Alexander, was killed at Fort Charles, Salcombe. It was thought that the enemy planes were targeting the anti-aircraft guns, and had just got lucky.

Other raids damaged Stoke Fleming, Kingsbridge, Beesands and Aveton Gifford. I went to all these sites soon after they were hit and organised repairs. Our teams of builders were splendid and they were able to make sure the buildings were either pulled down or made safe. Alec came with me and did a lot of work on maintenance and bomb damage repairs. He learned the business the hard way during this time. At eighteen, his evenings were spent in the Home Guard, so he too had his hands full.

Having completed his training, Peter was returned to England to re-join his squadron flying Spitfires as he had longed to do. He was very much on the front line through until Armistice Day. These young men were the aces, the best of British pilots, getting to grips with the enemy to try and prevent their bombs from reaching England. The very best of these pilots had developed a technique in which they actually used their planes to tip the wings of flying V12's to send them off course. There were very few pilots with the necessary skill and daring to use this manoeuvre. We learned a long time later that Peter had been responsible for bringing down two V12's over Kent in this way. He made light of these wins. It was not until years later, long after the award of his Distinguished Flying Cross medal that I learned the details of his bravery and of his safe landing of a blazing Spit. How a nineteen year old boy had these reserves of courage amazed me.

Citizens were encouraged to be vigilant in seeking out potential "saboteurs" and "enemies of the realm". Both the Home Guard and the Police were zealous in following up any sightings of suspicious persons. In the autumn of 1943 I took two of my police troop to investigate reports that flashing lights had been spotted on two consecutive nights on farm land near Soar Mill, 1 ½ miles from Salcombe.

After spending most of the first night in a hedge full of brambles to no avail, we trailed wearily home at dawn with nothing to show for it except a good haul of mushrooms which we shared out between us. Since eggs were now rationed to one a person each week, it said a lot for our honesty that we passed a hen house without helping ourselves to any eggs.

The next night was memorable mostly because in the pitch darkness I stumbled upon and nearly bayonetted a cow. The kerfuffle we made, both man and animal simultaneously convinced that they were under attack, brought the rest of the patrol running. When they saw what had happened, they were beside themselves with merriment at my expense,

The third night was more successful but almost as amusing. I was wearing my Home Guard hat, and had taken Alec with me as well as one other reservist, Jim, a non-local. It was a drizzly night and there was only a thin moon visible. Dotted separately around the field, each hidden in the shadows of the hedge for several wet, demoralising hours, we were eventually rewarded by the sight of a light on the other side of the field.

We must have spotted it about the same time, for we all crept forward together. Jim, who was a big, heavy man was first at the scene, and he jumped the figure and wrestled him to the ground.

Panting a little for it had been a long run across the muddy field, Alec and I reached the scene seconds later and threw our combined weight on the struggling man to help hold him down. It was then we heard his muffled voice from underneath us. Rather than the German accent we had anticipated, we distinctly heard the broad Devon: "Bugger I bey, what you be a-doing of?" as I realised we were sitting on Farmer Cole.

The fact remained that he had been showing a light, and though he explained that he had been having trouble with foxes in the hen house we had seen the night before, I still had to caution him. It was amazing how many times farmers, convinced that using a lantern in one of their own fields did not contravene black out regulations, still laid themselves open to prosecution. No matter how many times you told them that it had been scientifically proved that a single beam of light as narrow as a pencil was visible up to thirty miles away at night, they still seemed to believe that breaking the black-out did not matter if it was on their own land. We explained patiently to Farmer Cole that there had been several cases of isolated farms bringing attack on themselves in this manner, and even one instance in which a stack of bombs had been dropped on a smallholding outside Plymouth which had literally obliterated the farm and all its occupants, but we all knew that only the threat of court action and a possible severe fine could make farmers obey the regulations. As it was this time we issued a stern warning – and did not turn down the bag of eggs we were offered.

I was finding Alec indispensable to the firm, and as the time came for him to join up, I was aware I would miss him badly. He had a natural gift for architecture and was a very good artist. I could see that with him working with the firm, we could branch out into more elaborate house design. My dream was still to have both my sons in the business. Alec was pulling his weight well with the men and each day I grew more used to having him around.

But I was living in a fool's paradise. My younger son's papers came, and a few days later he was ready to report to barracks. He was now 18 ½. He was to spend fourteen weeks at Newquay doing the basic ground work for pilot training. One of his school friends from Truro had recently spent a couple of days at "The Tower" after completing his basic training, and we knew that he was expecting to be sent to Rhodesia, but we had no idea if

Alec was to follow the same route.

The knowledge that both boys would be in danger weighed heavily on us both, but Elsie took it hard and wept often in these days.

I had some petrol and told Alec I would take him down to Plymouth to catch his train, as I could combine the trip with getting hold of some supplies that the builders' confederation needed.

We approached Plymouth from the high ground, and instinctively looked across the water to the city. I knew that Plymouth had survived 31 bombings so far. Fred had described to me on one of his recent visits home how the city had taken another pasting, but nothing could have prepared us for the scene of utter devastation we encountered as we came over Laira Bridge.

It was so very much worse than the last time I had seen it when I took Peter to his train. I drove slowly along a track that had been cleared through heaps of rubble and stone and piled up masonry. Gangs of men were still working, lifting stones by hand and levering lintels and twisted metal girders aside. All around was a scene of devastation punctuated here and there by a few intact houses, which seemed somehow by comparison to make the desolation even worse.

The sight of wrecked houses which had partially collapsed with wallpapered walls, fireplaces, a staircase leading nowhere, kitchen tables and chairs, or a sofa, even pictures still hanging intact on the walls, was terrible. The bombs had not discriminated. Mighty public buildings had been reduced to ruins, as had the smallest terraced houses. There were gaps in rows of buildings and teetering columns of brick chimneys surrounded by collapsed walls.

Alec's face was pale as he looked around, and I saw his knuckles white as he clutched his case. I knew that he was thinking: "This is why we are fighting" and I could not blame him. This damage to infrastructure was terrible, and it was aimed at destroying morale. I know I was very far from being alone in my determination never to let it achieve its purpose. All across the city, despite the people I saw standing shocked amidst the rubble, the few sad piles of possessions that had been rescued, the heart breaking sight of a small boy with a bloodied bandage around his head and an injured dog in his arms, I saw signs that the people of Plymouth were not downhearted. Instead their spirit was inspiring.

The rank smell of raw sewage from fractured pipes hung in the air. Now and then we drove through a spray of water from a burst water pipe. Everywhere we looked we saw soldiers, navy men and volunteers just getting on with the job, shoring up buildings, producing sandwiches or mugs of steaming hot tea, offering comfort or helping those who had been bombed out. I saw an old lady sitting in a rocking chair amid the destruction, and in my rear view mirror I glimpsed a man hand her a dusty, dishevelled looking cat which had been pulled from the wreckage, and I thought that at least one person had been reunited with a loved one that day.

I dropped Alec off and said goodbye to him, fulfilled my commission for the builders, then parked and walked through the streets to the WVS Canteen in George Street, where I had arranged to meet Fred for lunch.

Until recently my brother had been able to hitch a lift on Navy transport two weekends in four to get home to Salcombe, but heavy bombing had put a strain on all services personnel in the city, and he had had to stay in the dockyard. It had been some weeks since I had seen him, and the sight of him sporting a bandage under his service cap as he made his way through the packed tables, was concerning.

He told me what had happened as we queued for corn beef sandwiches, explaining that he had been in the centre of the city some days before when the air raid siren sounded. The nearest shelter was about fifty yards away, and he was hurrying to it, when he heard the enemy planes already overhead. There was no time to reach the shelter and so he took cover behind a heap of masonry, donning his tin helmet and hunkering down. He said he counted four explosions that rocked the ground around him, deafening him, but the fifth which came a little after the others, had bowled him over and thrown him into the collapsing masonry, gashing his forehead and temporarily winding him.

By the time he stood up, he said, as we joined the second queue for tea, the street had changed beyond recognition, but what had really shaken him was that the main air raid shelter which was the one he had been making for, had received a direct hit. It was the worst number of casualties in one raid that Plymouth had suffered. But it was a lucky escape for my brother, who told me that he had a stiff scotch in the Naafi afterwards courtesy of a Wren who had a secret stash.

I left my brother and started for home. I was barely moving, picking my way through the rubble when suddenly I heard a sharp bang on the side of the car, followed by a child's howl. I clapped on my brakes and climbed out to find a small girl sitting in a heap of bricks nursing an elbow.

She had come from nowhere and I had not seen her. Almost immediately, as the child broke into ear piercing shrieks, people came forward to assure me that I was not at fault. A couple of passing ATS girls took charge of the child, checking her over and pronouncing her fine, despite her yells. Then a stout woman in a floral pinafore whom I took to be the child's mother, arrived, and before I could say anything, scolded the little girl for running into the road, boxing her ears hard and dragging her away. All was well I thought, mightily relieved. But just then a policeman in full uniform but covered from head to toe in plaster dust clambered over the rubble towards me, pulling his notebook out of his uniform pocket officiously as he approached. I had forgotten that the tax disc on my car was out of date.

My plea that I had been on Home Guard and Police duties for some nights as well as everything else, and my paperwork had merely been over looked, fell on deaf ears. Even balancing uncertainly on a piece of masonry in the middle of a destroyed city, this police constable was determined to do his duty, and though I was aware I would probably receive a fine, I was in a way glad that it was so. Plymouth got knocked to pieces that night and for the next few nights, but despite this a week or so later I received a letter from Plymouth Chief Constable with a warning regarding driving without a current licence and a request that I bring my renewed paperwork in for inspection within the week. Considering what Plymouth was going through I thought this efficiency was astonishing

On the way out of the city I passed the ruin of Charles Church. Fred had told me that the church had been hit, but actually seeing it in ruins was terrible. It had always been a monument to the city it protected, a part of Plymouth itself, its outline instantly recognisable.

On a whim I abandoned my car and picked my way over the rubble. An elderly woman in a red hat was kneeling in prayer on the stones in front of the wrecked altar. I was not a religious man but there was something so moving in her quiet homage amid the ruins, that I too bent my head and found myself saying the words of the Lord's prayer.

As I left I saw that several others had joined us. In typical English fashion we did not make eye contact, but somehow this spirit, this solidarity in refusing to accept that our church and our city was finished just because they were reduced to rubble, felt like a small victory over the enemy.

I renewed my licence and duly returned to a badly damaged Plymouth police station to face the music. Luckily I was let off, and just received a warning for my misdemeanour. At least I would not have to join the queues of accused attending court for offences such as showing lights or receiving contraband or meat off ration, as Elsie had predicted with a smile. She had teased me about my burgeoning criminal career, showing me a newspaper cutting about a woman in Ilfracombe who had been fined for putting too much sugar in the cups of tea she had made for her Methodist church canteen, assuring me that I would have been in good company in prison. At least this incident served to take our minds off Alec for a little while, but I found that I was lonely without him in the workshop. Like so many other parents, we could only hope and pray that our boys would come through their war service safely.

The R.A.S.C were transferred from the "Salcombe Hotel", but almost immediately their place was taken by a contingent of about 200 Royal Navy personnel. They brought with them a number of barges from the London Docks. Rumour had it that the barges were to be used in the proposed landing in France that we guessed must be being planned, and that the Royal

Navy sailors were to be trained for the invasion. The barges were a poor substitute for the landing craft that followed, but the officers and ratings who had been recruited to man them put in a good deal of training. This activity was known as "HMS Salcombe" to differentiate it from the Royal Naval Base, Salcombe.

We invited some of these officers to "The Tower" where our musical evenings were then in full swing. There were several good voices amongst them, and the young officers were very kind to Elsie, who, though she kept to her wheelchair, made an excellent hostess. Even when Elsie was not well enough to receive them we let it be known that they were welcome to use our sitting room in the evenings, and often the sound of the piano being played drifted over the neighbourhood. One or two of the men could play well, and often someone would go round to try and persuade Annie Lucy to join them and they would make up a little combo. Coming home late one evening from the workshop I found my mother in law crooning a swing song in the company of a group of delighted officers young enough to be her grandsons.

With Alec gone we were short-handed and I began working with the men more and more. I was tired and with tiredness came carelessness. I would have been the first to warn an apprentice against using the circular saw in such a condition, but I was the boss and I refused to listen even to Ern when he warned me to stay away from the heavy machinery. It was stupidity, but in a momentary lapse of concentration, I put my hand in the way of the blade and cut off the two middle fingers of my right hand.

It was while I was recuperating, doing light duties in the workshop, that the first of the RAF bombing raids over Germany began. Hitler had tried to break Britain's spirit during the Battle of Britain. He had bombed London on 57 consecutive nights, and had brought death and destruction on a large scale to so many other cities, but the British people had not surrendered.

Our retaliation when it came was terrible, Sir Arthur "Bomber" Harris was appointed by the Chiefs of Staff to carry out a campaign of "terror" bombing. The result was the "Thousand Bomber Raid". I saw on Pathe News the aftermath of the bombing of the ancient city of Cologne in which bombs and incendiary devices destroyed a third of the city in a single night.

The tide was at last turning. We waited now for the arrival of our American allies.

CHAPTER THIRTEEN

There were rumours that some American brass had been seen in the South Hams, and that their presence had something to do with a Second Front. Since it was common knowledge that the whole of the coastal shoreline of Slapton Bay and Blackpool Sands had been mined, when a 4"naval gun had been placed at Torcross and another below Strete Village, incredulity greeted the information that a United States Navy captain had been seen walking on Slapton Beach. Alerted by locals, he had been recalled by loud hailer, fortunately without incident. Somehow the information that the beach was mined had not reached the American Navy. I heard this story from Frank. He and our late father shared a similar irreverence when it came to military blunders.

Hitler's advances in Russia were buckling under determined counter attack by the Soviet Red army who was now our ally. Fierce hand to hand fighting had held a starving Stalingrad that was reported to be little more than a mass grave, and Russian troops had smashed through German and Romanian lines, threatening the destruction of General von Paulus's 6th Army.

Luftwaffe raids resumed on the West Country at Exmouth and Torquay. Bombs fell on Salcombe on the nights of 12th and 13th March. Squadron 266 was charged with the prevention of the hit and run raids which were causing havoc in southern England. Spitfires of 317 Squadron, escorting Boston bombers were caught in mist over RAF Bolt Head, and short of fuel, had to force land or bail out over the cliff top airfield. The Commanding Officer was killed and five Spitfires were destroyed during that incident.

American troops were disembarked from Dartmouth and Plymouth during March. From 27th to 31st March troops of the VII Corps under the command of Major General J L Collins were landed on Slapton Beach in a simulated battle exercise involving the 101st Airborne Division, the 42nd and

506th Airborne Infantry, the 4th Infantry, two cruisers and four destroyers.

On 31st March a Luftwaffe bomb killed two people at Fort Charles. We did not know it then, but this turned out to be the last air raid that caused casualties in Salcombe.

The Americans carried out another beach exercise in mist and heavy drizzle in the middle of April. Soon after the first landing craft made the beach, HMS "Enterprise" opened fire but the worsening weather conditions curtailed the bombardment. During the exercise two LCT's collided resulting in damage to both.

There was a rumour going around that Hitler had vowed to hit every cathedral city in England in retaliation for the RAF raids on German factories in the Ruhr Valley. Bath, York, Norwich and many other cities were hit, and Exeter sustained massive damage. Other towns in the West Country including Bishopsteignton, Exminster and Totnes were also bombed. A new quota of steel air raid shelters had recently been distributed in Exeter which it was thought helped minimise casualties there. One of my Home Guard patrol visiting his elderly mother in the city, described suddenly finding himself in the midst of a shower of incendiary bombs. He had a lucky escape as Stukas dived and fired at civilians running for cover around him. The following night, the 24th April, he told me he had counted sixty bombers over the city. After the release of flares to identify their target, they dropped incendiary and high explosive bombs, the majority of which fell on residential areas. It was later discovered that devastating damage to the Pennslyvania District of the city had been caused by two huge Satan bombs. 73 people were killed and 1,000 properties damaged in that attack. There was a third successive raid on the morning of the 26th, in which three were killed and gas and water mains damaged. "Dellers" famous café and dancehall which Elsie and I had visited on a couple of occasions was among the damaged property.

It was heartening to learn that volunteers had coped remarkably well with the devastating results of the bombing. We heard that the WVS women had gone without sleep for three nights in their efforts to help, producing sandwiches, and strong, sweet tea around the clock to comfort the shocked and injured whose homes had been bombed.

The news from abroad at this time was good. On the Eastern Front, the deadly war of attrition that had resulted as the Germans tried to take Stalingrad had ended with the surrender of the German Army to the Reds. There was enthusiastic talk now of a Second Front; then came heartening reports that the Americans were arriving in the West Country.

The Royal Engineers cleared Slapton Beach of mines by June 1943, but not until a farm collie had set off a mine which badly damaged the Royal Sands Hotel. The mines were left on nearby Blackpool Sands, and were not removed until October of that year. None of us could understand why the

Sappers had taken the time and trouble to lay the mines, only to clear them so soon afterwards. There were those who dreamed of visiting the beaches again to fish or swim, but there were still extensive coils of barbed wire prohibiting their use.

There was a Conference of Allied Leaders in Quebec in August 1943 which was reported in the newspapers. It concerned the proposed Allied landing in France, and dealt with the logistics of this exercise, the shore facilities which would be needed to maintain and repair the landing craft, the storage and supply of all necessary war materials, and above all the training of the American combatants. None of us knew then how much what was agreed at this conference would affect the South Hams.

In fact preparations were under way for the greatest invasion ever mounted. Our sleepy part of England was to be the scene of some of the most vital top secret strategic planning of the war, as the ports on the South and South West coasts from Portland to Falmouth became a battle training ground for American troops. The decision to land Allied forces in Normandy necessitated training untested troops on beaches that as closely as possible matched the landing zone designated "Utah". The South Hams landscape was closest in physical characteristics to the coast of France, and the area was also the most convenient leaping off point for the Channel crossing. Slapton Beach, which had already been the subject of landing practise was now deemed to be the ideal choice. With its Ley behind, separated from the sea by a narrow strip of land, it was identical to "Utah".

But the success of the whole operation depended on a blanket secrecy. It was vital that Hitler did not learn the exact location of the proposed Second Front landing. So much of what later happened during Operation Tiger, stemmed from Eisenhower and Churchill's blind determination not to compromise that landing.

The Americans were now expected almost daily, but despite it being common knowledge it was officially still a secret. The subject of their arrival spawned many very amusing cartoons in the local and national press. One I particularly liked showed two old Devon farmers talking in front of a bucolic scene of a typical Devon village dwarfed by a field of thousands of tents all laid out in the very definite shape of a giant stars and stripes flag. One farmer tells the other: "They won't let on who the camp is for."

On 16th August 1943 the first war time exercise involving the small but now steadily growing number of American troops in the area took place on Slapton Beach when the Royal Navy landed soldiers of Company "M" and the Headquarters Company of the 175 Infantry Division. The exercise was a peaceful affair, landing only troops and jeeps, firing blank ammunition. The British naval men in Salcombe joked that thanks to the skill of the Royal Navy, the Americans had been put ashore without getting their feet wet.

Aerial photo. Slapton Ley. 1943. D Murch

At the end of the exercise the men were marched smartly up to Slapton Village where they were picked up by British Army lorries. Locals watching passed news of this happening back to family members in Salcombe. Public opinion was rather scathing about the shortage of the wire mesh that would have stopped the heavy vehicles sinking into the shingle.

Once again our relations the Hannaford family were a rich source of information passing news and gossip from the butcher's shop in Slapton to Salcombe where our ration books were held. The weekly shop meant a chance for us to catch up on news from Slapton.

More good news was broadcast in July when the British Eighth Army, led by General Montgomery was reported to be beating back Rommel at El Alamein after a string of defeats. This was cheering stuff, and guaranteed to lift the country's spirits.

Then we received a telegram from the Air Ministry informing us that Alec had sustained severe injuries to his spine and leg in a plane crash. So far away from him there was little we could do except worry, but the matron in Bulawayo Hospital which was taking care of him, took the trouble to write to us, reassuring us that despite his injuries, our younger son was comfortable, and that it seemed likely that his leg, which they had feared might have to be amputated, would be saved.

Peter was now on ops flying Spitfires on the front line, and we were both worried stiff about him as well. They were difficult days.

On 29th September 1943 a number of United States officers and men came to Salcombe to prepare the way for an intake of what would soon become about 2,000 American personnel billeted in the town. The job of the U.S Naval Constructional Battalion in Salcombe was to set up an advanced Amphibious Base for the repair and maintenance of landing craft. No 8, Egremont Terrace, Devon Road was the first house to be requisitioned and occupied by the U.S Navy.

The barge organisation H.M.S Salcombe was transferred to Exmouth as H.M.S Tennyson, and the Americans began moving into the "Salcombe Hotel". A huge Quonset hut (an oversized Nissen hut) was erected on the site of the present swimming pool to house the men.

The U.S Navy Construction Battalion, known as "Seebees" began building a camp on the Rugby Football ground on the hill above town, which it was rumoured would eventually house 600 men. The buildings were British concrete slab huts, and we heard that there would be a galley area and mess hall built nearby. Provisions and refrigeration huts capable of feeding 2000 men were under way on the undeveloped land adjoining Kinsale, St. Dunstan's and Camperdown Roads, along with a 400 man Quonset hut camp. The refrigeration hut was later used by Salcombe residents for a while after the war for recreational purposes until Cliff House Assembly Rooms were refurbished.

It was common at this time to see American troops marching through the streets and moving about in the town. When the tide was low they used North Sands beach as a parade ground, much to the delight of the local children who always gathered to watch.

The "Salcombe Hotel" became the American Headquarters. "Cliff House" was used for messing and recreation. "St. Elmo's Hotel" became the hospital, and the Central Garage was soon a very busy workshop. By the end of November a further 52 properties had been requisitioned for accommodation, workshops and stores including all available hotels, garages and workshops, so that the Americans in total occupied 60 buildings.

The Town Quay had become the main centre for boat repairs.

Annie Lucy and Edmund had had a succession of American service personnel in residence at this time. Annie Lucy's English teas with home-made scones, jam and cream and fish paste sandwiches were very popular, as were her musical soirees. A Detroit captain introduced her to jazz, which she took to with huge delight. The trade was not all one way however. Visiting her one day I was amused to hear one young American officer speaking broad Cockney rhyming slang, having obviously been coached by my mother in law!

"The Salcombe Hotel" became the American headquarters. To right is Quonset hut. Front left, landing craft.

The U.S Base at Salcombe was officially commissioned on November 23rd 1943 with a parade outside the institute in Devon Road. Commander William H Henszey U.S.N.R was the American Commanding Officer, my brother Frank's counter-part. From the first they had a good working relationship.

The Americans had taken over all available workshop and boat storage space on Whitestrand, but the two rows of derelict 17th century cottages known as Harvey's Row running between the town quay and the Kings Arms Quay cramped their working area. Cmdr. Henszey talked to Frank about the possibility of knocking the cottages down. My brother raised the question with the Council, who gave their agreement for demolition work to begin immediately. The whole area, now officially re-named Whitestrand, became the centre of boat repair activity for the Americans with fixed and mobile cranes working around the clock, and twenty four hour arc lighting. The only time the floodlights were turned off was when the air raid warnings sounded.

From "The Tower" which looked directly across to the beach we could see considerable activity on the East Portlemouth side at Millbay about this time. The beach had been cut off from the land by coils of barbed wire and the Americans with the help of local civilian labour, had begun constructing a large concrete slipway, with cranes, winches and lifting machinery. The

After the demolition of Harvey's Row, the area became known
as "Whitestrand". The American troops used this area to service
and repair craft. Murch

American troops used their own transport to get across the harbour.
Civilians still had use of the Salcombe to East Portlemouth ferry at this
time.

Another centre of boat repair activity was the head of Shadycombe Creek
which had the advantage that craft could be worked on at any state of tide .

The slipway at Mill Bay was in operation by the end of November 1943.
From "The Tower" we watched landing craft being manoeuvred between
the two dolphins that marked the seaward end of the slipway, and over the
top of the massive iron cradle. The boats were secured to the cradle and
hauled up the slipway to be serviced or repaired as needed. As with
Whitestrand the arc lights were on almost continuously except when there
was danger from enemy aircraft. We got so used to the blaze of light
shining into the house from the other side of the estuary that after the war
the darkness was hard to get used to.

All sorts and sizes of vehicles now arrived in the town as the Americans
brought their equipment into Salcombe. The Two Hoots car park at the end
of Island Street was created by clearing the orchard around Gould Farm.
It was surface hardened and became the main vehicle car park and repair
depot, but jeeps and even tanks overflowed onto the foreshore area. At this

Work began on Millbay to establish a dock for landing craft.

time there was still no road to Batson as the reclaimed land built on the Council rubbish tip only extended for about 300 yards.

The Americans now began a series of practises, loading and off-loading troops in full combat gear from landing craft.

The 7th Beach Battalion practised a landing on Fisherman's Cove, storming the beach and entertaining locals on both sides of the estuary.

Some Salcombe men who had been crossing the harbour in the ferry on their way to work at Mill Bay had a ring side view of hundreds of marines in full battle dress charging up the sands with their rifles at the ready, which at close quarters they admitted to finding rather an alarming spectacle.

The following day the Americans again held an exercise in the Slapton area. Some of the landing craft came in over the Skerries, landing the troops near Torcross and the newly mine cleared Blackpool Sands.

It was about this time that members of both Devon County Council and Kingsbridge Rural District Council were seen in the outlying villages of Blackawton and Stokenham near Torcross. According to locals they had asked questions and examined premises, but no-one was any the wiser as to what they actually wanted. But it was now that rumours of a proposed

By 1944 Mill Bay beach was a scene of great activity.

evacuation surfaced in Salcombe. Current talk of a Second Front and the recollection of the military beach exercises of 1938 and August 1943 all provided grist for the idea that something big was afoot and that it probably would concern Slapton - but no-one could have foreseen what would happen next.

A long time later we learned that the Chairman of Devon County Council, Sir John Daw, had received a telephone call on November 4th as advance warning that an area of the South Hams was to be completely evacuated to make a training ground for the American troops. I know that Frank was part of a small group which was informed soon afterwards. I talked with him two days later and I could see that something was troubling him deeply, but he said nothing. All of them had been briefed early on that anything to do with the beach landings was top secret.

The first mention of the plans that I was aware of was at a meeting held at Stokenham "Victory Hall", which was attended by members of the local council, the Home Guard, police and several other volunteer groups. Maps were in place detailing the area involved, and the plans were explained together with details of the timings of the events. We all received the news in stunned silence. Never in our wildest dreams had we expected something on this scale. Most of the audience had friends or family in the evacuation area and I know we all found it hard to deal with on a personal level.

The second meeting was with the clergy from the churches in the areas to be cleared, which would also come under the compulsory evacuation order.

Men of the 7th Battalion practise landing on Fisherman's Cove

The church men were given details of the government's financial arrangements towards the cost of temporary accommodation and information about the payment of rents and storage of evacuees' furniture during the enforced absence. They were told that the evacuation had to be completed within six weeks.

Posters entitled "Important Meetings" were now pasted up around the area. Giving the dates of the meetings as Friday November 12th at East Allington Church and Stokenham Church, with the speaker Earl Fortescue , M.C, Lord Lieutenant of Devon, and Saturday November 13th at Blackawton Church and Slapton Village Hall, under the chairmanship of Sir John Daw. J.P, Chairman of Devon County Council, the posters contained the following information beneath a large heading "The Area Affected".

"The area described below is to be REQUISTIONED urgently for military purposes, and must be cleared of its inhabitants by DECEMBER 20th, 1943.

"All land and buildings lying within the line from the sea at the east end of Blackpool Bay in Stoke Fleming parish to Bowden; thence northward along the road to the "Sportsman's Arms"; thence west along the Dittisham-Halwell road to the cross roads ¼ mile east of Halwell Village; from this cross-road along the Kingsbridge road to the Woodleigh-Buckland cross roads; thence along the road to Buckland, Frogmore, Chillington, Beeson and Beesands to the sea, but excluding the villages of Frogmore, Beeson and Beesands. The roads forming the boundary are outside the area.

The parishes involved are the whole, or almost the whole of Blackawton, East Allington, Sherford, Slapton and Strete, most of Stokenham and parts of Stoke Fleming, Buckland-tout-saints and Halwell."

The meetings were packed. As one local put it bitterly: "They told us in church 'cos they knew us would not swear at "em there".

Afterwards knots of villagers gathered outside. All were shocked. Nobody could take in the enormity of what was to happen.

There were so many questions, but most of the farmers and villagers did not dare to approach the august personages and foreigners who had now forced themselves into their lives and assumed control of their destinies, so it was more often than not the responsibility of local police and Home Guard, to provide answers. Frank gave a briefing to all local volunteers, telling us that we could explain to those who questioned the move that live ammunition and shells would be used in the area which would place them in danger, but he stressed that the prime concern for all was not to alert the enemy to the invasion plan. In an attempt to lessen the risk of talk spreading it was decided that each village should have its own information centre.

Dazed and bewildered, the villagers struggled to make sense of it all. It seemed incomprehensible that whole families should be ordered to leave homes and farms that had often been in the same family for generations. It made no sense that they had to give up land that they were working in order to provide the essential food required by the Ministry of Agriculture. And all by 20th December... Six weeks to pack up a lifetime, to find somewhere else to live, different work to do when you knew nothing else.

The evacuation of the old and the sick particularly aroused considerable concern in the rest of Devon, for with the official announcement made public it was inevitable that the local newspapers got hold of it. Several protest meetings were organised, but nothing came to fruition probably because of pressure being brought to bear on the dissenters.

The order required the compulsory requisition of twenty five square miles of the South Hams countryside and the evacuation of all inhabitants, animals and farm animals from six parishes - three thousand people from seven hundred and fifty households. One of the greatest exoduses of a civilian population in our history was to start, bringing with it heartbreak and hardship that would scar the people of the area for generations. Six thousand head of cattle and twelve thousand sheep were to be removed, together with tens of thousands of tons of root crops and all farming implements and machinery. No official scheme was yet in place to offer accommodation to the people who were to be evicted from their homes.

Information leaflets were delivered to each affected household. Information centres were opened at Blackawton and Slapton, followed by similar centres in other affected villages. WVS volunteers did their best to address individual concerns and to help traumatised people. As families found somewhere to live the WVS was given responsibility for transporting them to their new homes. Many villagers found accommodation in Dartmouth, others were forced to travel further afield. Several went to Cornwall. One woman went as far away as Scotland. The task was the largest undertaken during the war by the WVS volunteer car pool and the heavy demand on local resources meant a severe shortage of petrol in the area for some time afterwards.

Finding containers for such a quantity of belongings was just one of the problems. Few villagers had ever travelled away from home before, and hardly any possessed suitcases or suitable containers. May Schofield made valiant efforts and many locals turned up trumps by bringing suitcases and storage boxes out of lofts; shops and offices brought boxes, local brewers and cider makers supplied barrels. But it was not enough, and an urgent call went out to all WVS Depots around the country, which soon led to a good supply of containers. The American Army supplied fifty transport trucks and a contingent of British sailors and American troops helped to load the lorries.

Mobile canteens were set up by the W.V.S to supply meals to the helpers; hot cooked food was sent over from Brixham's "British Restaurant". In Strete village the Ministry of Food set up a mobile kitchen, but the food was not very popular as a meal was based on a halfpenny's worth of meat ration per person.

As the evacuation continued village stores closed down. Emergency bread and milk deliveries were organised to supply the evacuated villagers and other nearby communities that had until now relied on the services and deliveries from village tradesmen. Notices gave the time and date of deliveries. "Last orders" were called at the "Queens Arms" in Slapton.

It rained continuously from the very start of the evacuation, and the lanes turned into quagmires. Lorries loaded with furniture sank up to their axles in the mud and tractors had to be brought in to pull them out. All the signposts had long since been removed as a precaution against German spies, and drivers who did not know the area became lost in the lanes. Since many of the houses were now empty there was often no-one to ask to find the way to individual farms and hamlets buried away down muddy by-ways. Added to this chaos was an outbreak of 'flu and chicken pox, which soon grew to epidemic proportions.

Though considerable efforts had been made to find homes for the evacuees, in the end three quarters of them found their own accommodation. Household pets were often taken by kind people outside the immediate area. If no homes could be found for them they were put down by the RSPCA. This caused considerable pain to many.

The removal of agricultural machinery and its storage was also a major problem. Some nearby farmers had room in their barns and offered to store farm equipment, or arranged the loan of it to be used on their own land. Cattle presented one of the biggest problems. There was a widespread belief that if cattle were taken from their old homes, they would die, so this was always going to be a difficult business. Many farms had built up bloodlines through generations, and could not bear to see their animals killed. Cattle sales were held in Kingsbridge, but the market was swamped. Then there was the problem of digging up and transporting vast quantities of root crops.

The churches presented their own unique problems. Many of the churches in the six parishes possessed a number of ancient and often very valuable artefacts. Blackawton Church had an irreplaceable Tudor rood screen that still retained its medieval colours of blue and vermillion, and this had to be removed and sent to Exeter Cathedral for safe keeping. East Allington Parish Church boasted a very fine carved oak screen, and a pulpit dating from 1547 and these were dismantled and carefully wrapped before being sent away to safety. One by one the treasures from the other churches were packed and removed. Items that were to remain were crated and carefully stored while the churches themselves were sandbagged and boarded up.

A continual line of transport was brought to the villages as trucks were loaded up with household possessions. Blackawton became blocked with vehicles, all floundering in a sea of mud. The villagers had never seen anything like it before. The inns and public houses served their last drinks and then closed. The final church services were held, and the doors of the churches were locked. To the door of each church was fastened this notice -

"To our Allies of the USA –

This church has stood here for several hundred years. Around it has grown a community which has lived in these houses and tilled these fields ever since there was a church. This church, this churchyard in which their loved ones lie at rest, these homes, these fields are as dear to those who have left them as are the homes and graves and fields, which you, our Allies, have left behind you. They hope to return one day, as you hope to yours, to find them waiting to welcome them home. They entrust them to your care meanwhile, and pray that God's blessing may rest upon us all.

Charles, Bishop of Exeter".

All the villagers had now left. The evacuation was completed by 20th December according to schedule. The helpers packed up and followed. The last of the volunteer workers left on Christmas Eve 1943 leaving behind them silent, empty villages. The battle area was now formally handed over to the United States Army.

Miles of barbed wire fencing was erected along the boundary of the area.

It was patrolled inside by American troops and on the outside by members of the Home Guard and other reservists. I patrolled it several times in the months to come. I found the deserted villages eerie and sad. Without predators the local wildlife increased. Each time I went on patrol the population of rabbits and pigeons seemed to have multiplied

Christmas Day 1943 would have been my parents Aaron and Ellen Murch's diamond wedding anniversary. We gave my now quite frail mother a small family party, and I was not alone in picturing my father's face wreathed in the proud smiles it would have worn had he been alive to receive the telegram from the king. We all knew that Aaron would have been convinced that King George would have written and posted the congratulatory missive personally. My father had had a wonderfully uncomplicated relationship with both his king and his God.

On 31st December 1943, ten days after all civilians had been moved from the battle training area battle the American forces began landing exercises concentrating on Slapton Beach. Frank briefed the Home Guard with basic information before each of the many test and training runs which continued for the next few months.

Luftwaffe planes flew over Plymouth again at dawn on 16th November, dropping bombs over a wide area of the city, Fred told us, during what was now an infrequent visit home. The bombs included incendiary, phosphorous and oil bombs, but it was the high explosive bombs that caused extensive damage to over two thousand homes, killing and injuring many.

There was now a gradual build-up of American troops in Salcombe. Ships and amphious landing craft began to fill the harbour. Small boats multiplied, running backwards and forwards from Whitestrand Quay and military vehicles clogged up the approach roads to the Two Hoots Car Park. Salcombe developed serious traffic problems especially when low loaders bringing in tanks, artillery guns or armoured personal carriers got stuck, but Dartmouth by all accounts had an even worse time. Frank delighted in a story of one elderly lady driver who had somehow managed to get her car caught up in an American convoy making its way to Slapton. She had refused to back up to allow the convoy to pass, and for a brief time there was a stand-off. But however determined the ancient Devonian was to hold her ground, she was no match for the American Army on the move. There was a crane in the rear of the convoy, and this was brought forward. After beseeching her in vain one last time to move her vehicle, soldiers fitted chains around the car, and with the old lady still inside, hoisted it up over a hedge and into a nearby field where they left it. I know both of us were thinking of Aaron and how he would have loved the story. As Frank said, father would have laughed 'till he burst his britches.

The presence of so many Americans in Salcombe altered the whole character of the town as their numbers equalled the entire civilian population. Used to austerity for so long, locals were astonished at the apparently unlimited stores the Americans brought with them. Lorry loads of rations and materials arrived, none of which seemed to be anyone's

Build up of American vehicles in Two Hoots Car Park.

particular responsibility. Such a vast amount of goods were brought in that I believed the rumour I heard that amongst them was an entire lorry load of chewing gum, ordered to counter sea sickness amongst service personnel unused to being on board ship.

For the children however, and a few of the local girls, the Americans were sent from heaven. The children followed them around hoping for chocolate. The girls wanted stockings, and were drawn to young men who came from a land of plenty with none of the hardships they were enduring. The local males were not best pleased however and there were one or two incidents between Americans and Devon men.

Aware of the possibility of trouble Frank and Cmdr. Henszey did their best to make sure that the fighting men of the two nations were kept apart. But on one notable occasion men from the Royal Navy and United States Navy ships met in the "Ferry Inn". Shore patrols from each navy intervened promptly, managing to separate American and British troops. Making sure that they left by separate exits the military police marshalled their respective charges down to the ferry steps and aboard hastily summoned transport back to their ships. Deprived of the chance of a good scrum, the two navies gave vent to their frustration by each trying to out sing the other. As the jolly boats left the ferry steps lusty bellows of "Rule Britannia" was countered by an equally loud rendition of "The Star Spangled Banner" that echoed behind the boats all the way back up the estuary.

Though there were a few problems such as when some American marines were encouraged to partake liberally of scrumpy, having been

My brother Frank.- Lieutenant Cmdr. Francis Murch R.N.V.R. Resident Naval Officer, Salcombe. Awarded the American Legion of Merit. 7th Sept. 1945

blithely assured that it was just apple juice, it was generally agreed that the behaviour of all the forces stationed in the town was exceedingly good. Though Frank sometimes privately bemoaned the Americans' lack of discipline – a hard thing for a Royal Navy man to swallow – I know he also appreciated their tact and their genuine desire to play their part in the protection of his beloved town.

In January 1944 men of the 6th and 9th Battalion – the Beach Masters who would be responsible for ensuring that the landing craft could unload combat ready troops – moved into the hut camp that had been prepared for them.

Frank and I met often sometimes officially, sometimes just as brothers. He was punctilious in never telling me anything, even in confidence, that was not something I should hear, but I knew he felt strongly that all the exercises that had taken place had only highlighted the work that needed to be done to improve communications between the Allied and U.S navies and The Airborne Forces. It was exactly these failings that would contribute to the horror of the next exercise, codenamed Operation Tiger.

Peter returned from Canada just before his twenty first birthday. On a brief leave which he spent at home, I gave him the remaining half of the

Commander William H Henszey. U.S.N.R. Commanding Officer
U.S.N.A.A.B., Salcombe. Photo. Given to Frank.

garden adjoining "The Tower" so that he could build his own house. He told us a great deal about Vancouver which he had obviously fallen in love with. He several times mentioned a Canadian girl named Ruth, whom he had often sailed with. He had a photograph of her in his wallet, and the whole family were quietly confident that this would become a serious relationship. Her picture showed an attractive big boned girl with a broad, open expression. It was the face of a girl I instinctively liked. But even to Elsie Peter did not say much more.

I had given Jim Camp notice of termination of our partnership twice before but withdrawn it at his urging. This time I determined to stick to it. After negotiations we settled that I would give him £1,000 for his share of the business. This was a good deal for him as the firm currently had very few assets and little work, but it was also the best thing for me, though it meant that I had to start again almost from scratch. But I preferred it that way. For the first time since we had become partners, I would now be free to run the firm the way I wanted.

Frank spent a great deal of his working day dealing with the logistics of moving American traffic around the town, but his job also entailed pacifying local residents who were understandably concerned that the massive concentration of US troops and equipment might endanger the town.

The US military high command were reluctant to meet with all the separate Civil Defence authorities within the area, and it was left to Frank to negotiate a deal with the American Officer Commanding to work within the structure set by the South West Civil Defence regional organisation to counter some of the civilian fears. All knew that the massing of troops and equipment carried with it the very real danger of a German super-blitz on the area, and with that came the ever present spectre of a gas attack. Arguing that Salcombe was a special case as it was amongst those areas designated an "Assembley Point" for Americans, Frank arranged for additional Anderson and Morrison shelters to be secured and erected around the town.

The harbour became busier and busier as the weeks passed and more and more vessels and ever larger contingents of men arrived.

Once more it was a cartoon that depicted this situation exactly. In the background an American soldier disappears into the distance with his arm around a young English woman. In the foreground two elderly Devon spinsters are gazing longingly after them. One says to the other: "Don't despair, Gertrude. I heard there's another thousand coming in next week".

To meet the perceived need many more Civil Defence and National Fire Service personnel were now drafted into Salcombe, further straining resources. The WVS addressed the problem of worries concerning gas by re-issuing advice about preparing a safety room. Women went from door to door collecting blankets to make sure all householders had the necessary equipment to build themselves a gas protection room. I saw May Schofield coming up the street and slipped out, but she caught me as I came back and I had to hand over two spare blankets. It was impossible to resist May's bright cheerfulness even though she must have been so worried about Grey, then serving in the Far East. Despite being so busy, she still made time to visit Elsie, and I was very fond of her.

Fuel tanks were constructed at Snapes Point and Shadycombe as yet more vessels were brought into the harbour, necessitating the laying of numerous moorings by the Royal Navy from Mill Bay to Gerston, near Kingsbridge. The construction and enlargement of marine facilities, the slipways and the wholesale clearance of storage areas, in addition to the increased number of boats and amphibious craft in the harbour and anchored up past The Bag towards Kingsbridge, was ample evidence that massive military action was being planned. Locals gradually became aware that they were seeing the beginning of the "Second Front", and a spirit of cautious optimism developed.

As usual the police and Home Guard were notified of the next exercise to be conducted by American troops. This one, code named "Tiger", was scheduled to take place between 26th and 29th April 1944. For this exercise the convoys were to use extended swept channels to simulate conditions as they would be for the landing in France. It was only later that we learned that the covering naval force would consist of the Tribal destroyers HMS "Ashanti", HMS "Athabaskan", HMS "Haida" and HMS "Huron" as well as coastal forces of Plymouth Command. The Task Force Commander and the Commanding General VII Corps, 4th Infantry Division were deployed on USS "Boyfield". The Second in Command was on LCH95.

I knew that the Naval Base had been on duty all night and I was sure that both Frank and Commander Herszey were there as they always were during exercises, but it was not until the following morning that we received news that the convoy had been attacked by EBoats.

It was much later that we found out that the fleet had not gone to Slapton as we presumed, but to an area 14 miles off Portland Bill, nearly 40 miles ENE of Slapton, where they had run into the Eboat pack that had devastated them.

The information must have come direct to Frank and Cmdr. Henszey, but word that there were a great number of casualties first reached the locals when LST 289 struggled back to her home port of Dartmouth, the only vessel to do so. Her seriously injured were transhipped on to be taken to the 228th Field Army Hospital in Sherborne, but there were other less seriously injured who were landed temporarily while they were awaiting shipment. It was these traumatised young men who spoke of hundreds of dead and injured left in the water in the wake of the attack.

The actual number of casualties was known to be very large, but it was to be years before the smoke screen was lifted and a figure of 700 was mooted, years later before that estimate was upgraded, perhaps to as high as 1,000 American casualties. But right from the start the treatment of the injured and the quick, unceremonious burial of the dead, was spoken of with disgust by locals. I know that Frank was upset by it, but the official line was that complete secrecy was paramount. After the war he told me that orders had been issued to doctors and paramedics to treat the injured as if they were cattle, not to talk to them, not to listen to what they had to say, at all costs to prevent them from telling what they had seen, so that advance warning was not given to the enemy. And that, to those who had lived amongst those carefree, almost childlike young men, was almost harder to bear than the garbled stories that later emerged, blaming the British for not transmitting the message about the EBoat presence, when much later it was acknowledged that in fact it was the Americans who had not been on the correct channel to receive the warning. There were so many faults but perhaps greatest amongst them was the problem that had already been established a year or more before, which hinged on the communication difficulties between the troops of the two nations.

The incident cast its shadow over the town. Commander Henszey and my brother worked tirelessly to accord the dead and injured within their jurisdiction their rightful care, but overall hung an impenetrable web of secrecy. In the days afterwards, when burnt, mangled bodies were still being pulled from the water the military police spirited the bodies away quickly.

The Americans now began a series of exercises. Troops were marched through the town to Whitestrand and then embarked on amphibious craft loaded with equipment. The number of times these craft were embarked and disembarked until finally the officers appeared satisfied with the performance, puzzled everyone until it was realised that it was embarking and disembarking that they were practising. The flat bottomed LST's then wallowed their way out to sea presumably on exercises in which the Royal Navy warships which could be seen in the Channel also played their part. The sound of heavy gunfire from ships onto shore came from the Slapton area several times over the months from December 1943 through to March and April 1944. At least two of these dummy runs used live ammunition.

We did not know then that we were seeing practise runs for landing in Normandy but the town was alive with anticipation. One of the tales doing the rounds of Salcombe at this time concerned a young ARP warden who had come across three men in bulky overcoats with binoculars lurking on the cliff top while on patrol. When challenged, it transpired that the three men were none other than General Eisenhower, General Montgomery and Winston Churchill!

It was now belatedly recognised that the South Hams was a high risk area, which worked in our favour as most of our remaining evacuees were taken back up country. I had from time to time heard news of the three children I had taken out to the farm at Shadycombe, and I was interested to learn from the farmer's wife when we met in the street that though the two girls had been returned home, the older boy had opted to stay in Devon as he had developed a real affinity for farming.

The Royal Navy laid numerous moorings to cope with additional craft. By May one of the biggest problems to be overcome was the shortage of water for all this influx of personnel. Salcombe had always had a problem with water supply, especially during the summer months when the town's population was swelled by visitors. Now, with the town full to overflowing with troops and volunteer forces, demand exceeded the flow to the reservoir.

At a conference with the Chairman of the Water Board, and American and British Naval heads, it was suggested that a booster pump be installed near South Brent, a few miles south of the water works at Bala Brook. It was an idea that had come up several years earlier when Frank had first become Chairman of the Council, and raised the problem of an emergency water supply to the town, and now it was agreed that it should be implemented.

Accordingly a pump was obtained from the U.S stores in Exeter, where everything seemed to be available, and this was installed. An electric generator was exchanged for a second water pump from the U.S Naval Hospital at "St. Elmo", in Sandhill Road, to further boost the mains water supply.

The next problem was the thorny one of how to get the water to the ships, as the one water boat the town possessed had been wrecked following the bombing in which Mrs Chadder-Blank had been killed.

A scheme was worked out and Cmdr. Henszey obtained all the canvas fire hoses he could from Exeter. With traffic stopped, the hoses were connected to the street hydrants and then laid down on Whitestrand. To reach the LST's moored three abreast in the centre of the harbour, it was necessary to support the hoses above the water on pontoons and boats. This worked, although movement of shipping interrupted supplies as the hoses had to be painstakingly disconnected and pulled back if a vessel needed to pass. The smaller vessels were supplied by a specially adapted landing craft.

At the beginning of 1944 the South Coast Area of England was designated a Prohibited Area and all but residents had to leave. In March, Defence Committees were set up, consisting of Naval, Military and Civil representatives with the R.N.O as Chairman.

The harbour was now the scene of constant bustle with increased troop movements. This had seemingly come to the attention of the enemy, and we now saw more German day and night reconnaissance flights over the area as well as increased Spitfire activity as our pilots from the base at Bolt Head chased them away. Radio broadcasts at this time reassured us that almost none of these German planes were reaching the interior of the country thanks to our daring pilots and our new radar system. But we were aware that Salcombe was under increased threat.

All contact between troops and civilians was now ceased and censorship tightened. No-one ever really knew whether it was "careless talk" or something more sinister, but I remember Frank telling me at about this time that of 20,000 letters intercepted in the area, 80% had made some mention of the top secret preparations in the harbour. Civilian movement was now heavily restricted, and I had to apply for travel visas for two of my workmen who lived on the other side of Kingsbridge. At the end of May all personnel were confined to their ships or bases to further tighten security.

Day by day now it seemed that there were more craft in the harbour. We learned to recognise the different landing craft: the LST's or Landing Ship Tanks which could carry up to 6 x 40 ton tanks, or 400 personnel; the LCR's the Landing Craft Rockets fitted with 1,000 x 5 inch rockets; the LCT's which carried up to 4 x 40 ton tanks and troops; the LCA's or Landing Craft Assault vessels, holding 30 men; the LCI's the Landing Craft Infantry, capacity 200 men; the Rhinos, Causeways and Blisters, all forms of flat bottomed barges; the Tugs, SC's or Sub Chasers U.S, and the ML's the British high speed Motor Launches, similar in size and used as escorts.

But in the meantime, there was a brief period when the preparations for war were put on hold and the American sailors donned their best blue uniforms, and together with the troops of the 24th United States Infantry Division, the British Army, Royal and Merchant Navies, the Royal Air Force, A.R.P Wardens, Home Guard, Police forces, and massed ranks of volunteers, paraded through the streets of Salcombe and Kingsbridge cheered by packed crowds of well-wishers, in a public relations exercise entitled "Salute the Sailor Week".

On May 11th 1944, in the hospital that I had built in Kingsbridge, Edmund John Symmons' heart finally gave out and he died, aged 86 years. He had been Elsie's adored father, a good friend to me as well as my father in law, and I missed his wise counsel badly. His loss hit Annie Lucy hard, and I guessed that she would not long outlive him. She tried to carry on, desperate to support her beloved daughter, but we could see that despite her brave smiles, the heart had gone out of her.

On 2nd June 1944 4 Royal Navy ML's led by ML490 under the command of Lt. Cmdr. Searle whose primary job was to get a convoy to the right beach at the right time, left Salcombe Harbour. It was years later that I heard that Lt. Cmdr Searle's M.L had been equipped with a device known as QH, which was an embryo Decca Navigation System. The secondary task of this ML was to shepherd and protect the convoy against enemy attack on the way.

Around the harbour troops were now waiting on their ships. The weather worsened, and we guessed that the commanders would stay in harbour until it improved. In the Bag were a number of Landing Craft packed with infantry men who must have had an uncomfortable 24 hours.

Early on the morning of June 3rd, I was amongst several men called to Frank's office to receive a special briefing. I remember that there was an undercurrent of excitement and anticipation at the Base that in retrospect I felt was much greater than for a normal exercise. My orders as Sergeant, Home Guard were to lead a platoon of men on duty at the Battery above Splat Cove the following day when a big convoy was due to leave. There was however an important amendment to the orders. Frank told us that

EBoats had been seen operating off Start Bay, and that it was expected that attacks by enemy aircraft, submarines and EBoats would be launched on the convoy both en route and in the exercise area. But he stressed emphatically that if we saw any enemy shipping we were on no account to open fire, as the Americans had given strict instructions that nothing was to be done that might alert the German Keigsmarine to the fact that Salcombe was defended.

Late on the afternoon of 3rd June 1944 a convoy of about 60 vessels of all shapes and sizes left the harbour. It was raining heavily and fog swirled around the estuary. From our position on the cliffs we watched the boats heading out to sea, looking down on a sea of tin helmets. Some of the men packed shoulder to shoulder in the landing craft knew our position and waved cheerily up at us.

The boats took a long time to pass us. We commented as we always did about the way the flat bottomed landing craft pitched and rolled in the choppy ocean and the miniscule size of some of the craft. We estimated that some of the smaller boats were only making about 5 knots while the ML's minimum speed was 8 knots with one engine shut down We saw some of the faster boats circling continuously to keep the flotilla together. Several times as the boats steered out to sea, we saw a shower of sparks and guessed that engineers on some vessels were clearing engines that had been labouring too slowly. At one stage we saw what must have been a boat on fire, which we thought was bound to attract German attack.

We watched the boats heading in the direction of Lyme Bay, until they were just faint smudges on the horizon. With them gone there was nothing to see in the fading light except miles and miles of open sea. As children Frank and I had called Bolt Head, the "End of the World", because there was nothing beyond it except endless ocean. Hunkered down out of a biting wind my patrol scanned the empty waves, talked a little, and then ate the sandwiches we had brought with us, waiting for our relief.

The weather deteriorated. Later it was confirmed that this first convoy had been forced to take shelter in Portland Harbour, which itself was already overcrowded with vessels waiting to leave for France. A message was passed from Frank's office to advise us that the operation had been delayed by 24 hours. The boats remaining in Salcombe Harbour were forced to wait.

On the afternoon of the 5th June, a secondary convoy of 17 LCT's and an SC left Salcombe to rendezvous three miles south of the harbour with a convoy which had sailed from Plymouth. This Plymouth contingent we later learned, consisted of a further 14 LCT's, the U.S Destroyer "O'Brien" and two Mine Sweepers.

A little later in the day another convoy left the harbour with between 9 and 11 LST's, 3 U.S Army Tugs, a Rhino, 8 Causeways, 8 Blisters and their escorts. They were met three miles south of the harbour by 3 Anti-Submarine trawlers which again had sailed from Plymouth

Then they were gone, and the harbour was empty and silent, the town quiet and stilled as if a party that had been in full swing had suddenly moved on, taking the people, the music and the noise with it, leaving behind a sense of something momentous and exciting playing out just out of our sight and hearing.

Frank at "La Barranca" on the eve of D Day, 5th June 1944.

On Tuesday 6th June it was announced on the radio that the Allied Forces had landed in Normandy in the area designated Utah Beach, in Operation D-Day. The jubilation that followed the news was evident in the streets and shops, in the strained faces which now broke into smiles and laughter. It had been a very long time coming, but at last we were beginning to see the light at the end of the tunnel.

Most of the news was still subject to strict censorship and it was some days before more details were forthcoming, even then much of what was published was speculation. But the fact remained that the Allied Forces had landed in France.

Much later we learned that in darkness on DDay, 6th June, the augmented Salcombe convoy had arrived off Utah Beach escorted by 7 R.N ML's and a U.S PT boat. The accompanying warships had opened fire on the beach, then at dawn, the guns had fallen silent as waves of landing craft headed for the shore. Salcombe was proud of the part it had played, and the town was joyous. We had little heart for celebrations, but I think everyone felt that something very special had happened, and quietly, we felt ourselves in some small way responsible for it. We had played our part.

Frank told us that the intention was that the USN Base at Salcombe would move over to Normandy. One boat, the LC1507 did leave, but there were so many captured Germans in the landing zone in France, that there was room for no more vessels, so they were ordered back to Salcombe.

About a week later the first casualties from DDay were brought into the town. The number of returning American servicemen was smaller than it had been before the Normandy landings so the camp in the Rugby Football Ground was turned into a Prisoner of War compound for captured German and Italian prisoners.

The exercises were over but in the Battle Training Area unexploded mines and ammunition had to be cleared before the houses and farms could be returned to their owners. There was tremendous damage to property. I remember particularly seeing the ruined house at the Strete Gate End of Slapton beach as well as the now derelict Royal Sands Hotel and the partially destroyed Parish church and nearby Church House Inn at Stokenham. Farmers on the perimeter of the area were the first to return. The lucky ones were home by the autumn of 1944, while those near the beach, where the shelling had been heaviest were not allowed back until early in 1945.

Before the USN Advance Amphibious Base party arrived back, a large floating dock was brought to the harbour and moored off Ditch End. This was to be used in the repair of the larger landing craft. There was still a need for a great number of serviceable landing craft and any surplus were sent to the Far East.

Not all the Americans left Salcombe after V E Day. Those remaining were mostly specialist servicing and repair teams. Under the terms of the Lend Lease damaged boats had to be repaired before being handed back to our government. So many landing craft had been damaged in the exercise that it was not possible to handle them all at Mill Bay so the excess was repaired at Ditch End.

A parade was held on the Berry and Admiral Moon of the U.S Navy presented a Purple Heart medal to all the U.S. servicemen wounded in the action.

Ellen had been ill for some weeks with an unspecified complaint. She had grown thinner and noticeably frailer of late. We talked a lot in those days. We were so alike, but now Ellen's temper and her firmness of purpose had gone with the loss of Aaron. She was as she put it, without her companion, "like a ship without a compass". She had grown used to talking to Aaron, and she talked to him now as if he were still living, chiding him for not being there. Her sons had made their mark in the world, and she was proud. Now all she wanted to do was to join Aaron. One of the last things we ever talked about was her chair. She had forgotten at the end that Elsie was now in a wheelchair and she asked that she be given her chair. I had to promise that I would give it to her – and I had to promise that finally, I would have its leg mended. She gave me a ten shilling note that she had put aside for the repair together with the money in the old teapot that she had saved to pay for her funeral. She ruled her household to the end. I missed her more than any of the others.

There was only Annie-Lucy left. She was frail now, but she hung on to try and help her beloved daughter. I made a point of seeing her most days. She was not able to walk the short distance to "The Tower" but she wrote little notes to Elsie. She was waiting to die, and she died gently, kindly, falling asleep in her chair by the fire, a smile on her still beautiful face.

It was a common sight to see the troops parading in the streets and marching around the town. When the tide was low they continued their practise of using North Sands beach as a parade ground. With D Day over, the tension had eased, and the Americans socialised once again with the local populace. The mixing was overwhelmingly good humoured and many life-long friendships were forged. In those days it was the paper work of the clear up that most weighed Frank down. Mostly they were small incidents largely caused by the numbers of vehicles the Americans used. It seemed to the locals as if each US serviceman had his own transport. Moving vehicles to transport them on to other sites meant taking large vehicles down narrow lanes and between houses. 3 civilian pedestrians and five cyclists were injured; one farm dog was killed and a farmer in a horse and cart was in collision with a jeep. There were five cases in which landing craft damaged other boats or shore side buildings. A mobile crane on Whitestrand quay damaged the Food Office (now Normandy House) in June, and a U.S Marine Corps Major driving a bulldozer demolished a wall in November 1944.

Christmas that year was celebrated with traditional parties for children, though with the paper shortage other ways had to be found to decorate rooms. Food did not seem to be so much of a problem this year, probably because the Americans helped out from their ample stores. A few families had managed to get hold of an orange to put in their children's Christmas stockings, though no-one had a banana which had been absent from the shops for so long that many youngsters had never tasted one. The acute shortage of leather meant that shoes could not be repaired. Most people had more than one pair and so the holed ones were put aside for some unspecified time in the future, when perhaps there might once more be enough leather to have them repaired. For the others, wooden shoes were introduced. For a few weeks we heard the clatter of clogs in Salcombe, but since the wood used to make them was soft and wore out quickly, this proved not to be a solution to the problem, so for a while a variation of the old Boot Club was resurrected. For drinkers, things were very serious, as there was no beer or stout to be had. Luckily Devonians always had cider! But I don't remember hearing complaints. Somehow it was all part of the dawning realisation that ultimately whatever hardships we might be enduring, the war was winnable

Salcombe responded well to an appeal for books to replace the tens of thousands lost to the bombing by Plymouth libraries. Elsie and I both donated some in recognition of the city's courage in trying so hard to re-establish its normal daily life amid the awful damage it had sustained. The bombings and the subsequent necessary demolition and clearance of hazardous, shattered buildings meant there were vast empty spaces in the city. Few shops were able to be repaired immediately and as time went on plans were made to erect Nissan huts for the traders. One of the many problems facing the city was transport. So many buses had been destroyed in the bombing that it was not possible to find sufficient replacements, but some of the old tram tracks had survived, so a few trams were brought back into service. There were however some record catches of fish reported at this time, presumably because local fishing had been limited for so long that fish stocks had had time to build up.

On 17th February 1945, Frank received a Letter of Commendation from the Admiralty for his services in the planning and execution of duties for D Day.

Franklyn D Roosevelt the President of the United States died on 12th April 1945, and a memorial service was held in the Parish church of Holy Trinity in Salcombe on the afternoon of Sunday 14th April. My brother Frank, in his position as Resident British Naval Officer, was asked to read one of the lessons. Almost 500 U.S Navy personnel attended, together with what seemed like everyone in the town, so that many had to stand outside in the churchyard and adjoining street to hear the service.

The activities of the American Base at Salcombe steadily declined as the European war moved towards its close. On 7th May 1945 the United States Base in Salcombe ceased operations and there was an open air gathering in Courtney Park.

Commander Henszey, addressed the gathering: "Today we are offering our prayers and thoughts in Thanksgiving for the defeat of our enemy in Europe... You must pardon me if at this solemn occasion I officially announce that the U S Naval Forces will soon leave Salcombe. It has been a happy voyage for us. We will regret leaving this beautiful community. We came here as strangers, but we feel we leave as friends. You made us welcome and your friendship is deeply appreciated. I want to convey from the Officers and Men our deepest gratitude to each and every one of you and in particular to your Resident Naval Officer, Lt. Cmdr. Murch, whose often repeated phrase "We're one Navy" was underscored by his efforts and co-operation. Much has been under done, much has been over done, but we have done what we came for. There will be much talked about and much better left unsaid. Duty will soon call us elsewhere, but Salcombe will always retain a special place in our hearts"

And more than one heart I thought, glancing across to where Audrey Petit the first local girl to marry an American serviceman stood with her family, a smile on her face as she fixed shining eyes on her new husband standing amongst the ranks of men. She was to go back to America with him – but everyone was sure that one day he would come back to Salcombe with her.

All the properties the American troops had occupied had to be inspected and taken over by the R.N.O and all contents signed for. For safe custody the portable contents were removed to the hut camp in the Rugby Field and placed under armed guard before being returned to the Naval Stores and U.S Depots. There were two huts filled with furniture and goods which apparently did not belong to either the U.S, Naval or R.N Stores. After advertising to try and find the rightful owners C.I.C Plymouth ordered them to be sold and the proceeds distributed amongst Naval charities. There were a great many articles of protective clothing left behind as well. For several years fishermen and locals could be seen walking around Salcombe in United States Navy jackets.

All stores were returned to the British Base and the equipment dismantled. The base itself ceased to exist in August 1945.

In a simple, but moving ceremony, my brother was presented with a desk made in the workshops of the American forces. A brass plaque had been inset on the top, which read:

Presented to Lt. Cmdr. F Murch R.N.V.R; R.N.O Salcombe, Devon, from the men of the 29th and 97th U.S.N Construction Battalion. Wm H Henszey Commanding Officer U.S.N.A.A.B, Salcombe, Devon. M. W Vincentsen O in C 29th and 97th U.S.N.C.B.D. 1943-45.

Frank's final report gave his analysis of wartime Salcombe. According to his records 41 escapees had been brought in Salcombe, 16 civilians and 4 naval personnel had been killed in air raids, and an un-counted number injured, a few seriously, most with minor injuries. Amongst them was a New Zealand naval rating who had been visiting relatives in Salcombe. The number of casualties was actually remarkably small compared with the damage to property. The Airfield at Bolt Head was operational from 1941-45. Raids on the airfield had taken place between 1941-1943.

Frank reported to Dartmouth and was demobbed on 27th August 1945. He had to go to Plymouth to be fitted out with a demob suit and was given leave until the end of October. I drove him down. As a surprise to mark the occasion I had contacted Fred the day before and arranged that we would all three meet in the bombed out city. It was a sobering visit. The city we had known was in ruins. The number of dead was so great that a decision had been taken in some areas to bulldoze the bodies in the ruins. Because of this the centre of Plymouth where we walked was several feet higher than it had been before the war. Yet despite the horror and tragedy everywhere we looked we saw unmistakeable signs that the city was coming slowly back to life, with a courage that was humbling.

On 4th May 1946, my brother Lt. Cmdr. Francis Murch R.N.V.R received a letter from the Admiralty informing him that he had been awarded the United States Legion of Merit. On 24th July of that year he received the decoration at an investiture at the American Embassy in Grosvenor Square, London.

When peace came, bringing with it celebrations in Salcombe and Kingsbridge, few had any heart left to celebrate. The war was over, but at what cost? My only thought was that at least the boys would soon be home and be safe.

The firm now operated under the name of "J.C. Murch & Sons" in anticipation of my sons' return. I threw myself into my work accepting contracts for the smallest of jobs as we had done when we started out so long before. Re-building the war damage in the country began slowly. Government guidelines spoke of new and better housing being built, with electric cookers and washing machines fitted as standard, but there was no money to do it. We quoted for the erection of 12 houses at Camperdown Road. The figure was in the region of £19,000 for all the houses to include this high specification, but when I went to the Ministry to discuss the tender, I found that they had decided that the quotation was too high and so the cookers and washing machines had to be dispensed with. I refused to cut the quality of the construction, so after a lot of debate, a final figure of £1,275 for each building was finally agreed in July 1946.

Alec, now almost fully recovered from his injuries, came back into the firm after demob and eventually took over the business. He designed many beautiful houses around the estuary and as far away as South America, until a down turn brought our firm to bankruptcy. Peter who had not been happy working in the building trade, returned to the R.A.F. He later had an illustrious career, and retired as a Group Captain. Both of my sons retained their love of sailing all their lives. Alec married a girl from London, Peter a local girl from a South Pool family. Her ancestors were the Weymouths and Crispins in Batson, so yet another generation of these old Salcombe families were linked. My first grandchild, Virginia Elizabeth was born to Peter and Jess in November 1947. She was followed by Alec and Brenda's three children, Henrietta, Dominic and Benjamin.

Frank lived in Salcombe until he died in 1969. He and his wife Edith Lucinda Harnden remained in the home we had built for them. Frank's son

Arthur emigrated to New Zealand where he married Joyce Chapman. They have two daughters Celia and Francis. They are part of a growing clan of New Zealand family.

Fred left the sea and went home to tend his garden. His wife Mabel Rosevear still ruled the roost and Fred retreated often to the greenhouse where he entertained his grandchildren with his stories of the sea and his diving exploits. My younger brother died in 1974 aged 87.

In time Fred's son, David, went to sea. When he left the sea he turned historian. Together with his wife Muriel, he wrote several books about Salcombe. He founded the Salcombe Museum, and he fought for and achieved the monument to the Americans in Whitestrand and the re-naming of the street as "Normandy Way" in their honour. Muriel became a school teacher. She looked after Fred and Mabel and her own parents in their old age. Their son Julian became a Captain R.N, their daughter Nicola, a Practise Manager for the NHS. Both lived their early lives in Salcombe and were imbued with its history. Neither has children.

Like Frank, David's life was Salcombe. He was a genealogist who painstakingly traced the blood lines of the old Salcombe families. He was in touch with many of the American soldiers and sailors he had known as a boy growing up in the town, and he worked tirelessly towards a reunion for the Americans and the people of the battle affected South Hams. He lived to see the return of many of the American service men who took part in D-Day, and he witnessed their meeting with the families who had given up their lands for the war effort. So many of them had left Devon never to return to their former homes, but that day they came back and took their place amongst the other local families and stood in the rain with tears running unashamedly down their faces as they accepted the grateful thanks of the men who had despoiled their land in the cause of freedom.

Peter and Alec are gone now.

Of my grandchildren, Henrietta went on to marry and have three sons. Dominic currently lives in Portugal. He has two sons. Benjamin has just come home to live…Virginia…

I was not a good grandfather. I did not have a natural empathy or even love for my grandchildren, and I was not able to show them affection. I had visited Elsie in hospital daily for many years. In her last hours I stayed at the hospital to be near her. I held her hand and talked to her. I told her that I loved her. When at last she slipped away my world ended. My girl was no longer suffering. But there was no peace for me, only an aching void that could not be filled. With Elsie's going there was nothing left. I existed in a grey world in which the sun never shone. I resolutely shut everyone else out of my Hell. How could I relate to my grandchildren? Their chatter and their happiness were like salt in my wound. All I wanted was to be left alone.

I don't know how it happened but in the days following Elsie's death I found myself with my eldest grandchild. It was the first time Virginia and I had ever spent time together... she was about two and a half years old. The pain inside me was so raw that it drove me to Batson, to my childhood home and the emptiness of the newly converted summer homes filled with people I did not know. Bitter and angry, I stomped around the road to Snapes Point, pursued by devils, so eaten up with the pain of my loss that I didn't care if the child followed me or not. I realised later that she was perhaps the same age as I had been when Aaron first took we three brothers there. Mebbe I should have carried her because she was very small, but I didn't. It didn't occur to me to do so. Even when she fell and grazed her knee I did nothing. I barely glanced back. She didn't cry. I think she knew that she would get no comfort from me.

But as we stood on the headland and looked out over Salcombe harbour, over the little houses climbing up the hill, the church, the white gold beaches and the rolling green hills, across the diamond bright waves to the dark menace of Bolt Head and Start, and the magical open sea beyond, something changed. I glanced down into my grandchild's face and I saw my beloved Elsie there. I thought of the generations before and those still to come who had stood where we were standing, and I felt ashamed. I had closed my heart to so much. I had lost so much. I could not change, it was too late, but for the first time since Elsie's death, I reached out to another living soul. The child looked up at me and smiled. She slipped her hand into mine and then her eyes went back entranced, to the scenic beauty before her.

"Salcombe..." she said pointing a chubby hand out over the harbour.

The moment was fleeting, transient. I felt clumsy next to this little girl. I was afraid lest I say the wrong thing.

"...Salcombe," I agreed. Then almost to myself I added... "Home... the one place on earth where we truly belong..."

A far distant memory stirred in me. We walked a little further around the point until we looked up towards Kingsbridge. The breeze was sharp on this side of the hill and I took off my jacket and put it awkwardly around her, shielding her from the wind as my father had once done for me. I bent down towards her.

"These are the creeks," I said, spreading my hand as Aaron had done so long before and counting off the fingers... "South Pool Creek...The Bag...Frogmore Creek... my big finger is Kingsbridge, Blanksmill Creek, Collapit, Widegates leading to Kingsbridge... the Blessed Saltstone..." and she listened, her head on one side the way the maternal great grandfather she had never met had done, and I thought about her and the generations of Salcombe children and outsiders stretching on and on, who would one day stand here for the first time and marvel at this beauty, and I thought how powerful was this love of place, stronger than anything else.